*A Sight for Sore Eyes*
*II*

# *A Sight for Sore Eyes*
# *II*

*76 Prints from the*
*Department of Prints and Drawings*
*The Royal Museum of Fine Arts, Copenhagen*

EDITED BY
CHRIS FISCHER
JAN WÜRTZ FRANDSEN

*Statens Museum for Kunst, Copenhagen 1998*

# PREFACE

In 1993 the Department of Prints and Drawings celebrated its 150th anniversary as a public institution with an exhibition accompanied by a book like this one. *A Sight for Sore Eyes I* only included drawings, which are usually private notes created as part of a working process. They are rarely intended for the stranger's eyes and can be described as the most exclusive of all the arts. We now mark the inauguration of the rebuilt Statens Museum for Kunst with yet another exhibition, but *A Sight for Sore Eyes II* only shows prints and photographs, which are probably the most democratic art forms, as they are produced in a process aiming at multiplication. The idea is that the two books should cover the entire range of the Department's collection. As can be deduced from the title, we have primarily been governed by esthetic considerations, but we have also cast a sidelong glance at the quality of impressions, the rarity of the prints and other circumstances which make this particular copy of a more or less well-known print especially interesting for the specialist as well as for the broader public.

The present book was created in a collaboration among all members of the Department's staff, curators as well as student trainees. We have also been fortunate in co-operating with Arkady Ippolitov, Curator at the Department of Prints of the Hermitage Museum in St Petersburg, and Ernst Jonas Bencard, who has worked as Assistant Curator in the Department. We bring both of them our warmest thanks.

All the prints in the show have been through the skilled hands of our paper conservators Anne-Dorthe Rogild and Barna Bengtsson, and, as usual, the passe-partouts and framing have been made by our framer, Mogens Kristiansen. Special thanks to Thora Fisker for the beautiful layout. The translation from Danish has been carried out by Ernst Dupont, John Kendal, Annette Mester. Catherine Philipps has carried out the translatin from Russian, but the editors are to blame for all errors concerning technique and technical terms. The introductory essay is the hitherto most comprehensive account of the collection's history, but it is evident that much is left to be done in this field.

A book involving so many authors can never become homogeneous. Everyone has his own style and his individual way of treating the material. This reflects the tension and excitement which is the very incentive behind all new thought. Together with the quality of the works of art themselves the authors' enthusiasm has generated the present book. It is our hope that this enthusiasm is conveyed, if only in part, to the reader of these pages.

ALLIS HELLELAND
*Director*

CHRIS FISCHER
*Keeper*

# ABBREVIATIONS

## THE AUTHORS

|        |                       |
|--------|-----------------------|
| AI:    | ARKADY IPPOLITOV      |
| CF:    | CHRIS FISCHER         |
| CKC:   | CLAES K. CHRISTENSEN  |
| EJB:   | ERNST JONAS BENCARD   |
| IO:    | IBEN OVERGAARD        |
| JeG:   | JENNIE GUNNARSEN      |
| JG:    | JAN GARFF             |
| JM:    | JOACHIM MEYER         |
| JWF:   | JAN WÜRTZ FRANDSEN    |
| LS:    | LISBETH STADSHIL      |
| LWK:   | LIZA W. KAARING       |
| MBR:   | MIKAEL BØGH RASMUSSEN |
| SP:    | SUSANNE PETERSEN      |
| VK:    | VIBEKE VIBOLT KNUDSEN |

## BIBLIOGRAPHIC ABBREVIATIONS

| | |
|---|---|
| Bartsch | Adam von Bartsch, *Le peintre graveur*, Vienna 1808-1821 |
| Biörklund & Barnard | George Biörklund, *Rembrandt's Etchings. True and False*, (2.ed.), Stockholm, London, New York 1968 |
| Dutuit | Eugène Dutuit, *Manuel de l'amateur d'estampes*, Paris 1881-1888 |
| Hind | Arthur M. Hind, *A Catalogue of Rembrandt's Etchings*, (2.ed.), London 1923 |
| – | Arthur M. Hind, *Early Italian Engraving. A Critical Catalogue…*, New York 1938-1948 |
| Hollstein | F.W.H. Hollstein, *German Engravings, Etchings and Woodcuts c.1400-1700*, Amsterdam 1954- |
| – | F.W.H. Hollstein, *Dutch and Flemish Etchings, Engravings and Woodcuts c.1450-1700*, Amsterdam 1949- |
| Lugt | Frits Lugt, *Les marques de collections de dessins et d'estampes*, Amsterdam 1921 |
| –, suppl. | Frits Lugt, *Les marques de collections de dessins et d'estampes, supplement*, The Hague 1956 |
| Wurzbach | Alfred von Wurzbach, *Niederländisches Künstler-Leksikon I-III*, Vienna-Leipzig 1906-1911 |

# CONTENTS

*Fig. 1. Johan Christian Wolfen's inventory of the royal print collection with Christian V's mono-*
*gram (1690s); Wiedewelt's 10 volume "Catalogus..." (1788) and leather cases bearing Christian*
*VII's monogram containing series of prints glued together in rolls.*

# FROM DÜRER TO NAUMAN

## *The History of the Print Collection in the Department of Prints and Drawings, Statens Museum for Kunst, Copenhagen 1523 - 1998*

*By Chris Fischer and Mikael Bøgh Rasmussen*

Once upon a time The Department of Prints and Drawings at the Statens Museum for Kunst formed part of the collections of the Danish king. Its Danish name *Den Kongelige Kobberstiksamling* reflects not only its royal origins but also the fact that at the end of the 17th century, when the first inventories were compiled, it consisted mainly of engravings, which was by far the most commonly used printing technique at that time. Today, however, the old name is somewhat misleading, as the collection no longer has any direct connection with the Royal Family, and comprises drawings, etchings, woodcuts, lithographs and all kinds of works of art on paper.[1]

Not much is known for certain about the origin of the collection, but it is very possible that the first collection of prints was established under Christian II (1481-1559, reigned 1513-23) (Fig. 2). It is during his reign that we find the first evidence of a Danish monarch's interest in art, an interest that probably owed much to that great Renaissance prince's relationship to the German emperor Charles V (1500-1558, reigned 1519-1556), whose sister he married in 1515. It was to meet the Emperor and obtain his support in the serious conflicts taking place in the lands under Danish rule as well as to study the Netherlandish economic system as a model for his planned reforms at home that Christian II visited the Netherlands in 1521. Shortly after his arrival in Brussels he met the most famous artist in Northern Europe, Albrecht Dürer (1471-1528), and invited him a number of times both to draw and paint his portrait.[2] On 3 July 1521 Albrecht Dürer wrote in his diary: "Jtem hab dem könig von Dennenmarckt geschenckt die besten stuckh aus mein ganczen truck, ist werth 5 gulden" (Further I have presented the King of Denmark with the best pieces of all my prints to a value of 5 guilders).[3] Dürer both sold and made presents of many woodcuts and engravings on his journey, and it would appear from his diary that when he uses the word "truck", this means "kupffertruck", that is engravings (or possibly etchings), since woodcuts are designated as "holczwerk". Thus in all probability the gift to Christian II comprised a selection of engravings and possibly etchings that Dürer himself considered to be his best.[4]

We do not know what Christian II did with Dürer's gift - but he must have appreciated the prints highly, and it is likely that he included them in his library on his return home.[5] The library was presumably taken over by his successors when the King fell in 1523. Prints by Dürer are mentioned in the earliest inventories of The Royal Print Collection, and as the engravings and etchings by Dürer in the possession of The Department of Prints and Drawings today are quite unusually beautiful and early impressions, it is tempting to assume that they are among the sheets that derive from Christian II's meeting with the German artist. If this is the case, the Department's collection may be presumed to be the oldest, still-existing print collection in the world.[6]

There are, however, two circumstances that suggest that this may be wishful thinking[7]. One is that the print quality is equally good in all the Department's Dürer sheets, also in the latest, which were not executed until after Dürer's meeting with Christian II, and which the King could not possibly have received as a gift that June day in Brussels, and we have no information as to where they come from. Therefore the argument based on the quality of the sheets does not hold. The second circumstance is that around the middle of the 19th century the Department engaged in a comprehensive exchange trade in duplicates. It appears from the accession records that Dürer sheets, many of which existed in three or four copies, were often traded for prints not in the collection. There is, then, a theoretical possibility that sheets from the gift were included in such exchanges.[8] We are therefore compelled to conclude that there is no evidence that can help us to determine to what extent the Dürer sheets in our collection are those that Dürer presented to Christian II. There are, however, no indications that the opposite is the case, and the doubt concerning the present contents of the collection does not affect the fact that Christian II owned a collection of graphic works by the great German artist, and that his successors further developed the collection on this foundation.

In 1605 Christian IV (b. 1577, reigned 1588-1648) handed over his book collection at Copenhagen Castle to The University Library, which burnt down during the fire of Copenhagen in 1728. But fortunately - for The Department of Prints and Drawings - the gift seems not to have contained graphic sheets.

When his son, the Heir Apparent, Prince Christian (1603-1647), took over Nykøbing Castle, the dower house belonging to his paternal grandmother, Sophie (1557-1631), he also took over her book collection and any prints it may have contained. The Heir Apparent's collection thus came to comprise material that went back to the time of his grandfather Frederik II (b. 1534, reigned 1559-88), and which may also have contained parts of the oldest royal collections of prints.[9] The Heir Apparent was not particularly interested in books, but like his father he appreciated art and appears to have been a passionate collector of prints. He had assistants who bought for him abroad. In 1642 the bookseller Jørgen Holst delivered about 50 engravings by (and after) such artists as Rubens, Rembrandt, Teniers and Diepenbeck.[10] In 1644 the sculptor Francisco Duissaert sent him a bill for 97 rix-dollars for some "Coppers and other Pieces of Art that his Royal Grace the Prince has purchased from him". And in May 1646 Holst delivered some more sheets, among others, Rembrandt's "Ecce Homo, Original" for 2 rix-dollars and 3 marks.[11] According to Karl Madsen, this is the only time we hear of a Rembrandt etching being sold outside Holland during the artist's lifetime.[12] There must have been quite a lot of engravings in the Prince's collection, as can be seen from an extant bookbinder's bill for "9 books, large and small, with the engravings within", and during the Swedish War, when Lolland-Falster and Nykøbing was threatened by invasion, a joiner constructed a box in which the engravings could be safely transported to Copenhagen.

Prince Christian died childless in 1647, and a detailed registration of his estate was therefore carried out. In the inventory under the section on the library's "copper pieces" there are now as many as 13 volumes of engravings, among them Du Perac's "I vestigi dell' antichità di Roma" and a volume containing "Albret Dürer's etzliche Holtzschnitte"[13] In addition, we find under "Oeconomiae" a "Trachtenbuch", which is probably identical with Weigel's "Trachtenbuch", published in Nurenberg in 1577, and which can be followed from the first inventories of the collection of prints at The Royal Library right up to the present day.[14] These volumes were delivered to a groom in waiting and seem to have come into the possession of the Prince's father, Christian IV. What he had retained for himself when transferring his prints to the University Library in 1605 and what he later acquired was inherited in 1648 by Frederik II, the founder of The Great Royal Library.[15] We must therefore assume that the library also contained the deceased Heir Apparent's collections. The Royal Library, which was housed at Copenhagen Castle, was arranged on the basis of examples from abroad, and, besides printed books, maps and

*Fig. 2. Jacob Binck, Christian II. Engraving, 264 x 215 mm. (Department of Prints and Drawings).*

manuscripts, such a storehouse of learning would naturally also contain collections of graphic art, a collection of engravings. It is from the time of Frederik III that the collection of prints begins to take shape in earnest.

When Peder Schumacher (Griffenfeld, 1635-1699) took over the administration of the library in 1663, an inventory was made of its contents. The inventory ends with a collection of prints containing 73 items, the majority of which are prints glued onto folio sheets.[16] Unfortunately the contents of each individual volume are not registered, as not all of them have title pages, but among those that can be identified is Jacques Callot's *Misères et malheures de la guerre* from 1633,[17] which is still to be found in The Department of Prints and Drawings today.[18] The oldest written inventory of the collection of prints at The Great Royal Library is from around 1673. In its 8 pages the "Inventory of the Engravings"[19] lists 7,924 sheets, distributed over 80 numbers that all seem to designate volumes containing bound or mounted prints. Among these are:

*No. 1. A large book in Folio Regal Paper by Albert Durer, some*
*cut in Copper, some in Wood*                                          *325*
*No. 2. One ditto*                                                *142*
*No. 32. Various Albregt Durer's engravings in copper and wood.*      *83*
*No. 42. Various stories in wood by Albregt Durer..*             *6*

As will appear from the total number, 566 sheets in all, there must already at this time have been a large number of duplicates, no matter whether all the sheets really were by Dürer or not (in the course of time many sheets have been erroneously attributed to him). It is tempting to make the purely hypothetical assumption that No. 2 represents Dürer's gift to Christian II, as the number would correspond very nicely to the number of sheets mentioned above.[20]

In all probability Prince Christian's collection had been absorbed into the library's collection of prints at this time. It is very likely that No. 42 is identical with the Prince's volume of "etzliche Holtzschnitte", and No. 9: "Vestigi della Antiquità di Roma, Tivoli Pozzuolo et altri Luogi" must be identical with Du Perac's "I vestigi della antichità di Roma" in the inventory of the Heir Apparent's effects.[21] Quite a few of the other numbers are merely registered as "various prints by various Masters", but some are easier to identify,[22] for instance, No. 74: "Shilder tonneel van David Teniers" from 1660.[23]

During Schumacher's time at the library and on through the 1670s and 80s the collection of prints grew through purchases abroad carried out by agents like the painter Toussaint Gelton (d. 1680, active in Denmark 1674-80) and the court official Jodoch Herman Uhlich (1631-82). It must also be assumed that many of the engravings produced in the lands ruled by the Danish king also came to the collection.[24] The collection received what must have been a far from insignificant augmentation through the purchases made by the painter and architect Lambert van Haven (1630-95) on his travels in Germany, Italy, France and The Netherlands in the years 1668-70. On his tour he bought paintings, engravings, objets d'art and curiosities for the staggering sum of 5,500 rix-dollars. It appears from the accounts he presented to Christian V (b. 1646, reigned 1670-1699) that 216 rix-dollars were specifically spent on engravings:[25]

*Bought various engravings in Rome for/ His Royal Highness:*
*Prince Jørgen*                                       *41 (Rd), 1 (Mk), 8 (Sh).*
*Bought for my own studies engravings*          *52 (Rd), 5 (Mk), 10 (Sh).*
*[...]*
*Bought in Paris various beautiful and curious engravings*     *121 (Rd), 4 (Mk).*

Thus, the major part of the money for the purchase of engravings was spent in Paris. It must be presumed that these engravings were bought for the King. In Rome, noting the purchases on the King's account, van Haven bought engravings for himself and Prince Jørgen (George), Christian V's younger brother (1653-1708), who was undertaking the Grand Tour in 1668-1670.[26]

After his return in 1670 van Haven was appointed Court Architect and, in addition, made *Pictor Primarius*, the superintendent of the arts of the realm. At his death in 1695 his widow sold his large private collection of prints totalling c. 12,000 sheets to the King.[27] The collection is somewhat cursorily registered in the inventory that the Court Architect's brother-in-law Niels Pedersen Slange (1656-1737) drew up in connection with the sale, but gives nevertheless an excellent idea of the composition of the collection and the collector's interests.[28] Naturally it contained a large portion of ornamental and architectural engravings, but also numerous historical and mythological scenes as well as landscapes, mainly by or after the most famous artists of the time. The collection is modern in the sense that many of the engravings it contains had been published only a few years prior to and were probably acquired during van Haven's protracted travels. The main focus is French and Italian, but German and Netherlandish art is also well represented. The collection was an admirable source of inspiration and guide to trends in contemporary art.[29] The librarian of The Royal Library Johan Conrad Wolfen (1656-1730) signed for the receipt of the collection at the end of the inventory and then reorganised the collection, fortunately with both the inventory and a pen at hand, so that to a large extent it is possible to trace his rearrangements of the individual portfolios.

Wolfen's handwriting reoccurs in the next known inventory of the royal collection, a thin folio, bound in red morocco with Christian V's monogram stamped in gold on the cover[30] (fig 1). It is written in German and divides the collection into two sections: "Unge-bundene Kupferstücke", with 12,274 registered sheets distributed among 208 portfolios, and "Eingebundene Kupferstücke", with 9,861 registered sheets distributed among 94 volumes. From a comparison of the inventory of Lambert van Haven's collection with the "ungebundene" engravings and with the help of Wolfen's notes in the former it appears that by far the larger part of the "ungebundene" engravings correspond to van Haven's collection in a rearranged state.[31] The "eingebundene" engravings largely correspond to the content of "Inventory of the Engravings" from c. 1673, except for the fact that the number of volumes has risen to 14, partly because of new accessions, e.g., from Gelton, and partly because some of the older volumes have been split up into smaller units.[32] Wolfen's more thorough or different descriptions of the volumes mentioned in the c. 1673 inventory make it easier both to verify their provenance from the Heir Apparent's collection and - thanks to the greater amount of information - to identify the contents of the volumes and van Haven's portfolios in the collection today.[33]

Under Christian V the number of Dürer sheets had now risen to 751, plus a small number of unspecified sheets,[34] The increase from the 566 sheets around 1673 is especially due to Lambert van Haven, who contributed 170 sheets by Dürer and Cranach.[35] But in addition a little book has arrived containing 31 sheets of Emperor Maximilian's Triumphal Arch,[36] which may well have come into the King's possession thanks to his dynastic ties to the German princedoms.[37]

On Frederik VI's (b. 1671, reigned 1699-1730) foreign travels in 1692 and 1709 a large number of prints were acquired - despite the King's reputedly slight interest in art - for the King was accompanied by Wolfen, who although present in his role as the royal physician must have had opportunities of adding to the contents of the library. Judging from his work on the catalogue, Wolfen's interest in art or, at least, his knowledge of art must have been quite considerable. But as for the rest of the period up to the 1780s the material in the archives is too scanty too enable to follow the growth of the collection properly.[38] The audit of the library that was carried out in 1729 does, however, provide insight into the status of the collection. The audit was based on Wolfen's inventory from the time of Christian V. The 94 volumes in the old inventory have now grown to 144, mainly containing engravings or woodcuts. The 208 portfolios containing unbound engravings (those from Wolfen's inventory, i.e., Lambert van Haven's collection) are still in existence, but have been augmented with 81 portfolios. They probably contained the accessions that had taken place since the end of the 1690s together with sheets that had been separated from the collection as duplicates.[39]

It appears that a rearrangement of the collection took place in the following period, for, as we shall see below, most of the engravings had been pasted onto both sides of the sheets in 56 big folio volumes when the sculptor Johannes Wiedewelt (1731-1802) drew up a survey of the collection in the years 1783-86.

In the last two decades of the century a number of landmark events took place. In 1781 it became mandatory to submit copies of all books and prints to The Royal Library, which must have brought about a considerable growth even though the prints submitted in accordance with this decree went to the Danish Department rather than to the actual collection of engravings.[40] In the following years the library acquired two large collections of prints. One of them, which was acquired in 1794, had belonged to the director of the realm's stamped paper production Frederik Adam Müller (1725-1795). It contained 4,500 engravings depicting topographical motifs and aspects of Danish history. As this remained a special collection, which was never separated from The Royal Library, it will not be discussed further here. The other was the art collector and diplomat Joachim Wasserschlebe's (1709-1787) collection of prints (Fig. 3). The library was invited to buy it in 1781 and this gave rise to Wiedewelt's already mentioned survey. Joachim Wasserschlebe had been a legation secretary in Paris from c. 1731 to 1751. Here he frequented the company of the influential families and leading artists. He made the acquaintance of engravers like J.G. Wille, C.N. Cochin, Ch. Eisen and J.B. Massé and of painters, sculptors and architects, not least of the leading court artist François Boucher and of Louis Toqué, who painted his portrait. Through his close relations with the Danish ambassador in Paris and later foreign minister J.H.E. Bernsdorff (1712-1772) Wasserschlebe came to exert an influence on trade and industrial policy in Denmark and played a major role in the relations pertaining to artistic matters between France and Denmark. It was he who was responsible for bringing the sculptor J.F.J. Saly (1717-56, active in Denmark 1753-75) and the architect N. Jardin (1720-99, active in Denmark 1775-71) to Copenhagen, and when Danish artists travelled to Paris, it was Wasserschlebe who helped them to establish themselves. In the course of the slightly more than 20 years that he spent in the French capital he purchased books for Bernsdorff's library and close to 10,000 prints for himself. These were primarily engravings and etchings by contemporary French Masters, but the best Italian and German printers were also represented in his collection.[41] On the above-mentioned F.A. Müller's recommendation Christian VII (b. 1749, reigned 1766-1808) resolved on 24 January 1783 that the collection should be purchased. Today it constitutes one of the most important parts of The Department of Prints and Drawings. The sheets in Wasserschlebe's collection are of excellent quality. All the nuances of tone are preserved, and the sheets are untrimmed, with full platemarks and margins; they have not been mounted and there is no significant yellowing. Wasserschlebe knew the value of his collection and reckoned to get 20,000 French livres for it at an auction in Paris, but was obliged to surrender it to the King for only 2,000 rixdollars. The collection contains a broad range of 18th century French prints with representations of Boucher's work as its main attraction. Many of the prints use what were new techniques at the time, such as crayon engraving and aquatint. However, one could have wished for a broader representation of engravings and etchings after Jean Baptiste Greuze, Jean-Honoré Fragonard and Antoine Watteau,[42] a lack that was remedied by a generous gift of Watteau prints from The Ny Carlsberg Foundation in 1960 (cat. 35).

On 12 February 1783 shortly after the decision to buy Wasserschlebe's collection the King set up a commisssion consisting of F.A. Müller, the engraver J.F. Clemens (1749-1831), the sculptor Johannes Wiedewelt and the chief librarian Jon Erichsen (1728-87). Their task was to rearrange the already existing collection of Prints "in the manner that you find most suited to the fulfilment of our purposes, namely to the advantage of those who wish to make use of this collection and to the adornment of the Library, and thereafter to compose a proper inventory of the whole collection".[43]

In practice it was Wiedewelt, assisted by his cousin P.F. Zeise (1721-1806), who was responsible for the rearrangement of the collection. It took place in his home on Frederiksholms Kanal. Wiedewelt divided the collection into two parts: "Den ældre Kobber-Samling" [The Old Collection of Engravings] and "Den nyere Kobber-Samling" [The New Collection of Engravings]. The former consisted of 47,228 sheets mounted in 57 large white parchment volumes, in which the prints were glued onto both sides of the

IOACHIM WASSERSCHLEBE.
*Gravé en taille par son ami Jean Martin Preisler,*
*d'après le buste de Jacque François Joseph Saly,*
*fait à Copenhague en 1754*

J.M. Preisler del. et sculp.

*Fig. 3. J.M. Preisler, Joachim Wasserschlebe, after J.F.J. Saly's bust,
1754. Engraving. Platemark: 305 x 197 mm. (Department of
Prints and Drawings).*

pages. Wiedewelt had originally intended to break up the 56 volumes, but as the prints
were glued to both sides of the pages, he abandoned this idea. Instead the volumes were
given new spines and each of them was provided with a list of contents, a task that was
completed in 1786.[44] The loose sheets and Wasserschlebe's collection were placed in
"Den nyere Kobber-Samling". This contained 29,016 sheets, which were arranged in
accordance with Wiedewelt and Zeise's hierarchic system by country, school, artist
(alphabetically) and motif (biblical, mythological, historical, portraits, landscapes, ornaments) and were mounted in volumes.[45] According to the catalogue *recapitulatio* the collection now consisted of 131 volumes containing mounted engravings, 78 actual
engraved books and 3 cases for very oblong sheets.[46] In "Den nyere Kobber-Samling" the
prints were mounted on only one side of the folio pages, according to Wiedewelt to facil-
itate the replacement of individual prints if a better impression was acquired.[47] Wiedewelt
drew up a catalogue of the whole collection with an index of artists. The catalogue filled
9 volumes and is still to be found in The Department of Prints and Drawings[48] (fig. 1). It
also contained 423 drawings, but there were more in the library's collection of manuscripts.

At the completion of the catalogue in 1788, the collection contained 76,244 prints distributed among 268 volumes. In addition to these there were 36 portfolios containing duplicates, maps, defective prints and the like, which the Commission suggested should be sold, together with a collection of Danish sheets that had not been mounted because of their poor condition. It is therefore not possible to determine exactly how many sheets there were in all, but there must have been a considerable number of accessions during the 18th century. By comparing the number of sheets from Wolfen's inventory, which also included actual books, with Wiedewelt's total, we arrive at an increase of 54,107 sheets, which quite certainly does not cover the whole increase. Of the 54,107 sheets (at least) 37,267 were in "Den ældre Kobber-Samling" while, besides van Haven's and Wasserschlebe's collections, about 7,000 of unknown provenance were to be found in "Den nyere Kobber-Samling". Although it would seem likely that Frederik V (b. 1723, reigned 1746-66) was the person responsible for so large an acquisition, it is probable that he would have been particularly attracted to contemporary French art. And as modern French prints were precisely what Wasserschlebe's collection was able to contribute, the theory must be abandoned. It is possible that we must go back to the time of Frederik IV and Christian VI (b. 1699, reigned 1730-46) as - despite his pietistic views - the latter was interested in intellectual matters and, to judge from his building and decorating initiatives at the new Hirscholm and Christiansborg Palaces, apparently also in art.[49] Both kings had close family ties with Germany, and it may therefore be imagined that dowries or other royal exchanges of gifts contained prints.

We can be certain, however, that The Royal Library received a considerable accession in 1749 when the Gottorp library was brought to Copenhagen from Gottorp Castle in Schleswig together with the "Kunstkammer" of the Holstein-Gottorp dukes.[50] It is very possible that the reason why The Department of Prints and Drawings still to this day contains a number of unregistered duplicates is to be found in the fusion of the two superb royal libraries. The Gottorp dukes were renowned for their interest in the fine arts and science. One can catch a glimpse of the erstwhile splendour of their collections on visits to Rosenborg and The National Museum, and in The Department of Prints and Drawings, where Merian's uniquely beautiful botanical work in gouache, Codex Gottorp, is among its finest treasures. The Gottorp collection of prints was undoubtedly of a high standard, but a closer scrutiny of its contents has not yet been undertaken.

How much art on paper was lost when Christiansborg Palace burnt down in 1794 is hard to determine. In the 1830s the fire was remembered as the most destructive event in the history of the royal print collections. Thus, the keeper of the Kunstkammer Johan Conrad Spengler (1767-1839) stated that an entire book containing drawings by Philip Wouwerman fell prey to the flames.[51] Apparently part of The Great Royal Library, including a number of pictures, had been transferred to The Royal Reference Library, which was entirely destroyed by the fire.[52]

At the beginning of the 19th century Marcus Widerøe compiled a more easily accessible alphabetical index of artists for both collections of engravings. This occurred at roughly the same time as Frederik VI in 1810 bought the entire collection of drawings and prints formed by the late Lorenz Spengler (1720-1807), ivory-turner and keeper of the Royal Kunstkammer. However, this collection was not in The Royal Library. In 1812 a catalogue of Spengler's collection entitled "Fortegnelse over den Spenglerske Haandtegning- og Kobberstik-Samling" was drawn up.[53] It appears from the very detailed catalogue that there were 2,441 graphic sheets, 19 engraved books and 847 drawings. Practically all of them are stamped with Lorenz Spengler's collector's mark, L.S., and therefore easy to identify in the collection today.[54] These sheets, which are in a generally poor condition,

*Fig. 4. S.J. Dahl, Portrait of Just Mathias Thiele, Dresden 2.11. 1846. Pencil. 282 x 204 mm. (Department of Prints and Drawings).*

primarily give an impression of how an art historian of the time viewed the history of art in the various countries concerned. The collection contains both reproduction prints - and prints by *peintre-graveurs*, starting with Schongauer and Mantegna. For most artists, with the exception of the Dürer, there is only what one might call a more or less representative selection, so that the collection seems almost designed for study purposes, an important function for the keeper of a Kunstkammer at a time when illustrated histories of art did not exist.

Wiederwelt's reorganisation brought a certain order and system to the collection, so that a large part of it was now accessible for study. But according to Just Mathias Thiele (1795-1874) (Fig. 4), who had received a post as a "copyist" at The Royal Library, the collection was not as easy to approach as suggested by the sources. In his memoirs he writes that "it lay virtually unheeded, in an immense number of huge volumes [...] and in all the nooks and crannies of the library a number of large and small portfolios lay in inaccessible stacks, about which one only knew that they belonged to the collection of prints and were presumably left-overs from the reorganisation".[55] About "Den ældre Kobber-Samling" he relates that the prints were mounted "without a trace of the simplest order, childishly ornamented with silhouetted fragments, by which operation many of the most beautiful and rare original etchings had been sacrificed in the most meaningless fashion. It was said that this vandalism derived from Frederik V's childhood, but this work must have been too comprehensive and demanding for a little prince and must rather be ascribed to some idiot of a courtier who knew nothing about art".[56] Nevertheless it could be used for study purposes, and that is what the North German art historian,

*Fig. 5. W. Heuer, Portrait of C.F. von Rumohr, Stylograph after a painting by Wilh. Marstrand. 205 x 203 mm. (Department of Prints and Drawings).*

collector and gourmet, Baron Carl Friedrich von Rumohr (1785-1843) did when he came to Denmark in 1826 (Fig. 5). He was a friend of the young and later so important art historian N.L. Høyen (1798-1870) and associated with Prince Christian Frederik (the later Christian VIII, b. 1786, reigned 1839-1848), whose acquaintance he had made in Italy. Through repeated visits to the collection with Thiele by his side he formed an overview of its contents. In this process Thiele's interest developed into a veritable study, and he writes that von Rumohr's "surprise [was] as great as his knowledge - but his indignation was no less".[57] The following year von Rumohr wrote an article about the collection,[58] in which he stated, among other things, that especially "Den ældre Kobber-Samling" contained "invaluable things",[59] among them about 1,045 sheets of great rarity.

In 1829 the Lord Steward A.W. Hauch (1755-1838) was appointed Director of The Royal Library. Hauch approved of the idea of separating the collection of prints from The Royal Library. He therefore contacted von Rumohr without delay and asked the immensely active museologist Christian Jürgensen Thomsen (1788-1865), himself the owner of a large collection of prints, to draw up a memorandum[60] (Fig. 6).

Thomsen criticised the arrangement of the collection and pointed out what he considered to be its defects, focusing especially on the under-representation of Italian art in relation to French art, which thanks to Wasserschlebe's collection was extremely well represented.[61] He added: "It is quite deplorable and unacceptable that in the New Collection [which was the better arranged of the two and therefore more accessible] there are bad impressions and copies of sheets of which there are to be found excellent impressions, at times in a number of copies, and original engravings in the Old Collection".[62]

*Fig. 6. J.V. Gertner, Portrait of Christian Jürgensen Thomsen, 1850. Pencil on blue paper. 176 x 147 mm. (Department of Prints and Drawings).*

This is undoubtedly a reference to, among many other sheets, the not so good Dürer duplicates, which might be (yet another) indication of the fact that the sheets that were later exchanged came from the New Collection, while the finest examples derive from the Old Collection. In conclusion Thomsen suggested the establishment of an independent collection of prints, which - like the recently established Royal Collection of Paintings should be placed under Hauch.[63] Hauch had the memorandum formulated in such a way that it could be submitted to the Court in the summer of 1830. Its reception was undoubtedly made easier by von Rumohr's support for the project, and its initiators were successful in convincing the King and the authorities that the collection represented a great treasure that should be brought out into the light.

The proposal to create an independent collection of prints was not, however, entirely new. The engraver G.L. Lahde (1765-1833) had put forward the idea some years earlier and through an indirect approach had managed to get Frederik VI (b. 1768, Prince Regent 1784, King 1808-1839) to pay a visit to the imperial collection of prints in the "Hofbibliothek" during the Congress of Vienna in 1814 in order to form an impression of how such a collection should be organised.[64] Because of the library's lack of funds, space and staff with the required qualifications Chief Librarian E.C. Werlauff (1781-1871) was in favour of the proposal. He actually envisaged that the collection of prints could be sold to The Royal Academy of Fine Arts, which already possessed a small collection and the expertise necessary to arrange and maintain it.[65] But it soon became evident that the Academy had no possibility of raising a sum that came anywhere near von Rumohr's valuation of 50,000 rix-dollars in coin of the realm or 80,000 rix-dollars in sil-

19

ver.[66] It was therefore decided, as proposed by Hauch, Thomsen and von Rumohr, to remove the collection of prints from The Royal Library and establish it as an independent collection.

In 1831 a commission was set up charged with the task of formulating guidelines for what was to be included in the collection and how it should be arranged. The commission consisted of Hauch, Werlauff, Thomsen, Thiele and von Rumohr.

The commission did not deal in half measures. It was decided that not only the collections in The Royal Library, but also the King's own collections of prints and drawings should be included, as were prints and drawings from the collections of paintings at Christiansborg and Rosenborg, Spengler's collection, West's collection and the Helmstjerne and Numsen collections at Fredensborg. In 1845 the Royal Academy's collection of prints and drawings was also included.

A new and far-sighted system was introduced, based as far as possible on Johann Adam Bartsch's (1757-1821) normative work in 21 volumes, *Le Peintre-graveur* (1803-21), and on his experience from organising the imperial collection of prints at the "Hofbibliothek" in Vienna.[67] The system reflected the fact that the collection was no longer regarded as an encyclopaedic pictorial documentation in connection with a library, but as a collection of art. Two parallel principles were followed: qualitative assessment and chronological order. With respect to quality, the principle was to give priority to artists who had worked independently in the media of the graphic arts, the so-called *peintre-graveurs*, who appealed to the taste of the day by having a "painterly spirit".[68] Chronology permeated all the museum work that Hauch and Thomsen were occupied with in these years,[69] but for practical reasons it had to take second place with respect to the part of the collection that could be arranged in accordance with Bartsch's catalogue, which is not in chronological order, but had on the other hand been widely used as a reference work and an instrument for systematisation.[70]

The collection was hierarchically divided into main two parts: *peintre-graveurs* and engravers. The group of *peintre-graveurs* was divided into two sections, one arranged in accordance with Bartsch's catalogue, and the other containing sheets that had not been included by Bartsch. The latter were arranged according to country, school and artist in chronological order. The engravings were similarly divided into two sections. The first, *graveurs éminens*, contained the virtuoso engravers, who it was thought had to be presented in their own right. They too were arranged according to country, school and artist in chronological order. The second group contained reproduction prints, which the commission considered to have only documentary value.[71]

Now the various collections had to be integrated. The old volumes that constituted the Old and New Collections had to be broken up and the graphic sheets detached from the pages and arranged after the artist's name, glued "onto thicker paper dyed at the mill in a tone that harmonises with the typical colour of aged paper"[72] and placed in boxes. At the suggestion of von Rumohr, who had a good idea of the extent of the task, it was decided to start off by detaching the sheets in "Den ældre Kobber-Samling" as it was in a better state of order and therefore more accessible.[73]

Detaching the sheets turned out to be a difficult operation, even for the dexterous Thiele, who could draw on his experience with scissors and paste from his work in Kamma Rabek's box manufactory at *Bakkehuset* on Frederiksberg. The old glue proved to be extremely refractory, refusing to dissolve in tepid baths. But then one September morning, while Thiele was labouring in the kitchen, he was interrupted by the groom, who had got his horse ready for a ride. In his memoirs he writes: "I left the experiment, let the swimming engravings look after themselves for a while. After a good ride I returned,

*Fig. 7. Eight etchings by J. Porcellis mounted by J.M. Thiele. At the bottom Thiele's note according to which these etchings were the first to be detached from the pages of the old volumes in 1833. (Department of Prints and Drawings).*

firmly convinced that the sheets that I had left in the warm water would now be more than sufficiently dissolved, but that the damage would not be great as I had of course only chosen valueless sheets to experiment on. But - no! Everything was just right; with a light hand each sheet could now be pulled off the thick paper, ready to be treated and cleaned as if it was a patch of skin".[74] In the following days he refined the method by, among other things, placing the engravings on blotting paper and removing the last impurities and remnants of glue with a sponge before drying them between two pieces of blotting paper in an old press. The time had come to present the method to the commission. Thiele was given six sheets out of a series of twelve by the Netherlandish printer Porcellis so that the detached sheets could be compared with those that had not been touched[75] (Fig. 7). The result impressed the commission. In 1835 the collection of prints was finally separated from The Royal Library with Thiele as its Keeper. The collection was housed in the big room facing the Arsenal in the building then occupied by The Royal Library (Fig. 8). Now Thiele could begin work in earnest. The news of his skill reached the Court and Prince Christian (VIII) and his spouse visited the kitchen and spent hours watching this unusual form of scullery work. "Daily, almost from morning to evening, I stood like a washerwoman by the warm tub, and hundreds of sheets passed through my drying apparatus and my press. When von Rumohr occasionally came to Copenhagen, he was just as persistent as I was, and now I received instruction from his knowledge concerning all these detached sheets that had to be ordered... I worked on and on with only a couple of interruptions until with arthritis in both hands I had to console myself with the thought that this is the washerwoman's final fate".[76] In his eagerness Thiele totally exterminated all traces of the original arrangement of the collection. Not a single volume from "Den ældre Kobber-Samling" was preserved for posterity, and Thiele made no notes about how the individual sheets had been mounted. A few intact sheets have recently turned up among some thousand never ordered sheets in the hidey-holes of The Department of Prints and Drawings and give us an idea of the size of the volumes and how they were ordered. When compared against the oldest lists these pages reveal that the sheets were divided into two basic groups containing either prints by or after the great Masters or a comprehensive material sorted according to subject. The latter, which seems to have comprised all the visual sources of the time, ranging from topography, flora and fauna through biblical scenes to allegories and genre motifs, must have represented a "World Theatre", which as a forerunner of the encyclopaedias of modern times played a role in the education of the absolute monarch. Thiele, who regarded the prints as works of art, did not understand this system. Furthermore, his report that the volumes with the childishly "ornamented" sheets was a project from Frederik V's childhood might suggest that part of the collection had been used for the Prince's education, which had apparently been arranged in accordance with the most advanced educational principles of the day. We must assume that the influence of Johan Amos Comenius (1592-1670), who prescribed the broad use of visual material and the stimulation of children's powers of observation, had made itself felt at the Danish court.[77]

In 1843 The Collection of Prints and Drawings was opened to the public. With impressive skill and diligence Thiele had separated 37,634 graphic sheets from the book pages to which they were glued, had mounted them on cardboard and arranged them in 400 portfolios according to the name of the artist.[78] He also started writing a hand list, in which the contents of each portfolio were described sheet for sheet, a system that is still used today.

In 1851-52 the Collection of Prints and Drawings moved to the Prince's Palace, the present home of The National Museum. It was now possible to have a permanent exhibition of the most important graphic works, and there was a study room where the public could have drawings and prints brought to them. The publication of the collection was begun. Around 1860 a grant was made for the establishment of a photographic studio, and in the following years reproductions of the most important drawings were published[79] in 8 issues prepared by Thiele and Christian Piil, the photographer. Thiele also wrote a handbook for the use of visitors who wished to make a closer study of the collection.[80]

*Fig. 8. Plan of the great Royal Library before 1843. The Print Room can be seen on the left (The Royal Library, Department of Maps and Pictures).*

Together with the other curators of the small museums in the Prince's Palace Thiele was appointed director in 1861, and by the time he retired because of ill health in 1873 he had detached and cleaned almost 70,000 graphic sheets.[81]

Although it is not always possible to identify the sheets in the collection with the often very cursory entries in the accessions registers, these do give a good idea of the explosive growth in the new institution. The arrangement of the many thousand sheets from the already existing collections had a contagious effect on the acquisitions, and drawings therefore played a relatively subordinate role. With the oeuvre-catalogues of Bartsch and Nagler in his hand Thiele identified the old prints, crossed off what was already present and made lists of what was lacking. The duplicates were sold or used for exchange in order to achieve completeness.[82] The standard was Bartsch, who had not included Danish printers, so that the national-romantic movement, which led to a catastrophic concentration on Danish artists with regard to the acquisition of drawings, had very little influence on the collection of prints. Thus the growth took place particularly in the fields that Bartsch had concentrated on. Thiele purposively focused on completing the early Netherlandish, German and Italian schools, while English prints, which in Bartsch had shown relatively little interest, seem only to have been acquired as and when opportunity offered.

Immediately after the establishment of the collection as an independent institution in 1835 93 sheets by Italian and Dutch masters were bought at the auction after the engraver Lahde, who, as we have seen, was the first to suggest the creation of such an institution. The following year von Rumohr bought 30 etchings by Cornelis Bega, 15 by Rembrandt and a few sheets by other Masters in Lübeck, and in 1837 the collection began a series of exchanges with him. In return for duplicates of Dürer's woodcut of Maximilian's Triumphal Arch and a "Christ's head" the Print Room received 31 sheets. In May 1838 no less than 319 mainly Italian etchings arrived, and the exchanges continued in 1839, 1840 and 1841.

In 1841 a sale of duplicates from the collection was held.

Von Rumohr died in 1843, and Christian VIII had a sepulchral monument erected in Dresden as a memorial to the gratitude owed to him by Denmark. Von Rumohr had received many honours, but his wish of becoming the Director of the print room was never fulfilled, and this was perhaps the reason why he did not leave his art collections to Denmark as had been expected. At his auction in Dresden on 19 October 1846 and the following days more than 600 sheets by early German, Italian and Netherlandish artists were purchased, including Mantegna's two Entombments (B.2&3), "Bacchanalia with Silenus" (B.20), and one of the two prints of Caesar's triumphal procession (B.11), Schongauer's "Annunciation" (B.3) and some Passion scenes (B.9,14,20), Albrecht Altdorfer's "Rest on the Flight into Egypt" (B.5) and sheets by Fantuzzi, Cantarini, Claude Lorrain, Rubens and many others. The following year the first portion of the painter C.A. Jensen's enormous collection was bought, 236 Italian prints, followed by smaller purchases in 1848, 1852, 1853 and the acquisition of yet another large portion of 250 woodcuts and etchings in April 1868. C.A. Jensen's financial circumstances were catastrophic, and the death of his patron Christian VIII in January 1848 can only have made the situation graver. In 1849, at Thiele's suggestion, C.A. Jensen was made a conservator in the Department, a post he retained until his death in 1870. In the accessions registers he is regularly to be met, either as a purchaser or a donor, and it would seem that the collection acquired what it wanted while he was still alive, for very little was bought at his sale on 24 October 1871. At the sales of Captain G.D. Schaper (1775-1851) in 1853 and especially the two sales in 1855 the Department had the opportunity to make hundreds of excellent acquisitions. Schaper was the son-in-law and clerk of works of the architect C.F. Harsdorff (1735-99). The print room acquired a number of chiaroscuro woodcuts, a very large number of portraits, sheets by Canaletto, Caraglio and Zanetti, 4 prints by Mantegna including "The Descent into Hell" (Cat. 3), a vast number by Chodowiecki, sheets by Rembrandt, Jan Visscher, Beham and many great European printmakers.

Another great Danish collector of prints, whose effects were to set their mark on The Department of Prints and Drawings, was Thiele's close friend, the archaeologist and museologist Christian Jürgensen Thomsen. At his death in 1865 he left a collection of engravings and a coin collection that were considered to be among the sights of Copenhagen. His effects were sold off at a number of auctions; the first, at which relatively little was bought, was in 1865, and finally there were two in January and October 1867, at which hundreds of sheets were purchased, (cat. 20) among them a large number by English printers like Reynolds, Gainsborough, Stubbs and Opie. Titular Councillor of State Christian Frederik Holm (1796-1879) was also an ardent and knowledgeable collector of prints, who supported the newly established institution through gifts and exchanges or as its agent buying from foreign art dealers on his travels in Germany. Holm often bought prints for the collection from Börner in Leipzig, with whom he must have had a particularly close relationship since most of the institution's acquisitions from this well reputed firm went through him. Another German art dealer who regularly delivered prints was Harzen in Hamburg. On the other hand, there does not seem to have been much contact with art dealers on the English or Parisian markets in this period.

From 1862 Thiele had C.A.F. Strunk (1816-1888) at his side, first in an unpaid capacity and from 1870 as Assistant Keeper, a post in which he continued until his departure in 1887. Strunk's most important contribution to posterity was the compilation and publication of the standard work on Danish portraits, *Samlinger til en beskrivende Catalog over Portrætter af Danske, Norske og Holstenere* (Copenhagen 1865 & 1882), which is still used to this very day.

In 1874 the Director of The Royal Collection of Paintings and Sculptures, Otto Rosenørn-Lehn (1821-1892), also became the Director of the Print Collection, thereby fusing the two institutions in a "personal union". Rosenørn-Lehn was very uneasy about the location of the collection in the Prince's Palace. One of his first actions in his new post was to apply to the Ministry of Culture for permission to move the collection to a couple of empty rooms in Christiansborg Palace, close to the Collection of Paintings. But the Ministry would not agree and maintained its decision when with reference to the fire hazards in the old palace he later tried to implement the plan by offering to pay the moving expenses out of his own pocket. As late as in 1884 Rosenørn-Lehn tried to get his plan accepted, but less than a month later Christiansborg Palace burnt to the ground. The Collection of Paintings only narrowly escaped destruction, and there is no further mention of Rosenørn-Lehn's moving plans.[83] The 1880s saw an expansion of the staff of the Collection and the beginnings of a fixed hierarchic personnel structure with a Keeper and Assistant. Rosenørn-Lehn's position appears to have been of a titular nature, and he must soon have felt the need for further assistance, as from 1876 the Assistant Keeper at The Royal Collection of Paintings and Sculptures since 1870, Emil Bloch (1836-1914), was also attached as Assistant Keeper to The Department of Prints and Drawings. When Strunk left in September 1887, Emil Bloch became the actual head of the Department, while A.C.F. Læssøe, who had been working as an unpaid trainee, became Assistant Keeper.

Bloch was extremely efficient and systematic, and in the years after his appointment he carried out an expansion and partial tidying up of the collection, producing a guide to the collection in 1881.[84] He was also interested in history and in 1879 wrote a little book about the origins and development of engraving.[85] His rearrangement, which did not alter the system fundamentally or affect the first priority of the collection, the focus on the so-called *peintre-graveurs*, brought together the two parts of the section devoted to engravers so that all the artists were now in one place, insofar as the format of the sheets permitted. The earlier distinction between *graveurs éminens* and other engravers was abandoned, and some of the artists previously classified under *graveurs éminens* were instead placed under French *peintre graveurs*. A special section of Danish prints was established. New groups were also established containing: 1) sheets representing Danish history and topography, 2) ornamental prints, decorations, goldsmith prints, architectonic and topographical sheets and 3) portraits of lesser artistic interest arranged according to the person depicted.[86] In 1880 the Department contained 60,000 sheets distributed among 500 portfolios, which means that a considerable part of the collection still remained to be arranged and registered.[87] Thus, many comprehensive tasks remained, and that - because of the permanent insufficiency of resources - these tasks were never completed is indicated by the fact that as recently as in 1997 Chris Fischer and Claes Christensen were able to produce from the storage rooms of the Department an estimated 15-20,000 mainly Netherlandish sheets from the 16th and 17th centuries, which had remained unsorted after the great work of classification in the 19th century.

Bloch's new regime immediately made itself felt through the introduction of inventory records, a decided modernisation of the accession registration hitherto practised, since each new acquisition was now given its own inventory number and entry in the records stating artist, motif, technique, dimensions, state of conservation, place and time of acquisition and, when relevant, price. The Department's collector's marks were also introduced at this time.

After the burning of Christiansborg Palace the Ministry recognised that it was necessary to build a proper museum of art, and in 1892-96 the Statens Museum for Kunst was erected on Quitzou's Bastion at the corner of Sølvgade and Nørrevold with Vilhelm Dahlerup (1836-1907) as architect. When the building was finished, The Department of Prints and Drawings moved into its east wing, where it has resided ever since. At the opening of the museum Emil Bloch became its Director, a post he occupied until 1911.

*Fig. 9. G. Eickhof, Portrait bust of Gustav
Falck. Gesso. H. 42, 5 cm. Statens Museum
for Kunst inv. no.7205*

The next outstanding personality in the Department was Gustav Falck (1874-1955) (Fig. 9). He began as Assistant Keeper in the years 1912-1919, and after six years of study and travel he was appointed Director of the Statens Museum for Kunst in 1925, a post, however, that he retained for only five years. He resigned as early as in 1930, plagued by the administrative burdens that then as now threaten to blot out any intellectual life in the museum world.[88] Gustav Falck became Assistant Keeper the year after Karl Madsen had become Director of the Museum (Fig. 10), and he acquired Leo Swane as his Assistant (Fig. 11). Their arrival heralded a greater interest in the conservation of the prints. The first expression of this new focus was the introduction of window mats, a passe-partout of thick cardboard that prevents the work of art from being worn through rubbing against the glass of the frame or other mounts. However, it was only the most valuable sheets, the very best impressions of Dürer, Rembrandt and Goya, together with certain drawings that were mounted in this way. In course of time the method has been developed and improved so that the sheets are now provided with a false margin that is glued with the help of hinges to openable window mats, making it possible to turn the sheets without touching the original paper. However, many thousand works of art are still hinged onto simple cardboard mounts, and many of them go back Thiele's day.

Another expression of this increased focus on conservation was the abolition of the permanent exhibition of a broad representative selection from the collection. This practice had originated in the wish to illustrate the history of prints and drawings in a way comparable to that used for the Collection of Paintings and was, in fact, in full accord with practice in other parts of Europe. However, light has a damaging effect on paper, and in 1915 the permanent exhibition was replaced by a series of special exhibitions. These give the regular visitor a fuller impression of the wealth of art stored in the depots. Since the introduction of this form of exhibition The Department of Prints and Drawings has held

*Fig. 10. Arne Lofthus, Portrait of Karl Madsen. Before 1921. Black chalk. Owner unknown.*

270 special exhibitions, on topics ranging from the oldest prints to the most recent drawings, from monographic to thematic presentations.

A third innovation, which was introduced in 1912, was the waiving of the old rule that the Department did not buy works by living artists. It would seem that this change of policy was more due to Madsen and Swane than to Gustav Falck, since Madsen and Swane were both very interested in contemporary art, while Falck had a decided preference for the Old Masters. Yet another effect of the Department's new approach to art was reflected in the permanent loan scheme arranged with The Danish Museum of Decorative Art, by which the Department exchanged its fine collection of old ornamental prints and other sheets of decorative art (a number of them probably from von Haven's collection) for Danish and foreign lithographs in the possession of The Danish Museum of Decorative Art[89] (cat. 48). Prior to Falck's arrival at the Department lithographs had not been considered worthy of a place in the collection side by side with the old and time-honored techniques.

In this period the inventory records testify to a marked interest in drawings. With respect to prints Falck's discriminating interest in the Old Masters can be seen in the purchase of 52 sheets at Victor Mayer's sale in Berlin (November 8 & 10, and the following days). The new acquisitions included Dürer's "The Apocalypse", a number of sheets by Schäufelein and a unique French metalcut of Christ on the Cross from c. 1490. The acquisition of the rare block book containing symbolic representations of the seven planets took place during Falck's time as Director. It had been found in the library at Lerchenborg Castle in the spring of 1928 and was acquired by the Department with the help of a grant from The Ny Carlsberg Foundation (cat. 1). By way of contrast, Madsen's and Swane's presence is reflected in the first purchases of 19th and 20th century French prints: large portions of lithographs by Toulouse-Lautrec (1922, 1928 & 1929), Vuillard and Bonnard (1922), glass etchings by Corot and Daubigny (1922, cat. 46) and etchings by Matisse (1927). Johannes Rump's donation of modern French art to the Statens Museum occurred in 1927. It contained not only paintings and sculptures, but also a number of watercolours, drawings and prints, among other things, lithographs by Daumier, Daubigny and Max Liebermann.[90] But the most important new acquisition of prints was 31 sheets from Edgar Degas' collection, which were bought in 1923 from State Councillor Wilhelm Hansen for the tidy sum of 12,000 kroner and paid for in instalments over four years. Wilhelm Hansen, who at Ordrupgaard created what is probably the finest collection of French art in Denmark, had himself bought the sheets at the auction of Degas' effects in 1918, and it would seem that the sale was motivated by the need to reorganise his finances after the failure of Landmandsbanken in 1922.[91] The acquisition included 6 magnificent monotypes by Degas (cat. 51) and 6 etchings and 3 lithographs by Manet (cat. 50), Mary Cassat, Braquemont, Gavarni and Daumier.

Today we can be both surprised and disappointed that The Department of Prints and Drawings did not seriously profit from the strength of the Danish economy in the years immediately following World War I. Economic depression in the countries that had taken part in the war led to many private collections in England, France and Germany being put up for sale, and the art market was bursting with treasures; but the purchases account was small, and The Ny Carlsberg Foundation was not yet a major factor. Gustav Falck's boldness in buying expensive masterpieces did not have the same impact on The Department of Prints and Drawings as on The Department of Paintings.

Gustav Falck's period as an Assistant Keeper marked the beginning of the interwar interest in contemporary art, with an especial emphasis on modern French art from Impressionism and onwards, but modern Danish graphic art was also abundantly and broadly represented. The continuity of this acquisition policy was established between the two world wars. Leo Swane (1887-1958) replaced Falck when the latter left Denmark in 1919 and succeeded him as the Director of the museum from 1930-1952.[92] Viggo Thorlacius-Ussing (1891-1978) was initially Assistant Keeper, but after Swane's appointment as Director served as Keeper up to 1931, when, after a couple years in the Department of Paintings, he joined the board of The Ny Carlsberg Foundation. He was succeeded by Erik Zahle (1898-1969). After six months with Thorlacius-Ussing and a period as Assistant Keeper for the Department of Paintings he exchanged posts with Thorlacius-Ussing and thus became head of The Department of Prints and Drawings in the years 1933-35, after which he returned to the Collection of Paintings, leaving it again in 1949 to become Director of The Danish Museum of Decorative Art. Zahle was politically left of centre, and as a museum man his social commitment expressed itself chiefly in lectures and reviews of modern art in the daily press. Together with Jørgen Sthyr he authored an excellent study guide to the Department's collections, designed to replace Emil Block's handbook from 1881.[93] Zahle was followed by Jørgen Sthyr (1905-78), who had been Assistant Keeper since 1931 and functioned as Keeper from 1931 to 1956 (Fig. 12). But neither of these two men came to exercise a decisive influence on the Department's activities. Leo Svane ruled the Museum with a rod of iron and saw to it that the organisation of the collection and the acquisition policy that he had introduced together with Karl Madsen and Gustav Falck in the second decade of the century were maintained into the 1950s. One change did, however, take place. In 1945 The Royal Academy deposited its drawings and sketchbooks by C.M. Tuscher, J.E. Mandelberg and H.E. Freund besides

*Fig. 11. Hans Bendix, Members of the Gallery Comission: Leo Swane, Director, the painter William Scharff and Andreas Møller, Permanent Secretary. 28. 10. 1950. Pen and black ink, 430 x 410 mm. (Department of Prints and Drawings)*

some works with etchings by G.B. Piranesi and G. Vasi in return for the permanent loan of the Department's architectural drawings. This marked the definitive removal of a field that had never had the interest of the Department. In this period the grants were very small, but a resolute effort by The Ny Carlsberg Foundation made new acquisitions possible. Between 1935 and 1952 currency restrictions put a stop to the import of drawings and prints. This had an effect on the purchasing policy because books were exempted, and with the help of The Ny Carlsberg Foundation the Department established a considerable modern collection of superb French illustrated works. The Department succeeded in obtaining complete series of books containing original prints by Bonnard (cat. 56), Maillol, Marquet, Matisse and Rouault in addition to all the major works of Dufy (cat. 59), Luc-Albert Moreau and Segonzac. After the rescindment of the currency restrictions the collection, which by 1956 already numbered 150 volumes containing c. 2,100 lithographs, 1,500 etchings and 1,350 woodcuts, was further expanded. Today the only comparable collections are to be found in Biblioteque Nationale in Paris and The Museum of Modern Art in New York.[94]

The purchases of books of graphic art by French artists was a further development of the interwar focus on the acquisition of modern French prints, and in the years after World War II these were supplemented by large-scale purchases of individual sheets by the Impressionists and their immediate predecessors and successors as well as of sheets by 20th century classical modernists. In the decade 1946-57 alone almost 400 French sheets were acquired, a number that was exceeded in the same period only by the growth in the Danish section. Leo Swane's legendary antipathy to Pablo Picasso was no impediment to Sthyr, who in a close and discreet collaboration with The Ny Carlsberg Foundation during the last years of Swane's rule made considerable purchases of Picasso's prints, which were handed over to the Department as soon as Swane had retired. This made it possible for such works as Picasso's "Suite Vollard" to be included in the collection. On the other hand, the Department would have nothing to do with the German Expressionists. This was in continuation of a policy that actually went all the way back to Eckersberg's French-oriented classicism and had been reinforced by the strong repugnance felt for all things German that originally derived from the Schleswig-Holstein wars of 1848-1850 and 1864 and later from World War II. Like Falck, who had been his model, Sthyr was a distinguished connoisseur of Dutch art, but it was in the study of Danish prints that he did his most enduring work. In 1938 he wrote a lengthy article on the engraver Albert Haelweg,[95] and during the German occupation of Denmark and the following period he wrote the still normative work on the history of the graphic arts in Denmark: "Dansk Grafik 1500-1800", published in 1943 and "Dansk Grafik 1800-1910", published in 1949. It is therefore quite natural that this field received particular attention in that period. Sthyr had a succession of Assistant Keepers at his side: first Jørn Rubow from 1935 to 1943, who was later to succeed Leo Swane as the Director of the museum, then for a short period between 1943 and 1948 Aksel Rode, who was replaced by Erik Fischer. When Sthyr left to join the board of The Ny Carlsberg Foundation in 1957, he had increased the Department's collection by more than 8,500 inventory numbers despite the unfavorable economic climate.

His successor Erik Fischer (b. 1920) was to work in the Department until he was pensioned in 1990, interrupted only by a period as chairman of the committee for pictorial art under the Danish Arts Foundation in the years 1965-67 (Fig. 12). Erik Fischer's interests are many and his range of contacts correspondingly broad. He was one of the founders of the "International Advisory Committee of Keepers of Public Collections of Graphic Art", serving as its president from 1971 to 1976, and he has occupied important posts in the art world both inside and outside Denmark. In his period as Keeper The Department of Prints and Drawings achieved international status. Furthermore, he focused strongly on the Department's exhibition activities, not least after the rebuilding of the museum in 1966-69. The Director of the museum, Jørn Rubow, was much concerned that the rebuilding should give the Department better physical surroundings. Since it had moved into the Statens Museum for Kunst, the Department had suffered under an unacceptable lack of exhibition space and a study room that was so crowded with books that there was barely space for the public (Fig. 13). An attractive library was provided together with new offices, new depots in the basement and a number of exhibition rooms, some with artificial and some with natural light, making it possible to arrange a greater variety of exhibitions. Since the introduction of the alternating exhibitions it had been customary to accompany the exhibitions with handwritten, later typed, labels, but as the volume of information grew in step with the wish to give the public a

*Fig. 12. Inger Hjorth Nielsen, Museum Assistant, Erik Fischer, Assistant Keeper, later Keeper of the Department and Jørgen Sthyr, Keeper, in the Kunstforeningen, February-March 1955.*

broader orientation, the labels were supplemented with stencilled sheets for the free use of visitors. In 1976 the information sheets were replaced by so-called "pocket books" consisting of 16 pages containing a brief illustrated introduction to the theme of the exhibition. 70 such pocket books have been published to date. Larger and more carefully researched exhibitions are increasingly accompanied by actual catalogues. This growth in exhibition activities and in the amount of information provided was also the result of a much needed increase in the 1960s in the number of art historians on the staff. Inger Hjorth Nielsen (1911-1995) had been hired as Assistant as early as in 1954 and remained in her post until 1979 (Fig. 12). Hanne Finsen (b. 1925) became Assistant Keeper when Sthyr left in 1957. In 1973 she took leave of absence and in 1978 she became Director of The Hirschsprung Collection and Ordrupgaard. In 1965 a new assistant keepership was created for Jan Garff (b. 1936) and in 1974 Jan Würtz Frandsen (b. 1939) took over Hanne Finsen's post. In 1980 the post as Assistant was upgraded, and Vibeke Knudsen (b. 1949) became an Assistant Keeper.

In the period 1957-1990 the main focus was on the acquisition of contemporary Danish graphic art. Not least on the instigation of Jan Garff comprehensive purchases were made of prints by Aksel Jørgensen, Povl Christensen, Olivia Holm-Møller, Palle Nielsen, Sigurd Vasegaard, Dan Sterup-Hansen, Svend Wiig Hansen, Wilhelm Freddie, Eiler Bille, Asger Jorn, Richard Mortensen, Richard Winther, Bjørn Nørgaard and Per Kirkeby. Many of the more significant collective purchases were made in connection with monographic exhibitions in the Department. Up to Hanne Finsen's leave of absence in 1973 it was still mainly French art, Corot, Manet, Picasso, Braque, Vuillard, Bonnard and Matisse that dominated among the acquisitions of graphic art from abroad. The purchase of David Hockney's "Illustrations for Fourteen Poems from C.P.Cavafy" (cat. 69) i

1970 and of Goya's "Tauromaquia" (1st ed. 1816)(cat. 43), which was acquired with the
help of The Ny Carlsberg Foundation in 1975, are among the rare exceptions.

One of Erik Fischer's important achievements is that he was instrumental in persuading
the collector Herbert Melbye (1898-1976) to leave his important art collection and an
appreciable sum of money to the Statens Museum for Kunst. The collection consisted
essentially of several hundred drawings, watercolours and prints by French artists from
the 19th and 20th centuries: among other things, lithographs by Daumier, Degas, Manet,
Toulouse-Lautrec and Moreau, woodcuts by Vlaminck and etchings by Dunoyer de
Segonzac and Gromaire, an accession that helped the Department to bring not least its
collection of Segonzac up to a distinguished standard.[96]

The arrival of Vibeke Knudsen in 1980 marked the beginning of the collection of political and feminist graphic art from the 1970s. On the instigation of Jan Würtz Frandsen
attention was turned towards the leading German artists Baselitz, Immendorff, Kippen-
berger and others, who are particularly well represented in the portfolio *Erste Konzentra-
tion*. In the wake of the Bjørn Nørgaard exhibition in 1981 and with the exhibition *Offset
i dansk billedkunst* offset was also accepted as a form of artistic expression on a level with
the other graphic techniques (cat. 68 and 70). At the same time photography also entered
into the Department's sphere of interest in recognition of its growing importance as one
of the new forms of graphic art.

Along with his museum work Fischer taught history of art at the University of Copenhagen from 1964. Fischer, who held his lectures and exercises in the study room of the
Department, where students were confronted with original works, was an outstanding
teacher, and a couple of generations of art historians have been influenced by his methods and views on art. His teaching had an effect on acquisitions. Thus, Fischer's series of

*Fig. 14. Chris Fischer, Keeper, 1997 during the sorting out of prints left unsorted at the retirement of Emil Block in 1911.*

lectures on Dürer in connection with the 500th anniversary of the artist's birth led to the Department acquiring in 1971 a volume containing as many as three of Albrecht Dürer's illustrated books on the theory of art, namely "Underweysung der messung" (1525), and "Vier bücher von menschlicher Proportion" (1528) in the original editions from Nurenberg, as well as "Etliche underricht zu befestigung de Stett Schloss und flecken" (orig. 1525) in an edition from Arnhem, 1603. The acquisition was an important supplement to the Department's almost complete collection of Dürer's works.

In 1991 Chris Fischer (b. 1950) was appointed Keeper (Fig. 14). His special interest in the old masters is reflected in acquisitions of etchings by Benedetto Castiglione, Giambattista and Giovanni Domenico Tiepolo (cat. 36) and Albrecht Altdorfer (cat. 12). The first half of the 90s saw an increasing interest in new American art, primarily reflected in the purchases of Bruce Nauman's big graphic sheets (cat. 71) and Mike Kelley's and Richard Prince's photographs (cat. 72 and 74). American pop art, on the other hand, is not represented in the collection to any significant extent. Danish prints have been collected continuously. Let us just mention the large collection of trial impressions and studies by Denmark's great illustrator Povl Christensen, which was acquired in 1993, and the gift from Charlotte and Richard Mortensen's art collection in 1996, which supplemented the already rich collection of Mortensen's graphic works, so that it is now almost complete[97]. In connection with an exhibition of copperprints from Niels Borch Jensen's studio in 1994 the Department received a special appropriation to acquire a large number of prints by Danish and foreign artists produced in Denmark[98]. Today as hitherto, as far as the economic resources permit, the acquisitions policy aims at strengthening the collection through the purchase of important and rare works from the past and the present. A further aim is to ensure breadth in the representation of modern art (especially Danish), so that the collection can become a mirror of our time which will gradually develop into a historically important and, hopefully, interesting reflection of the artistic life of the past.

At the time of writing The Department of Prints and Drawings houses c. 200,000 graphic sheets with particularly good collections of early Netherlandish, German and Italian Masters and of French graphic art from the 16th, 18th and 19th centuries. Should one wish to point out special fields that have not been mentioned in the above, some obvious candidates for mention are the unusually rich collection of Rembrandt etchings[99] (cat. 31), the distinguished collection of chiaroscuro woodcuts mainly by Italian, German and Netherlandish Masters from the 16th century[100] ( cat. 8, 10, 13, 21) and the almost complete collection of Melchior Lorck's prints[101] (cat. 20).

The Department of Prints and Drawings possesses the biggest and most important collection of graphic art in Denmark, and the most important collection of Danish graphic art in the world. Nowhere else in the world can one find a so broad and many-facetted overview of Danish art from the 17th century right up to today.

1. On the history of the Department: C.F. von Rumohr & J.M. Thiele, *Geschichte der königlichen Kupferstichsammlung zu Copenhagen...* Copenhagen 1835; Emil Bloch, *Den Kgl. Kobberstiksamling. En Haandbog til brug for Besøgende i Samlingen samt Fortegnelse over de under Glas udstillede Blade*, Copenhagen 1881; Jørgen Sthyr and Erik Zahle, *Den kongelige Kobberstiksamling. Grafik og tegninger*, Copenhagen 1939; Jørgen Sthyr and Erik Zahle, *Den kongelige Kobberstiksamling. Grafik og tegninger*, Copenhagen 1946; Erik Fischer and Jørgen Sthyr, *Seks Århundreders europæisk Tegnekunst. Udvalgte Arbejder fra Den kongelige Kobberstiksamling*, Copenhagen 1953; Jørgen Sthyr, *Den kongelige Kobberstiksamling. Erhvervelser 1946-1957*, Copenhagen 1959; Hanne Finsen, "Kopenhagen Kupferstichsammlung im Statens Museum for Kunst", *Das Grosse Buch der Graphik. Meisterwerke aus 24 berühmten graphischen Kabinetten*, Braunschweig 1968; Hanne Finsen, *Nyt i Kobberstiksamlingen. Et udvalg af erhvervelser 1965-67*, Copenhagen 1968; Erik Fischer et al., *Europæisk grafik. Et billedudvalg fra Den kongelige Kobberstiksamling*, Statens Museum for Kunst, Copenhagen 1970; Chris Fischer et al., *A Sight for Sore Eyes. 53 Master Drawings from the Department of Prints and Drawings*, Statens Museum for Kunst, Copenhagen 1993; Chris Fischer, "En ren Øjenlyst", *Kunst og Antikviteter*, no. 7, 1993, pp. 4-5; Chris Fischer, "The Department of Prints and Drawings at the Statens Museum for Kunst in Copenhagen", *Grapheion, European Review of Modern Prints, Book and Paper Art*, 3rd-4th issues, 1997, pp. 8-15.

2. The painting has unfortunately disappeared, but the drawing can probably be identified as the large charcoal drawing by Dürer, signed and dated 1521, today in The British Museum, Department of Prints and Drawings, inventory no. 5218-48. For a discussion and reproduction of this drawing, see Else Kai Sass, "A la recherche d'un portrait disparu de Christian II, Roi de Danemark, peint par Albrecht Dürer en 1521", *Hafnia. Copenhagen Papers in the History of Art* 1976 (Comité international d'histoire de l'art. VII^e colloque international. *Les Pays du Nord et l'Europe. Art et Architecture au XVII^e siècle*. Copenhague 1-6 septembre 1975), pp. 163 ff., Copenhagen 1976.

3. Hans Ruprich, *Albrecht Dürer. Schriftlicher Nachlass, 1*, Berlin 1956, p. 176.

4. Erik Fischer, *Albrecht Dürer. Kobberstik og raderinger i Den Kongelige Kobberstiksamling*, Statens Museum for Kunst, Copenhagen 1971.

5. In contrast to the ruler of the Netherlands, Margaret, to whom Dürer also tried to present both prints and portraits, the King was both gracious and generous towards Dürer, which must be seen as a sign of his satisfaction with Dürer's work. Ruprich, *Schriftlicher Nachlass, 1*, p. 176 f.

6. Von Rumohr & Thiele 1835, p. 2, finds it "more than probable" that all the Copenhagen sheets are Dürer's gift to Christian II; Emil Bloch, *Albrecht Dürer, Tydsklands største Kunstner belyst ved egenhændige Meddelelser*, Copenhagen 1874, p. 44 is in no doubt that the sheets in The Department of Prints and Drawings are Dürer's gift, but in Bloch, *Haandbog...*, 1881, p. 2 he modifies his view, writing that there is every probability that they derive from Dürer's gift; Gustav Falck, *Fortegnelse over Dürers Kobberstik udstillede i Den kongelige Kobberstiksamling juli 1917*. Statens Museum for Kunst, Copenhagen 1917, pp. 2-4 finds it tempting to assume that at least some of these sheets are the prints that Dürer presented to Christian II.

7. Bernhard Hausmann, "Albrecht Dürer's Geschenke an den König Christian II. von Dänemark", *Archiv für die zeichnende Künste 5*, 1859, pp. 165-167, is the first writer to subject the problem of the gift to a critical examination and tries to identify the sheets that may be concerned on the basis of the fact that the sheets comprised by the gift actually exist. Fischer, *Dürer*, 1971 refutes Hausmann's observations. In Dürer's diary from the Netherlands there are several mentions of the value of the prints that he sold or gave as gifts. A particularly interesting basis of comparison is that on 20.8.1520 he made the Portuguese factors in Antwerp, João Brandão and Rodrigo Fernandez d'Almada, each a present of his prints to a value of 5 guilders, the same as Christian II received. Besides a little Infant Christ carved in wood the gift to the former, which is unspecified, comprised a number of items that are also found in other of Dürer's gifts and must be seen as an indication of the kind of print by which he wished to see himself represented: "ein Adam und Eva, den Hieronÿmum jm geheiß, den Herculem, den Eustachium, die Melanckolj, die Nemesin; darnach auf den halben bogen dreÿ neue Marien bild, die Veronicam, den Antonium, die Weÿnachten und das Creucz; darnach die besten aus den viertelbogen, der sind 8 stucklein; darnach die

drey bücher: unser Frauen leben, Apokalÿpsin und den grossen Passion; darnach den klein Passion und den Passion in kupffer. Das ist alles werth 5 gulden." Cf. Ruprich, *Schriftlicher Nachlass*, 1, 1956, p.154. "An Adam and Eve (B.k1), a Jerome in his hut (B.k6), Hercules (B.k73), Eustachius (B.k57), Melancholy (B.k74), Nemesis (B.k77); besides on half sheets three new pictures of the Virgin Mary (B.k36, k37 and k38), Veronica (B.k25), Antony (B.k58), Christmas Night (B.k2) and The Cross (B.k24); besides the best of the quarter sheets, 8 in all; besides the three books: The Life of Our Lady (B.t76-t93), The Apocalypse (B.t60-t75) and the large Passion (B.t4-t15); besides the small Passion (B.t16-t52) and the passion in copper (B.k3-k18). Altogether this is worth 5 guilders." The selection here might well be the same or almost the same as that received by Christian II the following year. The three books and the *Small Passion* are all woodcuts, which does not, however, invalidate the argument above that these gifts are also a matter of what Dürer himself would also briefly designate as "die besten stuck aus mein ganczen truck".

8. Although the quality of the impressions would undoubtedly have been excellent in a gift to a king, the state of conservation may have been poor after about 300 years. There is one entry in the acquisitions records that is interesting with respect to the question as to whether sheets from the gift to Christian II were surrendered, since the high quality of the prints is mentioned. On 1.12.1880 the entire Passion series (B.k3-k13) was given to Dispacheur Suenson with the explanation that though the prints were good, they were in a poor state of conservation and had in addition been trimmed. However, since the series that is still in the Department is of the same excellent quality as the other prints in the collection, this idea is not particularly probable.

9. This is, however, hypothetical.

10. A number of them are so well described in bills from Holst that it is relatively easy to identify them in The Department of Prints and Drawings today. Thus, for example, nearly all the mentioned pieces by David Teniers are to be found among the sheets placed under collocation nos. 103,47-65. Abr. v. Diepenbeck's "Mary and Joseph" is probably identical with P. de Jode's print after his "The Holy Family with Anna" (272,51), while his "The Crown of Thorns" is in Ballin's print (213a,4); cf. Otto Andrup, "Kunstnere ved Den Udvalgte Prins Christians Hof", *Kunstmuseets Aarsskrift* VII, 1920, pp. 90 ff.

11. Andrup, "Kunstnere...", 1920, p. 99.

12. Karl Madsen, "Nyt om Rembrandt", *Gads danske Magasin*, 1906-07, pp. 225-235.

13. Andrup, "Kunstnere..." 1920, pp. 100 ff. As Prince Christian was married to Magdalene Sibylle, the daughter of the Elector Johan Georg of Saxony, it seems likely that the volume of Dürer sheets may have come to Prince Christian together with her.

14. This book, which is still in The Royal Library, did not accompany the collection of prints when it was separated from the library.

15. Harald Ilsøe, "Den udvalgte prins Christian (V)s bøger og Det kongelige Bibliotek", *Levende biblioteker. Festskrift til Palle Birkelund 29. januar 1982*, Copenhagen 1982, pp. 78-82.

16. Archives of The Royal Library, E6. E.C. Werlauff, *Historiske Efterretninger om det store kongelige Bibliothek i Kiøbenhavn* (2nd rev. ed.), Copenhagen 1844, pp. 46 ff. Palle Birkelund, "J. Wasserschlebe og Det kgl. Bibliotek. Den kgl. Kobberstiksamlings tilblivelse", *Fund og Forskning i Det kongelige Biblioteks Samlinger* XVI, 1969, 55. Knud Bøgh, "Frederik III's bibliotek på Københavns Slot. Et rekonstruktionsforsøg", *Fund og Forskning i Det kongelige Biblioteks Samlinger* XXVI, 1982-83, pp. 70, 83.

17. Bøgh, "Frederik IIIs bibliotek...", 1982-83, p. 83.

18. Collocation no. 151,190-207. It is very possible that a large part of the other Callot prints of military subjects, which are today located around this portfolio in The Department of Prints and Drawings were contained under this number in the 1663 inventory.

19. *Fortegnelse paa Kaabberstøckerne*, MS. Archives of The Department of Prints and Drawings.

20. In Dürer's time 125 sheets and a small wooden sculpture were worth 5 guilders (see note 7). The same value could also have applied for this volume of 142 sheets if the 17 extra sheets (e.g., the *Apocalypse*) equalled the value of a small sculpture like the one mentioned in the gift to the Portuguese factor.

21. This may be one of two works, either Du Perac's "Vestigi della Antiquità di Roma, Tivoli, Pozzuoli et altri Luogi" from 1575, which was not handed over to the commission established for that purpose when The Department of Prints and Drawings was separated from The Royal Library in 1835 (cf. *Commisionen for den Kongelige Kobberstik-Samling*, Ms. Archives of The Department of Prints and Drawings, p. 14) or Aegidius Sadeler's copies after Du Perac's work, published in 1606. The latter are still in The Department of Prints and Drawings (portfolios 391 and 121-158).

Sadeler's copies are mentioned in Wolfen's inventory from the 1690s (se note 36) under "Eingebundene Kupferstücke", no. 54: "Alte Gebäud und Ruinen der stadt Rom, Tivoli und Puzuolo Von Sadler."

22. The inventory mentions, among other things, "A little thin book, in blue paper with engravings". A number of the sheets in The Department of Prints and Drawings bear traces of having been stuck onto blue paper. These sheets may derive from this volume.

23. This book was created at the instigation of the Archduke Leopold Wilhelm of Austria and reproduced on 244 sheets his predominantly Italian collection of paintings in Brussels. The work was published in Brussels in 1660 in a Latin, a French, a Spanish and a Flemish edition. The copy mentioned is in Flemish and is today in The Royal Library, an example of the fact that those parts of the collection of prints that were books were not removed with the rest of the collection at the time of its separation from The Great Royal Library in 1835, but remained part of the library. This also appears from the protocol for *Commisionen for den Kongelige Kobberstik-Samling*, Ms. Archives of The Department of Prints and Drawings, p. 13, where the work figures in a list, drawn up in 1833, of books that according to the catalogue from the 1830s (see below) should be in The Department of Prints and Drawings, but which were not to be found among the works handed over by The Royal Library.

24. The royal household accounts from the time of Frederik II and Christian V also testify to the fact that the king both purchased and commissioned engravings for himself personally. The acquisitions between 1670 and 1699 are as follows: 29.10.1674: "Paul Clement, en Hollender, for kaaberstycker 10 r.", 5.8.1676: "en kobersticker, som overlefverte K.M. nogle koberstøcker om søeslaget [at Landskrona], 20 r.", 5.10.1676: "Ditmer conterfeir paa regnskab for et kaaberstøcke at lade forfærdige 50 r.", 3.2.1677: "Henning Lüdtzow til en kaabersticker 13 r.", 8.9.1679: "Conterfeir Gelton paa haanden for nogen koberstycker at forskrifve fra Holland 200 r.", 27.4.1685: "en kobersticker efter regenskab 72 r.", 16.4.1690: "Schøler bekommit til en kobersticker, som skulde afsticke medaillerne ved kunstkammerit, 24 r.", 14.10.1690: "til dend, som sticker kobberpladerne af kunstkammerit, er betalt paa regenskab 50 r oc til kobertryckern 58 r 2 m: 108 r 2 m", 26.11.1690: "dend, som sticker de koberplader paa kunstkammerit, foruden forrige endnu 50 r.", maj 1694: "H.K.M. har naadigst resolverit at gifve endnu til kober-

stickarbeidet vid kunstkammerit 170 r, deraf betalt 30 r.", 19.1.1695: "doctor Holger ræstn til kobrstickeriedvid kunstkammerit 80 r.", cf. Emil Marquard 8ed.), *Kongelige Kammerregnskaber fra Frederik III.s og Christian V.s Tid*, Selskabet for Udgivelse af Kilder til dansk Historie, Copenhagen 1918, pp. 123, 157, 161, 166, 210, 305, 380, 386, 388, 446, 455. If one compares the 200 rix-dollars, assigned to Gelton on 8.9.1679 in order to buy engravings in Holland with the 1,000 rix-dollars that van Haven's widow received in 1696 for a collection of over 12,000 sheets and some paintings, one must assume that either Gelton bought some very exclusive items very expensively or that the King got an extremely good bargain when he acquired van Haven's collection - the latter alternative is the more probable.

25. The accounts for his trip are located in the Danish National Archives.

26. It may be noted that Lambert van Haven's purchases cost roughly the same amount of money as Toussaint Gelton's in 1679 (see note 24). If we assume that they acquired more or less the same number of sheets for the money, we can make a very rough estimate of the size of the royal collection prior to 1670, when Lambert van Haven came home. About half of the engravings bought by van Haven were for the King, which means that the accession must have been approximately half as great as the accession represented by Gelton's purchases. As there are no other significant accessions registered between the "Inventory of the Engravings" from c. 1673 (see above, note 19) and the purchase of Lambert van Haven's collection in 1696 (see below, note 28), Gelton's purchases must have constituted the major part of the difference between the number in 1673 and the number in 1696 minus Lambert van Haven's c. 12,000 sheets. This difference is c. 2,000 sheets. If we subtract half of this figure from the 7,916 sheets registered in c. 1673, we arrive at a total of c. 7,000 sheets in the royal collection prior to Lambert van Haven's purchases in 1668-70. This estimate is, however, very loose, as it does not take into account the size, desirability and character of the sheets or for that matter changes in prices and the value of money in the 10 years between van Haven's and Gelton's acquisitions. As regards Prince Jørgen's (George) collection of engravings, it must have accompanied him to England when he married the later Queen Anne.

27. Marquard 1918, p. 474: 21.3.1696: "generalbiugmesters enke for skilderier, som kom til kunstkammeret, sampt kobrstyckr oc schetzr

til bibliotekid 1000 r." [the architect-general's widow for depictions that came to the cabinet of curiosities, as well as engravings and sketches for the library 1000 r.].

28. Jan Garff, *Malerier på papir. Olieskitser fra Lambert van Haven's samling*, Lommebog 66-67, The Department of Prints and Drawings, Statens Museum for Kunst, Copenhagen 1995, p. 1. Slange's inventory, "Fortegnelse paa Sal: General bÿgMesters effterladte Kaaberstÿcker, saa og Academishe Schetzer" is in the archives of the Department. It is dated 12.2.1696, the date of the transfer to The Great Royal Library. At the bottom of the document there is a receipt from librarian Johann Conrad Wolfen bearing the same date.

29. As a supplement to the engravings Lambert Van Haven made a large number of sketches after classical and contemporary sculptures and paintings, largely in oil. These are still in The Department of Prints and Drawings and were cursorily published in connection with an exhibition in the Department to mark the tercentenary of Lambert van Haven's death, 1995. Cf. Garff, *Malerier på papir...*, 1995.

30. Ms. Archives of The Department of Prints and Drawings.

31. This is further confirmed by Werlauff's note to the effect that in his day the inventory of Lambert van Haven's collection was located in the red morocco inventory bearing Christian V's monogram. Werlauff, *Historiske efterretninger...*, p. 106 f.

32. For example, No. 28 containing 31 sheets for Emperor Maximilian's Triumphal Arch by Dürer is very probably a new accession. Cf also note 37.

33. The comparison of the various inventories carried out in connection with the preparation of this article has apparently not been previously attempted, and the outline of a provisional concordance on which to base a more thorough study of the contents of the Old Collection is now filed in the archives of the Department. Such a study will, however, require resources that are not available to the Department at the time of writing.

34. This applies especially to "ungebundene" No. 84: "Großer Herren und Damen, item anderer Vornehmer Personen in Europa bildnüßen Von Titian, Rubens, Van Dyck, A. Durer, A. Wuchters etc.....74" and No. 87: "Vornehmer und gelehrter leute bildnüßen Von R.Urbin, titian, Rubens, Rembrandt, Sandraert, Steenwinckel, C. von Mander, C. Blomaert, A.Durer, Kilian, I Hond etc.....94" and to "eingebundene", No. 6: "Die 4.Evangelisten, die 5.-

Sinne und andere geist- und weltliche stücke Von Paolo Veronese, M.HeemsKerck, leonado da Vinci, J. Palma, A. Durer, Tintoretto, Dolendo und anderen....31". The number of artists' names that have to share the 199 sheets makes it improbable that Dürer would have been represented with more than a total of 10-20 sheets under these inventory numbers.

35. "Fortegnelse paa Sal: General bÿgMesters effterladte Kaaberstÿcker, saa og Academishe Schetzer", Ms. Archives of the Department, no. 248: "70 Geÿstl: historier af Albert Duren" and 249: "100 attskillige geÿstl: historier af Duren og L:GranaK". In all probability the major part of the latter number was by Dürer.

36. Wolfen's inventory from the 1690s, archives of the Department, "Eingebundene Kupferstücke", no. 28.

37. The Hapsburg King of Bohemia and Hungary, the administrator of Emperor Charles V's German fiefdoms, and later himself Emperor, Ferdinand I, commissioned an entire impression of 300 copies of the triumphal arch for himself in 1526, 7 years after Emperor Maximilian's death, in order to have sole control over the distribution of this propaganda material, which was of such great significance to the Hapsburg dynasty. The recipients were members of the dynasty, important connections among princes and the nobility and the most prominent of the Empire's administrators from among the citizenry. Cf. Jan-Dirk Müller, *Gedechtnus. Literatur und Hofgesellschaft um Maximilian I.*, Forschungen zur Geschichte der älteren deutschen Literatur 2, Munich 1982, p. 77 f. It is very likely that a book of this kind formed part of such a gift calculated to maintain friendly relations with the dynasty, but it is also possible that it was acquired by, for example, Toussaint Gelton for the funds that he received from the King in 1679 (cf. note 24).

38. The time available for the present work did not permit the thorough review of The Royal Library's accession protocols for the 18th century that this would require.

39. In Wolfen's inventory from the end of the 1690s a few duplicates occur, since there are works from "Eingebundene Kupferstycke" that are also found in the portfolios under "Ungebundene Kupferstycke". In the archives of the Department there is a loosely outlined catalogue designated "Protoc. p. 690. følgende Kaaberstykker ligger oven paa skabet" ["the following engravings are on top of the cupboard"], which lists 35 folders or portfolios containing drawings and engravings, single sheets and complete works. Here we reen-

counter a large number of the sheets that also figured in Lambert van Haven's inventory. It is possible that this is a draft from the 1729 audit, and that the sheets are duplicates or sheets that were separated for some reason during Wolfen's arranging and cataloguing work about 30 years earlier.

40. Birkelund, "Wasserschlebe...", 1969, p. 77.

41. Birkelund, "Wasserschlebe...", 1969, p. 69.

42. Birkelund, "Joachim Wasserschlebe und seine Kupferstichsammlung", *Schleswig-Holstein und der Norden. Festschrift für Olaf Klose*, Neumünster 1968 pp. 148-168; Jan Würtz Frandsen, "Joachim Wasserschlebe (1709-1787)", in Lene Bøgh Rønberg (ed.), *Lyst og længsel. Kærlighedsmotiver i fransk 1700-tals kunst*, Statens Museum for Kunst, Copenhagen 1995, pp. 107-109.

43. Birkelund, "Wasserschlebe...", 1969, p. 69.

44. Birkelund, "Wasserschlebe...", 1969, p. 71.

45. It is very possible that the system on which the work in The Royal Library was organised came from France, since the French way of organising a collection seems to have been introduced everywhere in Europe around the middle of the 18th century. This was due not least to P.J. Mariette's (1694-1774) organisation in the years 1730-35 of Prince Eugene of Savoy's (1663-1736) huge collection of engravings. In 1738 the collection with its 290 folios containing mounted prints went to the Hofbibliothek in Vienna (cf. Friedrich Ritter von Bartsch, *Die Kupferstichsammlung der K.K.Hofbibliothek in Wien in einer Auswahl ihrer merkwürdigsten Blætter*, Vienna 1854, p. IV). Mariette's was the most famous and also the most influential way of systematising a collection. J.A. Bartsch's system from the beginning of the 19th century, which is still used by, among others, The Department of Prints and Drawings, was also developed at the Hofbibliothek and is essentially based on Mariette's work.

46. *Catalogus over den nyere Kobber-Samling og nogle Tegninger i det Kongelige Store Bibliotheque*, vol .8, "Det totale Bedrag" (at the end of the volume). Ms. Archives of The Department of Prints and Drawings. In the records of *Commisionen for den Kongelige Kobberstik-Samling*, Ms. Archives of The Department of Prints and Drawings, p. 4, there is a reference in Hauch's preface to Wiedewelt's catalogue, but with a somewhat different result, inasmuch as "Den nyere Kobber-Samling" is here described as consisting of 112 volumes containing mounted engravings, while it is noted that there are about 100 actual books with engravings, which have come to the library as

books and should therefore remain there, and a large number of loose sheets. The discrepancy is apparently due to a lack of precision, for in a report of 26.1.1835 Thiele mentions that in 1831 167 volumes were delivered to the commisssion from The Royal Library. Here it is stated that "Den ældre Kobber-Samling" consisted of only 54 volumes. So there is a certain doubt about these matters.

47. Birkelund, "Wasserschlebe...", 1969, p. 71.

48. In all 8 catalogue volumes reference is made for individual artists to "Den ældre Kobber-Samling", if it contains sheets by the artist in question. In the ninth volume, which contains the index of artists, reference is also made to both collections.

49. The records of *Commisionen for den Kongelige Kobberstik-Samling*, Ms. Archives of The Department of Prints and Drawings, p. 3, contain the supposition that "the major part of the accessions to the collection took place under King Christian the Fifth and King Frederik the Fourth of blessed memory".

50. Werlauff, *Historiske efterretninger...*, 1844, pp. 158 f. In the period after the Royal Patent of 1713 regarding the transfer of the Holstein-Gottorp possessions to the Danish king, the Gottorp library began to trickle slowly into Denmark. This occurred partly in the form of loans that were later returned to The Royal Library and partly by the sending in 1735 of manuscripts and archivalia to Copenhagen. The library itself arrived in Copenhagen in September 1749 in 69 crates. Here a catalogue was compiled, from which first The Royal Library and then The Royal Reference Library (burnt in 1794) were to choose whatever was of interest to them. The remainder was sent to Sorø Academy.

51. Rumohr & Thiele, *Geschichte...*, 1835, p. 4.

52. Rumohr & Thiele, *Geschichte...*, 1835, p. 4.

53. *Fortegnelse over den Spenglerske Haandtegning og Kobberstik Samling. Forfattet i Aaret 1812*. Ms. Archives of The Department of Prints and Drawings (2 copies).

54. Jens Heinet Knudsen, "Lorenz Spengler's Collection of Drawings", Chris Fischer et al., *A Sight for Sore Eyes*, Copenhagen 1993, pp. 15-28.

55. This must be a reference to the already mentioned 36 portfolios that were left over after Wiedewelt's reorganisation. It is interesting to note how differently the commission responsible for separating the collection from The Royal Library assessed these loose sheets, which are described as a not insignificant amount of loose engravings in portfolios, among which there are also several of much

value. The records of *Commisionen for den Kongelige Kobberstik-Samling*, Ms. Archives of The Department of Prints and Drawings, p. 4.

56. Just Mathias Thiele, *Af mit Livs Aarbøger 1826-1874*, Copenhagen 1917, vol II, pp. 25-26.

57. Thiele, *Af mit Livs Aarbøger ...*, Copenhagen 1917, vol II, pp. 25-26.

58. *Morgenblatt für gebildete Stände* 1827, no. 41.

59. Quoted from the records of *Commisionen for den Kongelige Kobberstik-Samling*, Ms. Archives of The Department of Prints and Drawings, p. 4.

60. Jørgen Jensen, *Thomsens Museum. Historien om Nationalmuseet*, Copenhagen 1992, p. 100.

61. Jensen, *Thomsens museum...*, 1992, p. 100.

62. Jensen, *Thomsens museum...*, 1992, p. 100 f.

63. Jensen, *Thomsens museum...*, 1992, p. 101.

64. Birkelund, *Wasserschlebe...*, 1969, p. 78.

65. The catalogue of this collection, *Catalog over Det Kongelige Maler Billedhugger og Bygnings Academies Kobberstik-Samling*, which seems to be more or less contemporary with the catalogues of "Den ældre Kobber-Samling" and "Den nyere Kobber-Samling", and which like these appears to have been drawn up by Wiedewelt, but later continued by other hands, is in the archives of The Department of Prints and Drawings. It contains 653 prints and 82 engraved books, some of which are very small.

66. It is interesting to note in this connection that in 1789, when the English naval surgeon James Wright visited Copenhagen and saw the collection, it was valued at 140,000 rix-dollars, cf. Birkelund, *Wasserschlebe...*, 1969, p. 73.

67. This experience was recorded by Bartsch in the manuscript *Ueber die Verwaltung der Kupferstichsammlung der k. k. Hofbibliothek*, with which von Rumohr was probably familiar.

68. Thiele & Rumohr 1835, p. 5: "die werthvolleren Kupferstiche [seyen] eigenthümliche Erzeugnisse des Geistes und der kunst, welche nicht ohne Gefahr für deren Genuss und Aneignung können mit den mechanischen Nachbildungen geistloser Kupferstecher vermengt werden; wie solches nach dem alten Plane geschehe und geschehen müsse. [...]die Zeitgeneossen, seit Erscheinung des bekannten *peintre graveur* [haben] so ganz ausnahmslos sich dafür entschieden, den wichtigsten Theil des gesammten Faches, die Kupferstiche, welche von Malern oder auch nur in malerischem Geiste gearbeitet sind, von allen übrigen durchaus abzusondern, oder als eine ganz eigene Classe sie aufzufassen. Denselben dierin sich anzuschliessen, sey rathsam, des Austausches, der Ergänzung willen; auch damit Reisende schneller auffinden können, was jedesmal in unsrer Sammlung für sie ein

höheres Interesse besitzen sollte."

69. Jensen, *Thomsens Museum...*, 69. 1992, p. 101.

70. Thiele & Rumohr 1835, p. 5 f.: "Obwohl die systematischen und sonstigen Schwächen dieser grossen Arbeit [Bartsch's *peintre graveur* and *Catalogue de Rembrandt*] der Commision nicht entgangen waren, hielt sie dennoch den Vortheil für überwiegend, den die Befolgung eines allbekannten und vielbenutzten Katalogs in mehr als einer Beziehung ihr gewährte: indem sie die Arbeit des Anordnens erleichterte, der aus besonderen Gründen eine nahe Grenze zu setzen war; indem sie den Gewöhnungen der Kenner und Liebhaber entsprach, welche siet langer Zeit jenem wichtigen Hülfsbuche sich angeschlossen haben."

71. Rumohr & Thiele, *Geschichte...*, 1835, p. 6 f.

72. Records of *Commisionen for den Kongelige Kobberstik-Samling*, Ms. Archives of The Department of Prints and Drawings, p. 9

73. Records of *Commisionen for den Kongelige Kobberstik-Samling*, Ms. Archives of The Department of Prints and Drawings, p. 17.

74. Thiele, *Aarbøger...*, vol II, p.31.

75. The sheets are mounted together and are identifiable by the record written on the mount in Thiele's hand.

76. Thiele, *Aarbøger...*, vol II, p. 34.

77. We owe the reference to Jan van der Waals.

78. Bloch, *Den Kgl. Kobberstiksamling...*, 1881. In the records of *Commisionen for den Kongelige Kobberstik-Samling*, Ms. Archives of The Department of Prints and Drawings, p. 19 ("Allerunderdanigste Indberetning. 26de Januar 1835"), it is stated that from early summer 1834 to the summer of the same year Thiele had removed, cleaned and together with the rest of the commission preliminarily arranged close to 30,000 sheets. Clearly, the work was advancing rapidly. On the following page it is explained that in the course of spring 1835 the commission expected to have arranged and remounted the most important part of the collection, namely the c. 10,000 prints by the older *peintre-graveurs*, which could be arranged in accordance with Bartsch's lists.

79. The publication, *Cabinet Royale d'Estampes à Copenhague*, was issued yearly in the period 1862-1869, cf. Ida Haugsted, "Kobberstiksamlingens første fotograf", *Kunstmuseets Årsskrift*, 1990, pp. 22-40.

80. Just Mathias Thiele, *Catalogue de la 1re Section du Cabinet Royal des Gravures à Copenhague...*, Copenhagen 1844; Just Mathias Thiele, *Haandbog i Den kongelige Kobberstiksamling*, Copenhagen 1863.

81. For further material on Thiele, cf. Th. Stein, *Just Mathias Thiele i hans Forhold til Kunstaka-*

*demiet, Thorvaldsens Museum og Kobberstiksamlingen*, Copenhagen 1897; Søren Plum, "Lille Idas far", *Politiken*, 13 Dec. 1995; Jørgen Birkedal Hartmann, "Dagli "annali" di Just Mathias Thiele biografo di Thorvaldsen", *Lazo ieri e oggi. Rivista mensile di cultura, arte e turismo*, anno XXXII, no. 3, 1996, pp. 78-82.

82. In 1844 Thiele edited a catalogue of duplicates and wanted sheets, *Catalogue de la 1re section du Cabinet Royale des Gravures à Copenhague suivi d'une liste de Doubles en échange*, Copenhagen 1844.

83. Notes on the history of The Department of Prints and Drawings in the 19th century by Bjørn Westerbeek Dahl (Ms. Archives of The Department of Prints and Drawings); Chris Fischer, "The Department of Prints and Drawings. A Brief Historical Survey", Chris Fischer et al., *A Sight for Sore Eyes...*, Copenhagen 1993, p. 11.

84. Bloch, *Den Kgl. Kobberstiksamling...*, 1881, p. 4 f.

85. Emil Bloch, Blade af Kobberstikkunstens Historie, Copenhagen 1879.

86. A large number of the ornamental prints are today deposited at The Danish Museum of Decorative Art. Bloch, *Den Kgl. Kobberstiksamling...*4, 1881, p. 142 remarks that many of them are very rare, and that the collection, which dates back to the time of Christian V (i.e., derives from Lambert van Haven), is therefore very valuable.

87. We know that already in the 1780s there were more than 76,000 sheets plus an unknown number distributed among 36 portfolios, and that there had been a very considerable growth following the establishment of the Department as an independent institution in 1843. The latter is described in Bloch, *Den Kgl. Kobberstiksamling ...*, 1881, pp. 6-9.

88. Jørgen Sthyr, *Gustav Falck*, Aarstiderne, vol. 3, no. 2, 1943, pp. 33-36.

89. Jørgen Sthyr & Erik Zahle, *Den Kongelige Kobberstiksamling...*, 1939, p. 38.

90. According to the deed of gift the donation comprised 101 paintings, 20 sculptural works, 7 ceramic works, 107 drawings, 15 watercolours and one lithograph, but it appears from the records that there were many more prints. Cf. Villads Villadsen, "Rumps samling af moderne fransk kunst", *Johannes Rump, Portrtæt af en samler*, exh. cat. Statens Museum for Kunst, Copenhagen 1994, p. 91.

91. Wilhelm Hansen also bought a number of paintings at the Degas Sale. These and other purchases were financed by a consortium created for the purpose of buying and re-selling works of art. The consortium had taken a loan from Landmandsbanken, and when the bank failed in 1922, Hansen decided to sell 76 paintings in order to settle the debt, cf. Marianne Wierenfeldt Asmussen, *Wilhelm Hansen's Original French Collection at Ordrupgaard*, 1993, pp. 24-31, 61-66.

92. Leo Swane, *Ved mit Vinduesspejl*, Copenhagen 1955; Peter P. Rohde in *Information* 13. 2. 1952; Bertel Engelstoft in *Politiken* 24. 1. 1968; Harald Olsen, "Leo Swane", *Kunstmuseets Årsskrift*, LIII-LVII, Copenhagen 1970, pp. 1-5.

93 Erik Fischer, "Erik Zahle", *Kunstmuseets Årsskrift*, LIII-LVII, Copenhagen 1970, pp. 6-11. For the guide to the Department's collections, which appeared in two editions, in 1939 and in 1946, cf. note 1.

94. Jørgen Sthyr, *Den Kgl. Kobberstiksamling. Fortegnelse over franske bøger illustreret med originalgrafik af kunstnere fra det 20. århundrede*, Statens Museum for Kunst, Copenhagen 1956.

95. Jørgen Sthyr, *Kobberstikkeren Albert Haelweg*, Kunstmuseets Årsskrift, XXV, Copenhagen 1938, pp. 5-69. In book form as a Festschrift, Copenhagen 1966.

96. Erik Fischer et al., *Den Kongelige Kobberstiksamling. Herbert Melbye's samling. En illustreret oversigt*. Statens Museum for Kunst, Copenhagen 1977.

97. For a catalogue, cf. Jan Würtz Frandsen, *Richard Mortensen: L'oeuvre graphique 1942-1943. Catalogue raisonné avec une introduction en danois et français*, Copenhagen 1995.

98. Vibeke Knudsen and Niels Borch Jensen, *Made in Denmark. Kobbertryk fra Niels Borch Jensens Værksted*, Lommebog 65, Den Kongelige Kobberstiksamling, Statens Museum for Kunst, Copenhagen 1994.

99. Rembrandt's etchings are almost completely represented in the Department. They were recently conserved and exhibited in 1996 together with loans from Rijksprentenkabinet in Amsterdam of the few works that the Department did not have; cf. Jan Garff, *Rembrandts raderinger*, Lommebog 70, Den Kongelige Kobberstiksamling, Statens Museum for Kunst, Copenhagen 1991.

100. Jan Garff, *Clairobscurtræsnit*, Lommebog 55, Den Kongelige Kobberstiksamling, Statens Museum for Kunst, Copenhagen 1991.

101. Erik Fischer, *Melchior Lorck i Tyrkiet / Melchior Lorck in Turkey*, Lommebog / Pocketbook 49-50, Den Kongelige Kobberstiksamling, Statens Museum for Kunst, Copenhagen 1990.

*Copper plate and print. C.F. Clemens (1748-1831): Princess Louise Augusta. 1785. Engraving after a painting by Jens Juel (1745-1802). (Department of Prints and Drawings).*

# PRINT TECHNIQUES

By Jan Garff

Distinction is traditionally made between four basic forms of print: *woodcut, engraving, etching and lithograph*. From a purely technical point of view these four forms represent three essentially different printing methods: *relief printing* (woodcut), *intaglio printing* (engraving and etching) and *planographic printing* (lithograph). These three methods form the basis of the following brief description of the fundamental print techniques and some of the most important variants of them.

## RELIEF PRINTING

*Woodcut* (cat. 11, 52, 55, 58, 61, 62 and 66) is the oldest printmaking technique. It is impossible with certainty to establish when and where it came into existence, but as early as the latter half of the 14th century producers of textiles used carved wooden blocks for stamping patterns onto fabric, and literary sources from the end of that century mention so-called blockcutters in Germany and France. The first dated woodcut is from 1418.

Until the middle of the 18th century woodcuts were produced with blocks of either pearwood or walnut. On a planed, smooth surface the artist drew the design he wanted to print and multiply. Sharp knives cut away the wood in places that in the final print would appear as white areas or lines. When such a block is inked, only the areas that stand out in relief will attract the ink. The block and a sheet of paper are then put under heavy pressure in a press, the ink leaving a reversed, stamped image on the paper. This is the most common procedure, although there are early examples of the motif being transferred to the paper by being rubbed with a folding stick or with light strokes of a brush. In rare cases the artist may avail himself of a thin doughy substance as mount for the image (paste print), and the block of wood may be replaced by a metal plate which is exposed to a veritable hailstorm of strokes from a puncheon. Such *metalcuts* were popular in the 15th century, whereas another form of relief printing: *linocut* has gained ground mainly in the present century. The simple and classic form of woodcut has been in almost continuous use throughout the entire history of printmaking, variants being popular for relatively short or longer periods. One of these is *xylography*, which was first used at about 1770 by the Englishman William Blake, but which was ousted by mechanical reproduction methods about a hundred years later. In contrast to the blockcutters of the early days, who used blocks of side grain, xylographers work with burins on hard end grain, normally of boxwood, in order to obtain the most precise and detailed rendering of the picture possible.

The techniques mentioned above all rely on the contrast between black and white; however it was not long before woodcuts coloured by hand emerged; this satisfied the natural need for colours in pictures, although it broke with the basic principle of printmaking: speedy and cheap multiplication of a picture. Probably as a consequence of this, *hand-coloured woodcuts* (cat. 1) were soon replaced by *colour woodcuts*, in Germany at about 1500, and somewhat later also by *chiaroscuro woodcuts* (cat. 8, 10, 13 and 21), separate blocks being used for each colour and shade. Recently new variants have emerged, such as relief etching, produced by means of a metal plate and an acid bath containing a mixture of nitric and pyroligneous acids.

## INTAGLIO PRINTING

Technically speaking, an *engraving* (cat. 2-6, 9, 12, 15, 18, 20, 22, 23 and 27), corresponds to a woodcut in the sense that the artist must work manually on a hard surface with sharp and pointed tools. The fundamental difference between the two methods lies in the fact that the grooves the engraver's burin produces in the plate will be visible in the finished print. When the laborious engraving work has been completed, the plate is inked and wiped immediately afterwards, so that ink remains only in the grooves. The print is made by passing the plate and a sheet of dampened paper through a press. The picture will stand out in slight relief, and the contours of the printing plate will be discernible as a platemark on the paper.

Closely related precursors of engravings are the so-called *nielli*, produced by goldsmiths since the beginning of the 15th century in deep engraving on small silver plates, the grooves being filled with black pigment. It is a short step from there to printing pictures on paper, and once the invention had been made, new variants appeared in rapid succession. As a supplement to pure *line engravings*, whose lines usually taper to fine points at either end, the beginning of the 16th century saw the introduction of *punch* or *stipple prints*, the picture being entirely based on a dense shower of dots made with punches or roulettes. This technique was particularly popular in England from about 1770, when Italian born Francesco Bartolozzi and the Englishman W.W. Ryland imported a French variant: *colour stipple*, which is especially suited to imitate miniatures. This was preceded by *colour engravings*, invented by the German J.C. le Blon, which rely on Newton's theory of the primary colours and their mixing in light, and which are produced by means of three plates: one blue, one yellow and one red. This again was preceded by yet another technique: *mezzotinto* (cat. 42 and 45), which was first used by another German, Ludwig von Siegen, who from 1642 and onwards created a number of sheets of great painterly beauty. To achieve the effect desired, the artist must use a serrated rocking tool to furrow the entire plate so densely with grooves that the surface ends up having a completely uniform, rough character. All that in the final print must appear as contours or light areas is then smoothed out with a scraper. The result is that there will be no lines. The picture arises from the meeting of deep velvety black and lighter silky tones. To some extent the mezzotint is a precursor of the colour engraving, and was further developed especially in 18th century England in the form of the *colour mezzotint*, which gradually ousted *hand-coloured engravings*, although such engravings remained in demand well into the following century. Probably on account of the general popularity of graphic art and the ensuing demand for impressions in larger numbers, the 19th century saw a temporary use of *steel engravings*, whose only dubious advantage is that they will wear practically for ever. The plate is extremely hard to work on, and artistically the result is rarely worth the while. The technique fell into disuse when a method was invented to *steel-face* copper plates, thus ensuring them greater durability. Generally speaking, all the intaglio techniques mentioned above are no longer used for artistic expression.

*Etchings*, however (cat. 14, 17, 24, 25a-c, 28, 29, 33, 34, 36, 39, 41, 47, 49, 67 and 69), which have been known since the beginning of the 16th century, are still highly popular. The earliest works in this technique were made on iron by German artists, Daniel Hopfer and Albrecht Dürer among them, but as the stains of rust that will crop up on *iron etchings* leave black smudges on the paper, iron was abandoned in favour of copper or zinc. After the plate has been heated, it is covered with an acid-resistant etching ground, which normally consists of wax, asphalt and resin. Whereas the engraver will have to work painstakingly with the burin in the hard surface of the plate, the etcher may freely draw his design in the etching ground with his needle - as easily as with a pencil on paper. When the design is complete, the plate is immersed in an acid bath, usually containing nitric acid, which bites into the areas of the plate which have been laid bare by the etching needle skating across the ground. The amount of time the plate has to remain in the bath depends on the strength of the acid and how deep and dark lines and areas the artist wants the print to have. The plate is then rinsed in water to stop the mordant from biting further into the material, the ground is removed by means of methylbenzene, the plate is cleansed with turpentine and the first proof can be made. From there the process is quite similar to the one used for engravings: inking, cleaning and finally the printing of the plate. Etchings hold obvious advantages over engravings: the artist can work more freely and is able to make corrections by re-covering (parts of) the plate with ground or exposing it to a second biting. On the other hand, etchings lack the extreme precision of engravings; occasionally, therefore, the two techniques are combined (cat. 26, 35, 37, 38, 40 and 44). An engraving may be begun by a slight acid biting, which loosely sketches the principal contours, which are then reinforced with a burin, or the artist may prefer to let the two techniques work directly together. In the same way the special effects of an etching may be reinforced by means of a pointed instrument, the artist scratching and scraping directly on the plate (cat. 16, 19, 30, 59 and 60) or an etching may be made entirely in this way. In the latter case the work is called *drypoint* (cat. 31) to emphasize the contrast to etching, which is the result of a chemical process. Engraving and drypoint are thus closely related techniques, but whereas the engraver meticulously removes the copper shavings (the burr) made by the burin furrowing its way across the plate, the etcher leaves them standing. This means that the lines - at least in the first few prints - appear broader and more blurred than in an etching, but this calculated effect is gradually weakened by the hard wear the plate is exposed to during the printing process. Naturally only a  limited number of quality sheets can be printed in this way.

Towards the end of the 18th century *colour etchings* gained ground, culminating in the following century. Either a single plate is selectively inked in different colours, or several plates are inked each with its own basic colour. The starting point is normally a special form of etching: *aquatint* (cat. 50, 53 and 75). The invention of this technique goes back to 1765 to the Frenchman Jean Baptiste Le Prince. The plate is dusted with powdered resin or asphalt; it is then heated from the back until the powder adheres to the plate, which now looks almost like a half-tone block. When the plate is later briefly immersed in an acid bath, only the areas not protected by the ground will be bitten. This results in a finely scarred surface which in the print manifests itself as vibrating interplay between small black and white dots. Normally they are so dense that the total impression is of a network of richly varied greys. Before the plate is grounded, the artist may apply his design to the plate as a line etching; since the technique is best suited for summary presentations, the various figures of the picture are normally designed in the aquatint ground with a brush. To obtain such a wash-like effect, a fairly strong solution of equal parts of concentrated nitric acid and water is used; the areas which in the final print are to appear pure white must be protected ("stopped out") with varnish.

This technique has many variants. One of the most common is *sugar aquatint*, produced in the following manner: the design is executed on a grounded metal plate with a brush and a liquid consisting mainly of sugar and gum arabic; the plate is then covered with a thin layer of varnish and immersed in hot water. The sugar dissolves and swells and in the course of a few hours it breaks through the protective film of the ground. Areas affected by the sugar swelling are vulnerable to the subsequent attacks of the acid. By repeating the process the artist may obtain a great variety of greys; the areas which have most often been brushed over with the sugar solution appear as the darkest parts in the final print. This technique was further developed in France by Jean François Janinet in the form of *colour aquatints*. Like the black-and-white version, this one may be confused with the *crayon manner*, which had been invented in 1757 by another Frenchman, Jean Charles François. The purpose was to find a method which would produce deceptive fac-similes of red and black chalk drawings. The invention fused two well-known tech-niques into one: engraving and *vernis mou*, which is really derived from the etching technique, but instead of working directly on the ground, the artist draws with a pencil on a sheet of paper placed on a plate prepared with a soft etching ground. When the paper is cautiously peeled off, parts of the soft ground will adhere to the back of the paper. This means that all the drawing process has transferred to the ground will now have attained a porous character, which after being bitten will leave grained lines in the finished print. A multi-colour variant of this technique is called the *pastel manner* and is, like so many other intaglio processes, a result of the graphic experimentation of the 18th century. The possibilities of the various techniques are still being explored today, and this often results in the creation of individual variants so sophisticated and complex that even an expert may have difficulty in defining what techniques have been used to achieve the final product.

**PLANOGRAPHIC PRINTING**
*Lithography* (cat. 43, 48, 54, 56 and 71) is the most common planographic technique. The method is often called flat or plain printing. These designations actually indicate how the method differs fundamentally from the two other basic graphic forms: the design is transferred to the paper from a flat surface. Formerly such a surface was a finely polished slab of porous limestone. Today specially treated fine-grained zinc or aluminium plates are generally used, occasionally also lithographic paper. Normally, the design is drawn on the surface with greasy chalk or ink. The ink may also be brushed or sprayed on to the surface. From here the process may take various courses - there are many methods and no general rules. But the decisive principle of the technique is always the chemical fact that water and grease repel each other. To put it briefly, the stone or plate is washed in an acid solution and then in a pure solution of gum, the design is wiped out with turpentine, the hardly discernible traces are brushed over with asphalt varnish, rubber and varnish are removed with a wet sponge, and the damp surface is inked; the ink, which is only attracted and held by the greased areas, is transferred to the paper in a lithographic press. The method was gradually developed in Munich between 1796 and 1799 by the German Alois Senefelder, who also invented a number of other, now partly forgotten planograph-ic techniques. The natural next step was *colour lithography*, which has now almost totally ousted the former monochrome type. One variant is *transfer lithography*, which offers the artist the advantage that there is no reversion of the picture, which is otherwise always the case. The design is made on specially prepared transfer paper which is laid face down on the lithographic stone, thus transferring the image. The print will therefore be a non-inverted reproduction of the original. This advantage for the artist does not necessarily mean that it is also an artistic advantage: the structure of transfer paper inevitably leads to more coarse-grained effects. Finally brief mention must be made of the most widespread form of planographic printing, *offset lithography* (cat. 68 and 70), which was first used in the United States in 1875. Well into the present century this new printing technique

chiefly served practical industrial purposes, and for about a hundred years it was - not unreasonably - considered a reproduction method that had nothing to do with original graphic art. From the beginning of the 1970s, however, the technique was used also artistically, at first in the country of its origin, later in the rest of the world, and it is now generally accepted as a form of original graphic art along with the more classic processes. Just like the transfer lithographic method, offset-lithography does not reverse the design in the final print. The original method transfers the design from film to printing plate by exposure to light. It is further transferred to a rubber blanket which prints it on paper. In this way the design is not in the reverse in the final print. Today it is even possible for the artist to draw and paint directly on the printing plate, which entails larger artistic freedom than ever before.

Within the comprehensive sphere of art on paper there exist a number of methods which can at best be called "kinds" of graphic art but which, despite mutual differences, have one thing in common: they cannot, with one exception, in any way be called printed graphic art. Even so, they are often confounded with this phenomenon, and some of them must therefore be mentioned here. The oldest among them is silk *screen printing*, also called *serigraphy* (cat. 65), a term coined in the United States at about 1940, which has again gained ground in the latter half of the present century, and which is now also widely used for industrial, non-artistic purposes. Screenprinting can be executed in two essentially different ways. One consists in drawing or painting with lithographic ink or chalk on a fine-mesh screen, originally of silk or organdie, nowadays also of synthetic material, fixed tautly over a wooden frame. The screen is then covered with a thin film of paste (filler); like water, paste is repelled by grease, so the lines and areas that make up the design will not be covered and may therefore be removed again (for instance with paraffin), when the paste has dried. The frame is then placed on a sheet of paper, and with a scraper (squeegee) the ink which has been formed into a thick roll is drawn across the screen. In the places where the paste has been removed, the ink is pressed through the screen on to the paper below. In contrast to traditional graphic print processes there is no reversion of the design. The method here described is called negative and corresponds - not quite unexpectedly - to a positive one, in which the areas that are to appear white in the final picture are covered with filler. The squeegee is drawn across the screen, pressing the ink through the uncovered areas. Instead of a filler a special film may be used, cut into stencils fastened to the screen. Generally this technique corresponds to the principle behind stencil prints. Just as with screenprinting, there is no real printing process; the design is simply cut out in cardboard, placed on a sheet of paper, and the uncovered areas inked. The contours will have sharp edges, as if cut out - in cardboard!

Fundamentally, all graphic print processes aim at multiplication. Not so *monotype* (cat. 32 and 51), which - as indicated by the name - confines itself to one single print. From a practical point of view the method is inadequate and recommendable only for aesthetic reasons. Monotype was first used some time in the 17th century, by the Italian G.B. Castiglione among others. Instead of creating his design directly on a sheet of paper, the artist paints or draws it on a smooth surface, the most classic form being a blank copper plate. From there it is transferred to the paper in an ordinary printing press or by being rubbed by hand. At best a few, often gradually deteriorating, prints can be made, sometimes called "ghosts" or "relatives". The design may be touched up again and another few prints made. It has been a matter of debate whether such prints can actually be called graphic prints. Perhaps they should be looked upon as a form of *Abklatsch* or *contre-*

*épreuve*, designations for prints which artists sometimes make of a charcoal or chalk draw-ing, for instance as a step in a graphic production process. Such an inverted picture may give the artist a good impression of what the final print will be like. By transferring it to the stone, block or plate he is using, he can apply it directly in the graphic process and end up with a non-inverted final product. Even farther from traditional graphic printing is *glass print* (cat. 46), which is nothing but a photographic print on sensitive paper of a glass plate in whose opaque film the artist has scratched his design with a point or needle. By means of a stiff brush he may also make toned areas. In French the technique is sim-ply called *cliché-verre* (glass cliché or glass negative), a very precise and unbiassed name for this specific graphic print variety, which goes back to the late 1830s in France, where it gained artistic recognition during the latter half of that century. A further development is the *photomechanical graphic process* (cat. 73), which is growing more and more popular. Because it bears an outward resemblance to the oldest print technique, woodcut, it seems to add an extra dimension of time to the history of graphic art.

*76 prints from the*
*Department of Prints and Drawings*

**1** **UNKNOWN ARTIST** *Dutch, active about 1460*
*Venus. c.1460. Page 5 from a Dutch block book on the seven planets.*

In the spring of 1928 assistant librarian Carl Dumreicher was going through Count Christian Lerche's collection of books, when he stumbled upon an old parchment cover "merely used as a well-protected hiding place for highly different and loosely inserted sheets of paper". Among the sheets were seven well-preserved, hand-coloured woodcuts; six of them were held together by a piece of brown string, the seventh being loose. Together they constitute a complete "Planet Book" with symbolic representations of the celestial bodies of Saturn, Jupiter, Mars, Sol, Venus, Mercury, Luna - in that order, the sun and the moon having taken the positions of the planets Uranus and Neptune, which had not been discovered at the time.

Soon the librarian's find proved to be of unique value for the world of books and art history. A Berlin Planet Book (Neues Museum), almost identical with the Lerche specimen, had so far been regarded as unique and published as such by Friedrich Lippmann in 1905. However, a close comparison of the two works revealed that only the woodcuts of Jupiter and Mars were identical, the rest demonstrating several differences of style, technique, and - not least - quality, to the disadvantage of the Berlin edition. It was therefore concluded that the newly found Danish copy was intact, the German one being a conflation of two prints from the original edition and five almost contemporary copies after it. Naturally, the question was carefully pondered whether they had been done directly after the Danish copy, but ultimately the idea had to be abandoned because of a single delicate detail soon to be disclosed.

Without digressions the seven woodcuts all follow the same compositional pattern. Inscribed in a circle at the top is the planet god or goddess in question, flanked by two smaller circles displaying the zodiacal attributes of the celestial body. Like flying streamers, scrolls present information on who is who. Below, small overcrowded plots display various everyday occurrences in stylized and steeply sloping landscapes, documenting some of the activities people born under a certain sign, so-called "planet children", are predestined to perform according to medieval astrology. Handwritten Latin texts on the versos of the sheets sum up the astrological implication of the signs in question. We are informed that the celestial body in the present sheet, Venus, is female and positioned in the third house of heaven. It is cold, moist, temperate, loves female clothes and ribbons of gold and silver as well as "ballads, amusements and jests". In itself it is lighthearted, has a charming voice, beautiful eyes and eyebrows, ...has a body which is smooth, full, and of medium height.

The woodcut is not an actual illustration of the text, which was probably added at a later date. In her hands Venus holds a mirror and a bunch of flowers, and an atmosphere of blissful luxury and leisure is reflected in the thorough cleaning process in the bathtub behind the well-provided table, and in the singing and music of the many musicians for the pleasure of two decorous loving couples. As appears from the corresponding Berlin sheet, there originally was a third couple - not quite as decorous - among the trees on the right. Almost every trace of their horizontal exercises has been deleted in this version, which therefore can not have served as model for the Berlin copy.

JG

*Handcoloured woodcut.*
*Platemark: 269 x 181 mm.*
*Sheet: 280 x 188 mm.*

Only known copy.
Verso: At top a text of ten lines in Latin: "Venus ... in se." (pen and brown ink).
Provenance: Library of Castle Lerchenborg, Zeeland; acquired here 1928, purchased by the Ny Carlsberg Foundation.
Inv.no. 10458.
Selected literature: Carl Dumreicher & Sofus Larsen, *Et Blokbogs-Fund i Danmark*, Aarhus 1929 (facsimile edition printed in 300 copies, of which 100 in trade): M.J. Schretlen; "Blokbogen 'De syv Planeter' ", in *Kunstmuseets Aarsskrift* 1929-31, bind XVI-XVIII, Copenhagen 1931, pp.1-15; W.L. Schreiber, *Handbuch der Holz- und Metallschnitte des XV. Jahrhunderts*, 3. Auflage, Stuttgart 1976, p.55f., pl.138; Jan Garff, "Ubekendt kunstner, Mercurius (ca.1460)", in *100 Mesterværker*, Statens Museum for Kunst, Copenhagen 1996, p.32f., repr. (English edition: *100 Masterpieces*, ibidem 1996, p.32f.).

**2**  MASTER E. S.  *German, active around the upper Rhine c.1450 - 1470*
*The Virgin Mary with the playing Christ Child and Saints Margaret and Catherine.*

The Master E.S. is known to have made more than 500 engravings, a large number of which have survived. Although it is clear that he was of decisive importance for the development of engraving in Germany in the second half of the 15th century, his name has been forgotten. His dated engravings - 14 in number - are all from 1466 and 1467. Together with stylistic similarities relating him to, among others, the pioneer in the German Renaissance, Konrad Witz (d. 1447), the watermarks in the paper used and the Alemannic dialect of the inscriptions on some of the sheets indicate an area of activity around the upper Rhine and in Switzerland. Thus he was active in the same area as Van Meckenem and Schongauer, the other leading engravers in Germany at the end of the 15th century. In his later years he drew inspiration from and made copies of works by Netherlandish artists like Rogier van der Weyden and Dirk Bouts. The Master E.S's technique is far more heterogeneous and varied than that applied by his contemporaries and his successors, which can probably be explained by the fact that he absorbed impressions from so many different sources. The result of this eclectic experimentation with techniques was that E.S. developed the art of engraving to a hitherto unknown refinement in the variation of line and modelling and was thus able to render materials and surfaces far better than his predecessors. According to Geisberg *The Large Hortus Conclusus* is the culmination of the Master's early work.

The motif of Mary in the Rose Garden was prominent in Rhenish painting, especially in Cologne, during the 15th century, but it was to be found throughout the entire western part of Central Europe between Northern Italy and Flanders. As devotional pictures for the cult of the Virgin Mary they and similar variations on the Virgin and Child motif became extremely popular, which is also indicated by their mass production in engravings. The function of the devotional picture was private and personal meditative contemplation of the sacred. As a rule devotional pictures contained a number of symbolic or allegorical elements. They turned the contemplation of the sacred into an eternally new journey to its many aspects. As regards "the enclosed garden" (*hortus conclusus*), all its elements are to be understood symbolically in relation to the Virgin. The garden itself, its wall, its gate, its roses, each of these represents different sides of Mary's holiness: her virginity, her function as a gateway for the divine, her identification with the Rose of Sharon, etc. This complex of Marian symbolism dates back to the theologian Honorius of Autun and his interpretation of the *Song of Solomon*. This concentration of textually founded meaning into every single detail on the basis of the view that the Bible's text is generally symbolic, metaphorical and allegorical may seem somewhat unnatural or incomprehensible to the modern viewer. In its day, however, the motif appealed to a broad public for - one must assume - the selfsame reasons, although its sweet, smiling sensuality probably made a not insignificant contribution to its popularity.

MBR

*Engraving.*
*Sheet: 219 x 162 mm.*
*Trimmed to platemark.*

Lehrs, 83.
A few scratches in the plate.
Provenance: Old property. Most probably part of Den Ældre Kobberstiksamling.
Inv. no. GB 1074.
Selected literature: M.Geisberg, *Die Anfänge des deutschen Kupferstichs und der Meister E.S.* (Meister der Graphik II), Leipzig 1909, p.77f.; M.Lehrs, *Geschichte und kritischer Katalog des deutschen, niederländischen und französischen Kupferstichs im XV. Jahrhundert*, Vienna 1908-1934, Vol.II (1910), 153f., no.83; *Meister E.S. Ein oberrheinischer Kupferstecher der Spätgotik*, exh., Staatliche Graphische Sammlung München / Kupferstichkabinett Berlin, Staatliche Museen Preußischer Kulturbesitz, Berlin 1987.

**Master E. S.**
*The Virgin Mary with the playing Christ Child and Saints Margaret and Catherine*

**3** ATTRIBUTED TO **ANDREA MANTEGNA**   *Italian, Isola di Cartura? 1431 - Mantua 1506*
*Christ in Limbo.*

Christ's visit to Limbo is treated in the apocryphal gospel of Nicodemus. Here we read that Jesus delivered a number of Old Testament prophets and patriarchs who had not been damned but who could not enter Paradise until God had sacrificed his Son to expiate the sin of Adam and Eve. The visit to Limbo became an emblem of Christ's justice and his victory over death, and it was incorporated into the Creed despite the fact that there is no mention at all of the episode in the New Testament. Mantegna treated the subject several times, perhaps under the impression of Jacopo Bellin's drawing in his sketchbook, now in Paris, and Donatello's dramatic relief in Florence. This print shares many features with these works: the descent into Limbo passes through a gateway in a rock, the gates have been torn off their hinges and lie in pieces at Christ's feet. The Saviour is stretching out his hand to the just; Adam and Eve, standing on the right, are represented as old and emaciated, devils are flapping around blowing horns, a male figure is holding his ears against their ear-splitting noise. The man with the Cross is the Good Thief Dismas, whom Christ promised to take with him to Paradise. There has never been any doubt that the engraving was executed on the basis of a drawing by Mantegna himself. Hitherto, scholars have believed that the engraving was carried out by a member of Mantegna's workshop because the graduations in the shaded areas are not as delicate as those in prints known to be by Mantegna, but in the catalogue for the Mantegna exhibition in New York in 1992-1993 David Landau argued that it was the Master himself who did the engraving. There is nothing mechanical or uncertain in the way in which the figures are treated. The print is based on a reversed pen drawing on parchment in the Ecole des Beaux-Arts, Paris. Although the figures are of exactly the same size, the distances between them are different, which is probably due the tracing having taken place in a number of stages, during which the paper became displaced in relation to the plate. There are variations in some of the details, and the figure of Eve in the drawing has not been completed. It is not very likely that Mantegna would have left the preliminary drawing unfinished if it had been intended for another engraver. It is also improbable that another artist would have taken liberties in relation to the preparatory drawing. The somewhat rougher quality of the print in relation to those known with certainty to be by Mantegna can probably be ascribed to the fact that it is not entirely finished. The delicate lines between the coarser parallel hatchings, which give the prints known to be by Mantegna their special tone, are in part lacking. The sky, the landscape and the rocks are represented in relatively little detail, and the slipped strokes and errors have not been burnished away.

The hypothesis that this is an authentic but unfinished print would also explain why a print like ours, executed after Mantegna's death, is far more fresh than the corresponding prints of the generally accepted and completed engravings. Mantegna of course pulled many impressions of the completed engravings, thus wearing down the plates already in his lifetime, while he pulled only a few trial impressions from the unfinished plates, which therefore produced good impressions when one began to reprint them after his death.

CF

*Engraving.*
*Sheet: 437 x 345 mm.*
*Trimmed at top and bottom and to platemark at the right and left.*

Hind, V, 9.
Watermark: Oval ?
Inscribed verso in pencil: "Mantegna/B.5".
Provenance: Captain G.D.Schaper; his sale, Copenhagen 5.3.-2.4. 1855, lot 363; acquired here.
Inv. no. GB 1075.
Selected literature: Jacquelyn L. Sheehan, in Jay A. Levenson, Konrad Oberhuber and Jacquelyn L. Sheehan, *Early Italian Engravings from the National Gallery of Art*, exh., National Gallery of Art, Washington 1973, p. 208, no.80; R.W.Lightbown, *Mantegna*, Oxford, Berkeley and Los Angeles 1986, p. 492, no. 216; David Landau, in Jane Martineau (ed.), *Andrea Mantegna*, exh., Royal Academy of Arts, London / Metropolitan Museum of Art, New York 1992, pp.258-272, no.67a,b; Chris Fischer, *Ruinmani*, Lommebog 68, exh., Den Kongelige Kobberstiksamling, Statens Museum for Kunst, Copenhagen 1995, pp. 9-10.

*Andrea Mantegna: Christ in Limbo. Drawing. École des Beaux-Arts, Paris.*

Attributed to **Andrea Mantegna**
*Christ in Limbo*

**4**  **SCHOOL OF MANTEGNA** *Italian, c.1495 - 1500*
*Virtus Deserta.*  *(Allegory of the Salvation of Mankind).*

This sheet is the lower part of an engraving representing an allegory of Ignorance and Reason. The upper half shows Ignorance enthroned, surrounded by a suite of prophets, pushing Mankind, represented by a naked female figure, towards the fall. The lower part shows the path to salvation, which is possible only with the help of Mercury, inventor of the sciences and patron of the arts, messenger of divine Reason.

While both halves form a conceptual whole, they are made up of two separate, complete and independent compositions. The engravings was executed on two sides of the same plate, printed on separate sheets and only then united. Thus Mantegna made a separate drawing for each composition. The drawing for the upper part is in the British Museum, London, while the drawing for the lower part has not survived.

This composition demonstrates with the clarity of a diagram two characteristic moments in the style of Mantegna and his school - archaeological knowledge and strict asceticism. Filled with numerous hints comprehensible only to the educated few, such works were intended for a narrow circle of educated humanists who were able to appreciate the new art.

To the left we see a female figure in the process of transformation into a laurel tree, with an explanatory tablet - *Virtus Deserta*. Her significance is indicated by a passage from *Dialogo della Virtu contro la Fortuna*, written by Giovanni Battista Alberti in 1450 - the world is so imperfect that Virtue, like Daphne, turns into a tree. In the centre, in a narrow ditch, pressed in by stone walls, is mankind, victim of its own blindness. Mercury, god of knowledge, is mankind's only hope, only with his aid can Man rise from that low state to which he has been led by blind Fortune and Ignorance.

Despite the multi-layered allusions to Classical mythology, the compositional scheme of this engraving recalls a canonical subject from Christian mythology, the Descent into Limbo. Mantegna himself turned repeatedly to the theme (cf. cat. 3). The semi-circular arch in the cliff which symbolises the entry into Hell can obviously be identified with the firmly closed door shown in the engraving we see here. Thus Mercury fulfills the mission of Jesus Christ, but there is clearly a cardinal difference between them. Mercury the Liberator nonetheless remains in the enclosed space, while in the Descent into Limbo the broken-down gates provide an exit to eternal freedom, which is heavenly bliss. Reason-Mercury, who liberates from the grasp of Ignorance, cannot give such freedom, and so Man nonetheless remains imprisoned by earthly life. Antiquity, associated with reason and with art, is but 'a vocabulary of flight', as Peter Greenaway entitled his essay on this engraving in the catalogue *Le bruit des nuages* - while for free flight one has need above all of faith.

Due to its high quality this engraving is usually ascribed to Andrea Zoan, In the catalogue of the Mantegna exhibition in London and New York (1992), it is attributed to Giovanni Antonio da Brescia and described as one of his best works, but it is almost impossible to identify the artist with absolute certainty since all thoughts on the technique and style of engravers in the circle of Mantegna are doomed to subjectivity. It is, however, evident that this print was created by an engraver very close to Mantegna, perhaps under his direct supervision.

AI

*Engraving.*
*Sheet: 305 x 436 mm.*
*Trimmed to platemark.*

Bartsch, 17.
Watermark: Indiscernable.
Inscribed in the plate on the overturned stele bottom left: "VIRTV / TI / ·S · A · I·" and on the tablet at an allegorical figure to the left:"VIRTVS / DESERTA".
Inscribed recto, bottom left in pen and brown ink with monogram: "AD"; verso, to the right of centre, below centre in pencil in Emil Bloch's hand: "Zoan Andrea / B 17" and at bottom edge to the right of centre in pencil and another hand: "396,1".
Provenance: Old property.
Inv.no. GB 1039.
Selected literature: F.M. Massing, *Du texte à l'image: la Calomnie d'Appelles et son iconographie*, Strasbourg 1990; David Landau, "Mantegna as Printmaker" and Suzanne Boorsch, "Mantegna and his Printmakers", in Jane Martineau (ed.), *Andrea Mantegna*, exh., Royal Academy of Arts, London / Metropolitan Museum of Art, New York 1992, pp.44-67; Peter Greenaway, *Le bruit des nuages*, exh., Musée du Louvre, Paris 1992.

*School of Mantegna: Virtus Combusta. Engraving.*

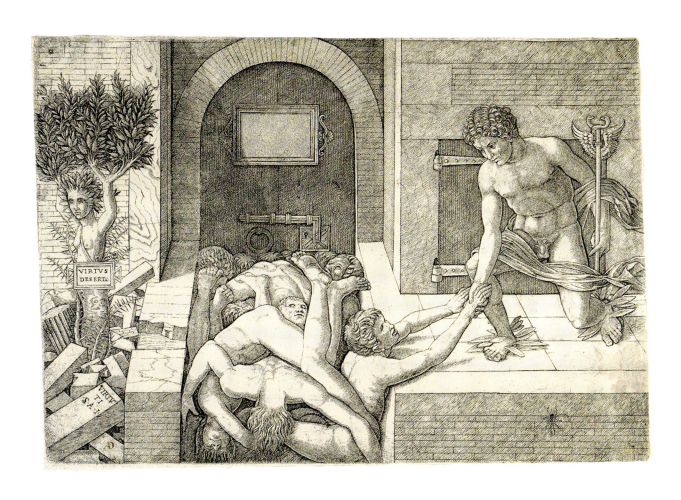

**School of Mantegna**
*Virtus Deserta*

**5** **ISRAHEL VAN MECKENEM** *German, Bocholt or Cleve? c.1445 - 1503*
*Ornament with lovers.*

The sophisticated art of filling a surface with complex, interlaced ornamentation was practised in Northern Europe from the early Middle Ages, especially in book illuminations, where it filled out a margin or constituted a decorative field for an initial letter at the beginning of a text. This decorative and playful form of art could also carry meaning and was to be found both in serious spiritual contexts and also in more mundane settings, such as wallpapers or friezes.

Van Meckenem, by far the most prolific (and for that matter also the most reproductive) of all graphic artists in the 15th century, executed a whole series of different decorative sheets, all of them characterised by a density of detail that seems to express a "horror vacui". In this compulsion to produce crowded, elegant total decoration Meckenem was continuing a late-Gothic tradition which survived into early Renaissance Germany more strongly than elsewhere in Europe. Van Meckenem's talent for the execution of these ornaments is seen not least in his ability to give equal value to figure and ornament, so that both are displayed in a flat relief-like space without appearing cramped.

In the interlaced thistle stems, which are symmetrically arranged, but nevertheless always individualised, various birds, animals and little naked humans are at play. Top centre an elegantly dressed pair of lovers are courting. They could be taken right out of one of the representations of "Liebesgarten" that were so common in that period, where the same kind of young, rich and beautiful men and women abandon themselves entirely to temporal desires - often in the company of a fool or a devil to indicate the foolishness and dangerousness of this sinful and apparently so carefree way of life.

Lasciviousness is in fact the keynote of this sheet. The many thistles surrounding the lovers were considered to be aphrodisiacs, and the little naked figures are partially represented as wild men, which suggests a satyric atmosphere. Some of the mannikins are enjoying the fruits of the plant, as are a dog and a crane. On the woman's lap lies a cat, a symbol of both vanity and lust, and the man is offering a fruit to the woman, which she is about to accept as if this was a new variant of the Fall of Man.

Thus, all the sheet's decorative and therefore apparently neutral elements prove to be imbued with connotations of sexual frivolity, leaving no doubt as to the moralising intention behind the beautiful ornamentation.

*MBR*

*Engraving.*
*Sheet: 171 x 246 mm.*
*Trimmed to platemark, except at the top, where there is a narrow margin.*

Bartsch, 205.
Signed in the plate top centre: "Israhel - V - M".
Watermark: Gothic P with a crown (Piccard XVI, 301-371: Burgundy, known c.1480-1510). A few barely discernable scratches in the plate.
Provenance: Old property.
Inv. no. GB 1076.
Selected literature: Max Geisberg, *Israhel van Meckenem*, Strassburg 1905, no.471, 218; A.Warburg, *Israhel van Meckenem. Sein Leben, sein Werk und seine Bedeutung für die Kunst des ausgehenden 15.Jahrhunderts* (Forschungen zur Kunstgeschichte Westeuropas VII), Bonn 1930, Taf.29.

**Israhel van Meckenem**
*Ornament with lovers*

**6**  **MARTIN SCHONGAUER**  *German, Colmar c.1450 - Breisach 1491*
*The Archangel Michael Fighting the Dragon.  c.1477/78.*

Martin Schongauer was the first great German engraver to emerge from anonymity. He achieved European fame already in his lifetime, and among the artists inspired by his style was Albrecht Dürer, who during his wanderyears decided to visit Schongauer in the city of Colmar only to arrive there shortly after the Master's death in 1491. Schongauer brought the technique of engraving to a stage that remained unsurpassed by his successors for many years. The technical brilliance of his prints, the statuary weight of his figure groups, the elegance of his lines and the strong expressions of his characters made them a model for a whole generation of artists, who kept them as workshop material either for inspiration or to be used as patterns for later works. In prints like *St Michael* one senses Schongauer's virtuousity in the convincing rendering of different kinds of surfaces by means of the burin. At the same time he bestows upon his compositions a rounded natural space. The composition emerges as a harmonious whole although the artist renders opposing strong and dynamic forces in both form and content.

The counterbalance between the Archangel's hand and the monster's claw on the shaft of the lance - placed at the centre of the composition - is in itself an image of the struggle and victory of the good and beautiful against the evil and ugly, where the clean form of the lance stands like a lever in terms of composition as well as meaning. The Archangel is imbued with a calm serenity that is typical of the so-called "international gothic". This serenity radiates from the idealised, stoical and assured face and is reinforced by the closed surface of the mantle and the clear-cut lines of its contour. The body of the monster beneath his feet, on the other hand, is presented in its writhing, stabbing, rattling death struggle as brutal, wild, split and utterly in conflict with itself; nothing is turned inwards and gathered together, everything seems to be falling apart. Its grotesque limbs express only desperate and powerless convulsions, and its surface is dissolved into pincers and claws, tentacles, thick hair and thorns.

MBR

*Engraving.*
*Sheet: 161 x 110 mm.*
*Trimmed to platemark.*

Good impression. A few scratches in the plate.
Bartsch, 58.
Signed in the plate, bottom centre with monogram of Martin Schongauer.
Provenance: Heinrich Anton Cornill-d'Orville (1790-1875) (Lugt, 529); his sale at Amsler & Ruthardt, Berlin, 4.4 and the following days 1903, lot 2001; acquired here.
Inv.no. 4729.
Selected literature: S.Renouard de Bussierre, *Martin Schongauer. Maitre de la gravure rhenane vers 1450-1491*, exh., Musée du Petit Palais, Paris 1991/92, no.91, 236; H.Krohm & J.Nicolaisen (ed.), *Martin Schongauer. Druckgraphik im Berliner Kupferstichkabinett* (Bilderheft der Staatlichen Museen Preußischer Kulturbesitz Heft 65/66), Berlin 1991, no.22, 119, Abb.36; *Le beau Martin. Gravures et dessins de Martin Schongauer (vers 1450-1491)*, exh., Musée d'Unterlinden, Colmar 1991, no.G100, 402f.; N.G.Stogdon, *Martin Schongauer* (Catalogue X), Hampshire 1996, no.20.

**Martin Schongauer**
*The Archangel Michael Fighting the Dragon.  c.1477/78*

**7** **ALBRECHT DÜRER**  *German, Nurenberg 1471 - Nurenberg 1528*
*The Great Cannon. 1518.*

*The Great Cannon* is a strange work of art. On closer inspection the apparently simple content becomes difficult to explain. The German lansquenet by his cannon, which is pointing in the direction of a little cluster of houses in a German landscape, where a horse is peacefully grazing in a field between a chapel for wayfarers and a church, does not really seem to fit in with the turbaned man in the foreground towards whom he is looking. The men gathered behind the Turk seem to be waiting for something to happen. There is a tense atmosphere in the composition, a quiet before the storm, as if the lansquenet, the Turk and the cannon are a threat to the little town below them, an incomprehensible and malevolent alliance.

At the time when this etching was made, the Germans and Turks were at war. After the fall of Constantinople in 1453 the Turks - the infidels - were on European ground, and the need for solidarity and resistance to this danger was becoming increasingly urgent, while internal European dissensions were making such a resistance more and more unlikely. The danger soon proved to be real. Only 10 years after the etching was made, the Turks had subjected Hungary and were beseiging Vienna.

The anxiety caused by the Turkish threat and the lack of reaction to it led to conspiracy theories especially in the German Lands. It is possible that Dürer has represented this concern about an unholy alliance in which Germans were used by the enemy against their own people. As so often with Dürer's single sheets, however, it is not possible to give a straight-forward interpretation, since Dürer was a master of hints, allegories and riddles that could stimulate the scholarly viewer to read the sheets not only as a visual but also as an intellectual exercise.

This copy is unusually well preserved and, furthermore, an early and perfect impression of great clarity with both platemark and margin. Iron etchings of this standard, without any sign of rust marks, are extremely rare.

MBR

*Iron etching.*
*Platemark: 217 x 327 mm.*
*Sheet: 233 x 337 mm.*

Early impression "before all rustmarks" (cf. Meder).
Bartsch, 99.
Watermark: High crown (M.31).
Signed in the plate, top left with Albrecht Dürer's monogram and dated "1518".
Provenance: Old property. Most probably Den Ældre Kobberstiksamling, possibly in the Royal collections since 1521 when Dürer presented King Christian II with a selection of his prints. Inv. no. GB 1077.
Selected literature: J.Meder, *Dürer-Katalog. Ein Handbuch über Albrecht Dürers Stiche, Radierungen, Holzschnitte, deren Zustände, Ausgaben und Wasserzeichen*, Vienna 1932, no.96, 108; Erik Fischer, *Albrecht Dürer. Kobberstik og Raderinger i Den kongelige Kobberstiksamling, Statens Museum for Kunst*, Copenhagen 1971, no.78; F.Anzelewsky, *Dürer-Studien. Untersuchungen zu den ikonographischen und geistesgeschichtlichen Grundlagen seiner Werke zwischen den beiden Italienreisen*, Berlin 1976.

**Albrecht Dürer**
*The Great Cannon. 1518*

# 8 LUCAS CRANACH THE ELDER  *German, Kronach 1472 - Weimar 1553*
## *St Christopher. c.1509.*

Cranach was one of the pioneers of coloured printing. In a letter from 1508 to Maximilian I, Emperor of the Holy Roman Empire, his secretary Konrad Peutinger writes enthusiastically of Cranach's woodcut from 1507 representing St George. It was printed in black and gold on blue-dyed paper, and Peutinger immediately saw the possibilities of starting a production of highly luxurious prints. He gave Hans Burgkmair from Augsburg the task of further developing this type of woodcut. The result was - thanks not least to Burgkmair's outstanding block cutter Jost de Negker - the first actual chiaroscuro woodcuts with different tone blocks: first a St George on horseback (1508) and later an equestrian portrait of Emperor Maximilian (1509-10). The coloured surfaces were produced with the aid of differently coloured blocks, which allowed the untreated white paper - in some case parchment - to shine through to produce the effect of heightening.

*St Christopher* is dated 1506 in early impressions, but this dating has been removed from our sample. It was not until January 1508 that Cranach received permission from his prince, Frederick the Wise, to use the winged snake as his coat of arms, and it is not found on any Cranach's works prior to 1509. So the original dating on the plate is probably too early and a manipulation on Cranach's part. The reason for this may have been vanity - a wish to appear as the actual inventor of the technique - and it is likely that Cranach used the dating in a competition to gain Emperor Maximilian and Frederick the Wise's favour with a view to further commissions for such prints. Thus, Burgkmair's experiments appear to have been made as prototypes for a production of imperial gifts to members to the Order of the Knights of St George with its associated Society of St George and Brotherhood of St George, which were strongly supported by the Emperor.

Like many other of Maximilian's often grandiose plans this production was never realised - it remained at the prototype stage. The Christopher sheet and the story attached to it do, however, indicate that in Germany at the transition from the Middle Ages to the Renaissance there was something akin to a policy for the arts, and that efforts were made at the very top level to develop the potential of the graphic arts as effective, serially produced propaganda. It was this potential, though at a much less exclusive level, that Cranach himself was soon to exploit in every conceivable form, once the Reformation got under way.

MBR

*Chiaroscuro woodcut with one line block and one grey tone block. The two blocks are not precisely adapted to each other. Image: 285 x 202 mm. Sheet: 290 x 209 mm.*

Late state. The original date (1506) has been erased from the block.
Bartsch, 58.
Signed top left in the line block with Cranach's signature and a winged dragon.
Provenance: Old property.
Inv. no. GB 1078.
Selected literature: Dieter Koeplin & Tilman Falk, *Lukas Cranach. Gemälde, Zeichnungen, Druckgraphik*, exh., Kunstmuseum Basel, 1974, Vol.I,63, Vol.II.,644f.; G.Bartrum, *German Renaissance Prints 1490-1550*, British Museum, London 1995, no.175, 172f.

*Lucas Cranach the Elder: St George and the Dragon, c.1507. Colour woodcut with two line blocks, one black, one in gold, on blue prepared paper, partly scraped to give the effect of high lights. British Museum, London.*

*The original date in the block. Detail from: Lucas Cranach the Elder, St Christopher, c.1509. Chiaroscuro woodcut with one tone block in reddish brown and one line block in black. British Museum, London.*

*Hans Burgkmair the Elder: The mounted emperor Maximilian I., 1508. Colour woodcut with two line blocks, one in silver and gold, one in black, on light red prepared paper. British Museum, London.*

**Lucas Cranach the Elder**
*St Christopher. c.1509*

**9**  MARCANTONIO RAIMONDI  *Italian, Argini c.1475/80 - before 1534*
**AGOSTINO DEI MUSI,** CALLED **VENEZIANO**  *Italian, Venice c.1490 - 1536*
*Lo Stregozzo. The Carcass.  After Giulio Romano ?*

*The Carcass* is one of the most mysterious Italian engravings of the 16th century. In turning to a subject linked with black magic, the artist whimsically intertwines Antiquity and medieval legends. Against the backdrop of a swampy landscape moves a strange procession. An old woman with flowing hair is seated on the skeleton of some unknown animal which forms a strange chariot, guided by four naked athletes. In front of her are a mass of woeful children, clearly intended for some cruel and bloody sacrifice. The strange cortege is accompanied by goats, a semi-naked boy blowing into a twisted horn, and other fantastical skeletons.

Swamps were always associated with dark forces, particularly in German legends. That the figure of the old woman dominating the procession is borrowed from Dürer's engraving *The Witch* (B.67) brings *Lo Stregozzo* even closer to northern medieval legends about witches. But unlike the northern witches' sabbath, most frequently depicting a gathering of witches of different ages hastening to pay their respects to the Devil, Marcantonio shows us a triumphal procession worthy of any Classical god. If it were not for the skeletons and the weeping children going to their deaths, the whole procession would recall some bacchanalia. The similarity with Classical processions has led to the suggestion that the engraving shows Hecate, dweller of the underworld and ancient goddess of black magic. But Hecate's chariot should be drawn by dogs, and the goddess herself was usually depicted as three-faced, with a burning torch, which leaves the identity of this witch with her magnificent cortege unsolved.

Nor do we know the author of the original composition. Michelangelo was a clear influence as many elements recall figures from his cartoon *The Battle of Cascina.* The figure of the youth in the foreground, holding the body of a child under his arm, is a version of a soldier in Raphael's cartoon (Paris, Louvre,) for the *Battle of the Milvian Bridge*, executed by Giulio Romano in the *Sala di Constantino* in the Vatican. The combination of influence from Michelangelo and Raphael, a tendency towards Classicism and at the same time a love of naturalistic details such as the depiction of the rushes and the flying ducks, all indicate that Giulio Romano may have been the author of the drawing from which the engraving was made.

The name of the engraver is also open to question. We know of four states of the engraving: with an empty tablet (the mark of Marcantonio); with the letters AV (Agostino Veneziano) engraved on the tablet; with the initials excised; and the last state, when the initials AV appear on the boy's horn. The link between the initials AV and the tablet indicate a collaboration between Marcantonio and Agostino Veneziano, such as in the engravings *King Solomon and the Queen of Sheba* (B.18) and *The Emperor Freeing the Slave Androcles* (B.196), but this engraving is very different to either of the others. The sheet was probably completed by Agostino Veneziano, who would seem to have touched only some insignificant details, for the style of the engraving is fully in keeping with the late works of Marcantonio himself.

The print reveals an interest in the magical side of the Underworld, in life after death, the dark, Dionysian source of Ancient mythology. This Dionysian approach was alien to the High Renaissance and it is in Mannerism that we see the birth of this idea, so important to the modern mentality.

AI

*Engraving.*
*Platemark: 305 x 641 mm.*
*Sheet: 311 x 644 mm.*

First state of four.
Bartsch 426[I].
Inscribed verso, bottom centre in pencil in Emil Bloch's hand: "Aug. Ven. B 426 I".
Provenance: Old property.
Inv.no. GB 1040.
Selected literature: *Raphael Invenit. Stampe da Raffaello nelle collezioni dell'Isituto Nazionale per la Grafica*, exh., Rome 1985, p.262; Bruce Paris, *Mannerist Prints. International Style in the Sixteenth Century*, exh., Los Angeles County Museum of Art 1988, pp.110-113.

**Marcantonio Raimondi**
and **Agostino dei Musi,** called **Veneziano**
*Lo Stregozzo. The Carcass*

## 10   UGO DA CARPI   *Italian, Carpi c. 1480 - Bologna 1532*
### *Diogenes.*   *After Francesco Mazzola, called Parmigianino*

*Diogenes* is Ugo da Carpi's major work, monumental in its dimensions and executed in the rather rough technique of the chiaroscuro woodcut, which heightens the effect of the masterly composition. The cynic Diogenes, who lived in the 4th century B.C., was famous for his contempt for man's material needs, which is why the philosopher is portrayed absorbed in his reading, very lightly clad and placed in front of the barrel that constituted his simple home. The plucked hen on the right is a reference to Diogenes' mockery of Plato, who had defined man as a featherless, two-legged creature.

As shown by the inscription at the bottom, the composition derives from Parmigianino and was perhaps executed after a drawing that has now been lost. Both Parmigianino and Ugo da Carpi were in Rome in the years up to 1527, when Charles V's troops took and plundered the city, which forced the artists living there to leave. Both artists went to Bologna, where - according to Vasari - this woodcut was produced. A second possibility is that Ugo da Carpi worked from a more or less contemporary print by Gian Giacomo Caraglio of the same motif. This possibility is supported by the fact that Parmigianino seems otherwise only to have provided compositions for chiaroscuro woodcuts to the printer Antonio da Trento.

In 1515 Ugo da Carpi applied to the Venetian senate for a copyright on his hitherto production of chiaroscuro woodcuts, claiming in his application to have invented the technique. Although it is more likely that the invention was made by contemporary German printers, Ugo da Carpi was probably the first Italian artist to work in this technique, which he perfected. In the earliest chiaroscuro woodcuts, which use only two blocks, the black colour corresponds to the motif more or less as in an ordinary woodcut. However, in woodcuts like *Diogenes*, which were executed with a greater number of blocks, the black colour corresponds to shading and only affords a meaning when printed together with the other coloured blocks and the areas where the white paper is revealed. Through this modulation of tones from light to dark, chiaroscuro, the woodcut comes to resemble a drawing on coloured paper, where the artist is able to work up and down in light and dark tones with the help of pen and ink, wash and pure white.

Ugo da Carpi probably started his artistic career as a painter in his own region, but without achieving much success, Thus, Vasari relates the curious but condescending anecdote that one of his paintings was done with his fingers. From about 1509 Ugo da Carpi was active in Venice, where he executed woodcuts for book illustrations, more or less freely copied from Dürer and Titian. Around 1517 he settled in Rome, where he reproduced Raphael's compositions in the new technique. His reputation in this field has led to a very large number of chiaroscuro woodcuts being attributed to him in the course of time. Today, however, Ugo da Carpi is only believed to have produced 14 woodcuts using this technique.

JM

*Chiaroscuro woodcut with four tone blocks in black, brown and two yellows. Sheet: 483 x 356 mm. Trimmed to the image.*

Second state of two.
Bartsch, 10.
Inscribed verso in pencil: "B XII. VI. No10."
Signed in the most bright of the two yellow tone blocks, bottom left: "FRANCISCUS / PARMEN. / PER UGO CARP."
Watermark: Crown above circle with oneheaded eagle.
Provenance: Old property.
Inv. no. GB 1079.
Selected literature: Jan Johnson, "I chiaroscuri de Ugo da Carpi/ Ugo da Carpi's clairobscur woodcuts", in *Il coniscitore de Stampe*, vols 3 and 4, nos 57-58, 1982, pp. 2-87, no. 15; Bruce Davis, *Mannerist Prints. International Style in the Sixteenth Century*, exh., Los Angeles County Museum of Art, Los Angeles 1988, no. 19 (with bibliography).

**Ugo da Carpi**
*Diogenes*

**11**  **ALBRECHT ALTDORFER**  *German, Regensburg c.1482/85 - Regensburg 1538*
*St Christopher. 1513.*

St Christopher carrying the the Infant Christ across a river was a vastly popular motif in German art throughout the 15th and in the beginning of the 16th century. It is already well represented among the earliest preserved prints.

Briefly recounted, the legend tells the story of the giant Christopher (the Greek root of the name means Christ-bearer), who seeking to serve the highest master in the world at first follows the Devil, whom so many fear, but realises that the Devil himself fears the sign of the cross. A hermit teaches him about the cross and Christ, and as a way of serving Christ Christopher is given the task of helping people across a river by carrying them on his back. One day without knowing it he is carrying the Infant Christ across the river and feels the weight on his shoulders becoming heavier and heavier as if he were carrying the whole world, until he is finally close to being pressed down beneath the waves. Christ then explains to him that he has carried more than the whole world since he has carried the creator of the world, after which he himself baptises Christopher in the river.

Christopher was the patron saint of travellers, and the motif was regarded as a lucky charm that could afford protection against a violent or unshriven death on the day that one looked at it. This appears from, among other things, the short passages of text that are occasionally to be found on the woodcuts. For travellers, therefore, it was practical to have small and transportable mass-produced pictures of St Christopher on them, which is undoubtedly part of the explanation of the frequency with which they appear in the prints of the period. At times the cult of St Christopher was so intense that it almost assumed the character of idolatory, as can be seen in Erasmus of Rotterdam's *The Praise of Folly* from 1509.

The woodcut is unique in Altdorfer's oeuvre and an impressive example of the experiments with the medium that he started on after Dürer's publication in 1511 of "The Three Great Books", which set new standards for the art of the woodcut. Only here with St Christopher does Altdorfer succeed in transferring his free and lively lines to the medium of the woodcut. The result is neither stiff nor more conventional than in his drawings. At the same time the characteristic traits of the woodcut are displayed in their full potential.

The dramatic use of upward-seeking lines in the tree, St Christopher's staff and the mountain ridge in the background give the composition a dynamic power, as if these inanimate elements were helping to press the giant to his knees - it as if the diagonals are pushing him down in the same direction as that towards which the little hand of the child is also pointing.

One of the most striking features of the woodcut is its effective economy of means, especially with regard to the mountain ridge. The reason for this may be that the block was originally conceived as a line block for a chiaroscuro woodcut, and that the tone block(s) was (were) never completed, possibly because the image of the line block was in itself so satisfactorily different and interesting.

MBR

Woodcut.
*166 x 120 mm. Trimmed to the image.*

Very good, early impression. Two small cracks in the block: bottom of St Christopher's mantle and in the frame bottom left and top right.
Bartsch, 53.
Signed in the block with Altdorfer's monogram and dated "1513".
Watermark: Unicorn.
Provenance: Old property.
Inv. no. GB 1080.
Selected literature: Hans Mielke, *Albrecht Altdorfer. Zeichnungen, Deckfarbenmalerei, Druckgraphik*, exh., Kupferstichkabinett Berlin, Staatliche Museen Preußischer Kulturbesitz, Berlin 1988, no.76, 160; D.Landau & P.Parshall, *The Renaissance Print 1470-1550*, New Haven & London 1994, p.202ff.

*Hans Holbein the Younger: Adoration of an image of St Christopher, 1515/16. From the humanist Molitor's copy of Erasmus of Rotterdam's Egkomion Morias seu laus stultitiae, Froben, Basle, 1515, Kupferstichkabinett Basel.*

**Albrecht Altdorfer**
*St. Christopher. 1513*

## 12 ALBRECHT ALTDORFER *German, Regensburg c.1482/85 - Regensburg 1538*
*The Large Crucifixion. c.1515/17.*

This engraving is not only unusually large for Altdorfer but also one of his crowning achievements as a printer. Both the anatomy of the figures and the pictorial space are realistically and coherently represented. By his use of figures with their backs half-turned or in three-quarter profile he creates a natural sequence of diagonals that lead the eye into and around the pictorial space. At the same time the most important axis of the drama leading from the crucified Christ to his grieving mother stands out clearly and strongly. Above the tight little group of mourners and spectators the figure of Christ on the Cross rises, suffering and compassionate, against the dark sky among the sparse trees, which seem to create a solemn, high-ceilinged room around the story. Jerusalem in the background has become a German town, Golgotha is a clearing on a hill in the German forests, whose thickets can be seen extending behind the figures at the bottom right of the picture. Together with the radiant aureole around Christ's head shining against the tremendous dark sky torn by lines of light, the bright sidelight imbues the print with a supernatural sheen.

Altdorfer's composition is permeated by his preference for the vertical, but the pictorial space is less confined than in earlier works. In *The Large Crucifixion* he succeeds in combining the grandness and atmospheric qualities of his German landscape fantasies with the clarity of space and figures characteristic of the Italian Renaissance.

The similarities to Mategna's prints are obvious in the draperies of the foreground figures, and the group around Mary can be traced back through a number of stages in Altdorfer's work to Mantegna's great *Deposition* (B.4). For the Masters of the Danube School, among whom Altdorfer was one of the most prominent, the rendering of the crucifixion from an oblique angle had been favoured ever since the paintings of Lucas Cranach the Elder. This treatment of the theme might also derive from Mantegna. In Altdorfer, furthermore, the use of this device makes the scene more dramatic and less iconic, more alive and less representative.

Altdorfer skilfully engages the viewer in the human drama. Nearly all the figures are oriented towards Mary, not towards Christ. Only Mary herself is looking up at her son and Saviour. She is the person with whom one identifies. With her one looks up towards the living crucifixus, who in the midst of the horror and grief is bringing victory over death and joy at man's reconciliation with God. The figure raised against the vault of the sky is alone, backs and eyes are turned away from Him, and yet it is He that gives the whole representation its celestial atmosphere.

MBR

*Engraving.*
*Platemark: 146 x 99 mm.*
*Sheet: 147 x 101mm.*

Very good and early impression.
Bartsch, 8; Hollstein, 9.
Signed in the plate, bottom right with Altdorfer's monogram.
Provenance: Kupferstichkabinett Berlin; extracted and sold as a dublet at Amsler & Ruthardt, Berlin 1.3. and the following days 1886, lot 51; Boerner, Düsseldorf, acquired here 1996. Inv.no. 1996-92.
Selected literature: E.Waldmann, *The Masters of Engraving and Etching: Albrecht Altdorfer*, London & Boston 1923, no.25; F.Winzinger, *Albrecht Altdorfer. Graphik. Holzschnitte, Kupferstiche, Radierungen. Gesammtausgabe*, Munich 1963, no.134; Hans Mielke, *Albrecht Altdorfer. Zeichnungen, Deckfarbenmalerei, Druckgraphik*, exh., Kupferstichkabinett Berlin, Staatliche Museen Preußischer Kulturbesitz, Berlin 1988, no.85, p.174f.

*Albrecht Altdorfer: The Deposition, from The Fall and Redemption of Mankind, c.1513. Woodcut.*

*Detail of Andrea Mantegna (attr.): The Deposition, c.1465. Engraving.*

**Albrecht Altdorfer**
*The Large Crucifixion. c.1515/17*

**13  HANS BALDUNG GRIEN**  *German, Schwäbisch Gmünd (?) 1484/85 - Strassburg 1545*
*Madonna with the Child and Angels in a Landscape. c.1511.*

Hans Baldung Grien belonged to the inner circle of artists who were influenced by Dürer's breakthrough in German art, and he is probably the most independent and interesting of Dürer's pupils. While Dürer may seem severe and academic, Baldung is often burlesque or grotesque, demonic or sensuous in a way that reveals him as an almost mannered heir of German Late Gothic's often extreme expressional register. In Baldung the common or normative nearly always gives way to the special and characteristic; his interest is the psychological and spiritual, and his representations often possess an informal liveliness and a playful use of unexpected, apparently unplanned and at times inappropriate details. The frivolous angels on the woodcut, and the enthusiastic Infant Jesus, who is receiving a fruit from one of them, create around the mild figure of the Virgin reading an atmosphere of intimacy and immediacy that few of Baldung's contemporaries could match. The motif is actually traditional: a variant of the typical Late Medieval and Renaissance Madonna in an outdoor setting, which the Master E.S. also produced a version of (see cat. 2). The placing of the sacred subject against the background of a characteristic landscape with local features produces a fusion of the divine and the human, the celestial and the terrestial, makes it easier for the viewer to relate intimately and sensuously to the divine, to participate in the sacred drama, which was one of the goals of pious contemplation at that time. If we compare Baldung's treatment of the motif with those of other artists of the day, for instance Dürer or Raphael, we are struck by the informality of the print, especially because of its markedly non-axial composition. This displacement from a central axis is typical of Baldung, whose pictures - though they may lack solemnity - seem more human and immediate, since the viewer does not feel as if he has been placed in front of a throne but rather as if he were a passer-by who discovers the sacred story in the middle of an otherwise familiar world.

The Department of Prints and Drawings owns a chiaroscuro drawing by Baldung on a reddish-brown background, which has close affinities to this sheet. Here too an intimate mood prevails. But since the figures are placed against a neutral background, the supernatural light created by the chiaroscuro technique emphasises more strongly than in the woodcut the unique and supernatural character of what the viewer is witnessing.

MBR

*Chiaroscuro woodcut with one line block and one grey tone block.*
*Sheet: 377 x 259 mm.*
*Trimmed to and partly over the image.*

Signed in the line block, bottom right with monogram.
Provenance: Old property. Most probably Den Ældre Kobberstiksamling.
Inv. no. GB 1081.
Selected literature: A.Shestack & Ch.W.Talbot, *Hans Baldung Grien. Prints & Drawings*, exh., National Gallery of Art, Washington D.C. 1981, no.22b, p.132ff.; G.Bartrum, *German Renaissance Prints 1490-1550*, British Museum, London 1995, no.60, 73f.

*Hans Baldung Grien: Mary reading with the Christ Child and playing Angels. c. 1511. Drawing. Department of Prints and Drawings, Copenhagen.*

74

**Hans Baldung Grien**
*Madonna with the Child and Angels in a Landscape. c.1511*

## 14 JEAN DUVET *French, Langres? 1485 - 1570 ?*
### *The Angel shows St John the River with the Water of Life. (Revelations, ch. 22).*

Jean Duvet's work constitutes in every way a sharp contrast to anything else one might find in 16th century French art. In this period pictorial art was almost exclusively linked with the king or the great families of the nobility, a court art distinguished by aesthetic sophistication, elegance and subtlety. In Jean Duvet's etchings, however, we enounter the works of a religious mystic, whose visionary expressivity and spiritual intensity make us forget his technical and anatomical weaknesses. These etchings take us beyond the court at Fontainebleu to a world that is in many ways related to medieval representations like the sculptures at Moissac and Suillac and which foreshadows the dream visions of the much later mystic, William Blake. Like Blake Duvet drew copiously upon the pictorial world of the High Renaissance and often quoted Raphael, Michelangelo and Dürer. This is not least evident in his major work, 24 scenes from the Revelations of St John, of which the present sheet is, unfortunately, the only one in our collection. The series was published in Lyons in 1561, but the first plate with the artist's self-portrait is dated 1555, and others may well have been executed before that date. Here Duvet has borrowed extensively from Dürer's woodcut series from 1498, but he had a quite different point of departure. While Dürer sought to expound the obscure and irrational text as clearly and comprehensibly as possible, Duvet accepted the visionary character of the text and created his compositions on the basis of this acceptance. He renounced any attempt at making them rationally credible, paying no regard to relations of space, perspective and scale. The figures are distorted or cut wherever he finds this necessary in order to underscore the symbolic or emotional impact of the picture. Duvet accepted the text quite literally and did not hesitate to make his composition severely symmetrical where this is indicated by the text, as in this sheet. The words of St John's text are as follows: "And he (the angel) shewed me a pure river of water of life, clear as crystal proceeding out of the throne of God and of the Lamb. In the midst of the street of it, and on either side of the river, was there the tree of life, which bare twelve manner of fruits, and yielded her fruit every month:... but the throne of God and the Lamb shall be in it; and his servants shall serve him: And they shall see his face; and his name shall be in their foreheads. And there shall be no night there; and they need no candle, neither light of the sun; for the Lord God giveth them light: and they shall reign for ever and ever.... And I, John, saw these things, and heard them. And when I had heard and seen, I fell down to worship before the feet of the angel which shewed me these things."

All the elements from the text are included. John is kneeling before the angel on a rock in the foreground, and in the clouds behind them John's vision is displayed to us just as it is described in the text: God's throne, from which the river with the water of life is pouring forth, stands in the middle of the city, the celestial Jerusalem, and we see the tree with its fruit and God's servants, upon whom the light of the Lord's countenance shines. In accordance with a later passage in the text the halo is circumscribed with the words: "EGO SUM ALPHA ET OMEGA".

CF

*Etching.*
*Sheet: 284 x 206 mm.*
*Trimmed to platemark.*

Second state of three. Bartsch, 35. Watermark: Cluster of grapes, 6 x 7 rows with Db in centre. Signed in the plate on the tablet bottom centre: "IOHA/NNES/FAC;DU/VET". Inscribed in the plate on the tablet bottom right: "HIST/ CAP.22/APOC", in the halo: "EGO SUM ALPHA ET OMEGA". Inscriptions: Verso in pencil: "1059/57", in another hand: "Jullien de la Boullaye 49/ B VII 35/ R Dv 49. CP5LII/ge M" ?, in a third hand: "26,80a" (collocation no.), in Emil Bloch's hand:"I 4576", in a fifth hand: "Lb", in a sixth hand, almost erased: "Apocalypsen 22", in red pencil an illegible tre-figure no. Provenance: F. Meyer, Dresden (Lagerkatalog XXVIII); acquired here 1903. Inv. no. 4576. Selected literature: E. Julienne de la Boullaye, *Etude sur la vie et sur l'oeuvre de Jean Duvet dit le maître à la licorne*, Paris 1876, no. 49; A.E.Popham, "Jean Duvet", in *The Print Collector's Quarterly*, VIII, no. 2, 1921, pp. 122-150, no. 49; Jean-E. Bersier, *Jean Duvet le maître a la licorne 1485-1570?*, Paris 1977, no. 40; Colin Eisler, *The Master of the Unicorn. the Life and Work of Jean Duvet*, New York 1979, no. 61.

**Jean Duvet**
*The Angel shows St John the River with the Water of Life*

## 15 GIOVANNI BATTISTA PALUMBA    *Italian, active c.1500 - 1525*
*Leda with the Swan.*

This is the technically and compositionally most advanced and, in addition, the most widespread sheet by a printer who has left no other traces than fourteen engravings and eleven woodcuts, most of them signed with the monogram IB and a bird. After much guesswork he has been identified as the artist Giovanni Battista Palumba, inasmuch as the "I" stands for John (Giovanni in Italian), the "B" for Battista and the bird for Palumba, which means dove. No further information is available about Palumba, so we are obliged to study his works to learn something about him. We know that Palumba must have been working in Rome around 1503, for he has produced a flysheet representing a pair of Siamese twins and a three-headed cat. According to the text below they were born in Rome in that year, and a flysheet of this kind would not have been produced much later than the time when these events took place. On the basis of this flysheet and the influences that can be detected in the 23 known works a picture emerges of a printer who was initially strongly influenced by Albrecht Dürer and to some extent developed parallel to Marcantonio Raimondi, later absorbing impulses from Filippino Lippi, Bernardo Pinturicchio, Baldassare Peruzzi and Cesare da Sesto, all of whom were working in Rome during the first decades of the 16th century. Stylistically Palumba developed from clearly circumscribed figures with a stress on surfaces and placed in front of a landscape to plastically modelled figures whose contours interact with the richly varied hatching of the shadows, the figures now being integrated into the landscape. *Leda with the Swan* marks the culmination of this development, and it is in this print that Palumba first uses cross-hatchings to characterise the deepest shadows. There is a general consensus that the print should be dated to about 1510.

The Neoplatonism of the Renaissance led to a strong interest in the legend of how Jupiter in the shape of a swan seduced Leda, the wife of the Spartan king Tyndareus. In the Renaissance the story was seen as symbolising divine love expressed through man's union with God. The union of Leda and Jupiter resulted in the antithetical pairs of twins Castor and Pollux, who represented harmony, and Helen and Clytemnestra, who stood for discord. In Palumba's engraving the erotic content is merely hinted at through the relation of the Leda figure to an antique represention of a kneeling Venus. The scene is first and foremost a depiction of family intimacy. The shells of the eggs from which the twins have been hatched lie in pieces on the ground. The amicable Castor and Pollux are caressing their mother or handing her a butterfly, while the discordant twins Helen and Clytemnestra are tugging at the feathers of their father, who is punishing one of them by nipping her hand. In the background can be seen a very precise depiction of the antique ruin of the temple to Minerva Medica. The cylindrical structure of the temple was considered to be the ideal form for a sacred building. In the 1490s it had been used as the model for the rotunda on Ss. Annunziata in Florence, and Peruzzi was strongly interested in it. But the elaborate and man-made building is crumbling under the effect of its encounter with its antithesis: time and nature, for just as man can only be united with God in death, so art can only be united with nature through its dissolution.

CF

*Engraving.*
*Sheet: 155 x 126 mm.*
*Trimmed inside platemark.*

Inscribed verso in pencil (20th century ?): "20 / no. 5794", in another hand (20th century): "Inv. no. 8649".
Provenance: Paul Davidsohn, Grunewald-Berlin 1839-1920 (Lugt and Lugt suppl. 654); his sale at Boerner, Leipzig, 22.-26.11.1920, Zweiter Teil, lot 1347, repr. tvl. XX; acquired here.
Inv. no. 8649.
Selected literature: A. Campana, "Intorno all'incisore Gian Battista Palumba e al pittore Rimpacta (Ripanda)", in *Maso Finiguerra*, I, 1936, pp. 164-81; J. Byam Shaw, "The Master IB with the Bird (Jacopo Ripanda?)", in *The Print Collector's Quarterly*, 19, 1932, pp. 272-297, 20, 1933, pp. 9-34 and pp. 168-178; K. Oberhuber, in J.A.Levenson, K. Oberhuber and J.L. Sheehan, *Early Italian Engravings from the National Gallery of Art*, exh., Washington 1973, pp. 440-454, no. 162.

**Giovanni Battista Palumba**
*Leda with the Swan*

**16  GIROLAMO FRANCESCO MARIA MAZZOLA** CALLED **PARMIGIANINO**
*Italian, Parma 1503 - 1540*
*The Entombment.*

In the second decade of the 16th century the provincial town of Parma developed into a centre of art on a level with Florence, Rome and Venice. This sudden flowering took place thanks to the inexplicable emergence of two artistic geniuses: Correggio and Parmigianino. Correggio saw the world expressed in colour, light and shade and exerted his main influence on the art of the late 17th and of the 18th century, while Parmigianino, who focused primarily on the decorative and rhythmic qualities of the line, was more in accord with the spirit of his time and immediately influenced contemporary art far beyond the Italian peninsula.

Parmigianino was the first artist to discover that shading could be used in a free and spontaneous manner. The technique was ideally suited to his artistic nature, since it provided him with the opportunity to develop the sinuous and supple line that distinguishes his elegant and energetic drawings. *The Entombment* is considered to be one of his best prints. It exists in two versions, which are reversed in relation to one another. In the other version the painterly qualities are more pronounced and there is more immediacy to the facial expressions, but in the version shown here the plate is shaded with greater assurance and technical skill. The lines are stronger as a result of a longer immersion in the acid bath. The modelling is more plastic, the expression more intense, and it is therefore generally thought that our version is the older of the two. Both versions must, however, have been executed within a relatively short period, since a number of preserved studies show that from the start Parmigianino had been working with the idea of reversing the motif. With respect to their dating it must be presumed that the two etchings were produced in 1530-31, since the forms of the draperies and the figure types are closely related to studies for the female figures of the ceiling vault at Santa Maria della Steccata in Parma, which Parmigianino embarked on early in 1531.

Compositionally both versions deviate from traditional versions of the Entombment, but in the version shown here Parmigianino has gone a step further. The body of Christ is laid out in all its youthful splendour, and Nicodemus is holding the crown of thorns above his head as if he were crowning the victorious Saviour with a laurel wreath. Through this gesture there grows out of the grieving crowd surrounding the dead Christ a consciousness that Death has been vanquished.

CF

*Etching and drypoint.*
*Platemark: 331 x 240 mm.*
*Sheet: 334 x 245 mm.*

Bartsch, 5.
Inscribed verso in pencil (19th century): "Mazzuoli/ B.5.I/ I. 2961", in Erik Fischer's hand: "47.3a" (collocation no.).
Provenance: Gerhard Schlegel; his sale, Copenhagen 17.4. and the following days 1899, lot 2633; acquired here.
Inv. no. 2961.
Selected literature: Konrad Oberhuber, *Parmigianino und sein Kreis. Zeichnungen und Druckgraphik aus eigenem Besitz*, exh., Graphische Sammlung Albertina, Vienna 1963, pp. 20-22, no. 43; A.E. Popham, *Catalogue of the Drawings of Parmigianino* I-III, New Haven and London 1971, vol. I, pp. 94-95; Sue Welsh Reed, in Sue Welsh Reed and Richard Wallace, *Italian Etchers of the Renaissance and Baroque*, exh., Museum of Fine Arts, Boston 1989, pp. 13-16, no. 9.

*Parmigianino: The Entombment. Etching.*

**Girolamo Francesco Maria Mazzola** called **Parmigianino**
*The Entombment*

**17** **ANTONIO FANTUZZI**  *Italian, Bologna c.1510 - 1550 -*
*Euanda throws Herself in the Pyre of Capaneus.*  *After Rosso Fiorentino*

The School of Fontainebleau, continues to amaze us with its enigmatic extravagance. "The Autumn of the Middle Ages", as French Mannerism was described by Walter Pater, is a mixture of the chivalrous courtly traditions and fashions of Italy and of Antiquity as perceived through the means of radical Italian Mannerists such as Giovanni Battista Rosso (Rosso Fiorentino) and Antonio Fantuzzi, respectively designer and engraver, of our print.

By their very psychophysical type they both belong to the first generation of Mannerists, eccentric in their art as well as in their behaviour.

Around the high flames of a pyre, in which a lifeless body lies spread, a strange group of mourners has gathered, expressing their grief without restraint. The half-naked woman with flowing hair, the streams of which recall the tongues of flame in the pyre, is entering the fire. Her stricken and mournful gaze is concentrated on the dead body. On the steps in the foreground naked youths have disposed themselves in uncomfortable poses, as if leading the viewer towards the action, the tortuous twists of their bodies seeming to force the viewer to experience and suffer himself the events taking place before him.

Hitherto nobody has come up with a convincing interpretation of the subject. I would, however, like to point out a scene which seems to fit our picture. It is found in the story of the love of Capaneus and Euanda, a legend from the so-called Theban Cycle. Euanda, the wife of Capaneus, a participant in the campaign against Thebes, learns of the death of her beloved husband too late and, arriving when the funeral is already under way, throws herself into the fire in grief. Her history became a typical example of a lover's selfless grief. It appears in Euripides' *Suppliants* from which it enters Apollodorus's *The Library*, Ovid's *Art of Love* and Virgil's *Aeneid*. The depiction of subjects from the Theban Cycle is very rare, but another engraver from the School of Fontainebleau, Domenico del Barbiere, produced an engraving from a drawing by Rosso (B. XVI, 358, No. 4) with a depiction of a warrior in a chariot falling into the earth with the inscription "Ampharao", i.e. indicating the legend of the death of Amphiratius, one of the heroes of the Theban Cycle. If it were not for the engraved inscription, scholars would have long searched for the subject, taking it for the more widespread subject of Curtius.

The use of the Theban Cycle by the artists of the School of Fontainebleau has not yet been explained by any concrete events, but the cruel tragedy of these myths, so popular in the art of the 20th century from Stravinsky to Pasolini, could not have been better suited to the eccentric tastes of the court of François I.

AI

*Etching.*
*Sheet: 267 x 409 mm.*
*Trimmed inside platemark.*

Bartsch, 26.
Watermark: Simple coat of arms with P[?] S.
Signed in the plate, bottom left with monogram: "-AF-".
Inscribed verso, top left in pen and brown ink: "348/3", above that an indistinct chiffer, bottom right in red chalck turned upside down: "264", bottom to the right in pencil in Emil Bloch's hand: "Ant Fantuzzi and: "B 26", below that: "R".
Collector's marks: Verso bottom left WV in a red violet circle, i.e. unknown (Lugt suppl. 2655[b]), bottom right Heinrich Füssli (1755-1829), (Lugt 1008).
Provenance: Heinrich Füssli (1755-1829), Zürich; acquired before 1887.
Inv.no. GB 1043.
Selected literature: Henri Zerner, *Die Schule von Fontainebleau. Das graphische Werk*, Vienna 1969, A.F.21, repr.; Eugene A. Carrol, *Rosso Fiorentino. Drawings, Prints, and Decorative Arts*, Washington 1988, pp.242-244; Bruce Davis, *Mannerist Prints. International Style in the Sixteenth Century*, exh., Los Angeles County Museum of Art 1988, pp.190-191.

**Antonio Fantuzzi**
*Euanda throws Herself in the Pyre of Capaneus*

**18   GIORGIO GHISI**  *Italian, Mantua 1520 - Mantua 1582*
*Venus and Adonis.  After Teodoro Ghisi.*

This engraving is united by its subject with two other engravings by Giorgio Ghisi on compositions by Luca Penna, *Venus, Pricked by a Rose Thorn* (B. 40) and *Diana and Endymion* (B. 43). As was rightly noted by L. Massari, the composition was created under the influence of Titian's *Venus and Adonis* (Prado), then well known from the engraving by Jacopo Caraglio. Whilst there are many compositional similarities in both engravings, the treatment of the subject in Ghisi's work differs sharply from that of Titian, Caraglio and from the whole tradition of depicting this scene. Titian's Venus seeks with her caresses to restrain Adonis from the hunt which promises to bring him to his death. This is the most common treatment of the subject, known from the paintings of Rubens and Poussin. At first glance, Ghisi's Venus also seems to be restraining Adonis by force, but a number of details allow us to give a different reading of the subject. Scholars have noted that the landscape in the background, where we see Adonis meeting his death, differs greatly from that in the foreground, being empty and harsh. This may symbolise Adonis's passage to the kingdom of the dead, while Venus's joyous, passionate embrace marks his return to earth, which puts forth luxurious vegetation. Adonis's somewhat startled look must be a reaction to the horrors of the underworld, of which he has been a recent witness. That the engraving shows not the canonical depiction of time characteristic in images from this myth - in the foreground Venus's warnings, and in the background the death of Adonis - but quite the reverse, with his death in the background, and in the foreground the joyous meeting of the lovers after Adonis's temporary resurrection - is supported by the fact that Adonis is shown resting his foot on the head of his enemy, the wild boar who fatally wounded him. At the lovers' feet is Cupid with a hare. The hare or rabbit was a symbol of fecundity and often accompanied Venus, but the hare is also a symbol of cowardice. Cupid's strange duel with the hare may symbolise the love which overcomes fear, including fear in the face of death.

Such a treatment of the subject is extremely characteristic of the art of the Mantuan court, where the leading artist, Giulio Romano, combined a love for archaeology with irony. His wall paintings in the Palazzo del Te remain to this day the unsurpassed masterpiece of such an interpretation of Classical mythology. Giulio in some sense followed the traditions of Andrea Mantegna, one of the most learned representatives of the *all'antica* style. Giulio brought to the global seriousness of the Renaissance a Mannerist play of meanings, and his art exerted a huge influence on the artists of his circle. This engraving is a typical example of the interpretation of Classical myths in the style of Giulio, combining humour, open eroticism and a conscious modernisation of mythology.

Ghisi's plate suffered many indignities: in the 18th century Venus's buttocks were covered with drapery for reasons of modesty, and in 1823 Pope Leo XII ordered that the plate, then kept in the Calcografia in Rome, be destroyed. This sheet is one of the few surviving examples of the print's first state.

At Chatsworth, in the collection of the Duke of Devonshire, is a fragment of a drawing by Teodoro with a figure of Cupid and a hare. The drawing of which this is a part was probably that used as a sketch for the engraving.

AI

*Engraving.*
*c.320 x 222 mm. Trimmed inside platemark.*

First state of four.
Bartsch, 42 [1].
Signed in the plate, bottom left abov a small stone: "GMF".
Inscribed in the plate on a table bottom left below Venus's foot: "TEODORO / GHISI / IN".
Inscribed verso, bottom right in pencil in Emil Bloch's hand: "Giorg. Mantuano / B. 42".
Provenance: Old property.
Inv.no. GB 1041.
Selected literature: S. Massari, *Incisori Mantovani del '500'. Giovanni Battista Adamo, Diana Scultori e Giorgio Ghisi dalle collezioni del Gabinetto Nazionale delle stampe e della Calcografia Nazionale*, Rome 1981, pp.204-205; M. Levis, S. Boorsch, *The Engravings of Giorgio Ghisi*, exh., The Metropolitan Museum of Art, New York 1985, pp.146-148.

**Giorgio Ghisi**
*Venus and Adonis*

**19  PIETER BRUEGEL I**  *Flemish, Breda (?) 1525/1530 - Brussels 1569*
*The Rabbit Hunt. 1560.*

In the 1550s Pieter Bruegel the Elder began depicting nature from sketches made directly in front of the motifs. Before that time most landscapes consisted of a mixture of observation recollected, experience acquired and pure fantasy. Only rarely were the pictures "actual landscapes".

There was a special category of so-called "world landscapes", far-reaching vistas of what was at the time considered god-created, but also mysterious nature, bearing richly varied evidence of man's industry on land and sea. Nothing was too great or too small to be registered in such a universal map of everything between heaven and earth. Formally speaking the majority of Bruegel's landscapes belong to this category.

Of the many graphic sheets that bear Bruegel's name, only one - the present sheet, *The Rabbit Hunt* - comes entirely from his own hand. In the left bottom corner he has written his easily forgeable signature and a practically illegible date, most often interpreted as 1506. Naturally this is chronologically impossible, so the nought has been read as an imperfect six, and a date of 1566 generally accepted. In 1975, however, Lutz Malke concluded, on the basis of a drawn copy in Paris (Fondation Custodia, inv.no. 6959), dated 1560, after Bruegel's no longer extant original, that the two last figures should be read as 60, as Bruegel's lack of graphic practice apparently had made him oblivious of the reversion which takes place when a print on paper is made from the plate.

A comparison between copy and etching reveals a number of both essential and minor differences. Something new has been added, other things have been altered or completely removed. This is just what happened to the rabbit which was sitting there, right in the middle of the foreground. It has now been spirited away and replaced by a rotting stump of a tree with jaws wide open like a ferocious animal. Left are only two rabbits, which the crossbowed hunter and his dog tensely concentrate on. If the etching (as first pointed out by Philipp Fehl) is an illustration of a certain proverb by Erasmus, the rabbit hunt must inevitably fail, for - as the proverb goes - the one who chases two hares will catch neither ("Duos insequens lepores neutrum capit").

If Fehl is not wrong, the etching has a double point, since the hunter is unaware that he is being chased by a halberdier, who is tiptoeing out of his hiding place behind a tree to the right. Using Lasse Söderberg's characterization of Arne Haugen Sørensen (Paletten, XXV, 3, Gothenburg, 1964, p.125), the huntsman may here be called a "persécuteur persécuté": a pursuer pursued.

Otherwise peace seems to reign in this spacious landscape, where the river quietly meanders through the fields and the castle towers on the mountain top. But it is no perfect idyll. There is a heavy and ominous contrast between the open unprotected panorama and the sombre threat of the fist-like rock formation. As if darkness and light were fighting an unequal struggle in this landscape, where power and human evil thrive. As a tacit reminder of the existence and possible victory of the good, the ivy undauntedly twines around the large dead tree, the worn-out symbol of transience, under which the fatal drama of folly unfolds.

JG

*Etching with traces of drypoint.*
*Platemark: 223 x 291 mm.*
*Sheet: 226 x 292 mm.*

Only state.
Inscribed in the plate, bottom left: "BRVEGEL 1506" (the two last chiffers indistinct); top right: "H cock excu".
Provenance: Old property.
Inv.no.  GB 1044.
Selected literature: René van Bastelaer, *Les Estampes de Peter Bruegel l'ancien*, Brussels 1908; Ludwig Münz, *Bruegel, The Drawings, Complete Edition*, London 1961, p.20; Louis Lebeer, *Catalogue raisonné des estampes de Bruegel l'ancien*, Brussels 1969; Joaneath A. Spicer, "The "Naer het Leven" Drawings: by Pieter Bruegel or Roelandt Savery?", in *Master Drawings*, 8, 1970, pp.3-30; Matthias Winner e.a., *Pieter Bruegel d.Ä. als Zeichner, Herkunft und Nachfolge*, Staatliche Museen Preussischer Kulturbesitz, Kupferstichkabinett, Berlin 1975, p.70 (under cat.no. 75; Lutz Malke); Christopher White, ""The Rabbit Hunters" by Pieter Bruegel the Elder", in *Pieter Bruegel und seine Welt, Ein colloquium ...*, Berlin 1979, pp.187-92; David Freedberg e.a., *The Prints of Pieter Bruegel the Elder*, Tokyo 1989, pp.15, 168 (cat.no. 62).

**Pieter Bruegel I**
*The Rabbit Hunt. 1560*

**20  MELCHIOR LORCK (LORICHS)**  *Danish-German, Flensburg 1526/27 - ? 1588 ?*
*Oval Arabesque. 1561.*

This beautiful little print shows Lorck from an almost unknown side as an ornamental artist. He uses the delicate radiating lines with great sophistication to raise the ornament from its background, allowing it to unfold its charms with an aery yet meticulous elegance. The arabesque is divided into an upper and a lower half, The basic structure proves to be identical in the two halves, and the ornament is perfectly symmetrical around the vertical and horizontal axes. However, the upper part has been elaborated by the addition of a multitude of small drops that evoke associations with buds and thereby emphasize the obvious reading of the arabesque as placed halfway between culture and nature, between mathematics and poetry, between geometry and life.

That the ornament is an arabesque and not a grotesque is characteristic of Lorck - the most marked feature of his work is probably the large amount of oriental, especially Turkish, motifs. Lorck was a member of the German emperor's embassy to Sultan Sulejman the Magnificent in Istanbul in the years 1555-59. Here he drew and documented everything that might be of interest for Westerners - the life of the people, the organisation of the army, new mosques or antiquities. A large number of these drawings are now in The Department of Prints and Drawings. Lorck never saw the completed product of his endeavours. His comprehensive "Turkish Publication" containing 128 woodcuts based on his drawings was not published until 1626. There are two copies of this book in The Royal Library in Copenhagen, and a large number of the woodcuts together with other examples of Lorck's prints can also be seen in The Department of Prints and Drawings. The woodcut is best suited to Lorck's style, some of his engravings even look like woodcuts. Nevertheless this delicate arabesque bears witness to the fact that the influence of an alien and sophisticated culture extended beyond a mere interest in motif and documentation.

MBR

*Engraving.*
*Platemark: 112 x 79 mm.*
*Sheet: 172 x 134 mm.*

Hollstein, 52.
Signed and dated in the plate: "1561  MLF" (Lorck's monogram).
Inscribed i  the plate surrounding the arabesque:" C E S T V S  I N D I S S O L V B I L I S A  M I C I T I A · "
Provenance: Christian Jürgensen Thomsen, Copenhagen (1788-1865); his sale, Copenhagen 21.1.1867, lot?; acquired here.
Inv. no. GB 1082.
Selected literature: Erik Fischer, *Melchior Lorck. Drawings from the Evelyn Collection at Stonor Park, England and from the Department of Prints and Drawings, The Museum of Fine Arts, Copenhagen*, Copenhagen 1962; Erik Fischer, *Melchior Lorck i Tyrkiet*, Lommebog 49-50, exh., Den Kgl. Kobberstiksamling, Statens Museum for Kunst, Copenhagen 1990/91.

**Melchior Lorck**
*Oval Arabesque. 1561*

**21**  ATTRIBUTED TO **NICOLO VICENTINO**  *Italian, active middle of the 16th century*
*Hope and Temperance.  From the series The Christian Virtues.  After Francesco Parmigianino.*

This sheet provides us with an opportunity - comparatively rare these days - to see an engraving in the state it left the press. Graphic sheets were passed from hand to hand and very quickly became worn. To preserve them, collectors often lined the engravings with sheets of thick paper, cut off worn edges, or simply stuck the sheets into albums, radically changing the appearance of the artist's original idea. The merits of engravings do not end only with the image. An important role is played by the colour and quality of the paper, the relationship between the area of the surface left clear and the image, the width of the margins. We have but a few sheets untouched by time, and this is one of them.

These two small woodcuts form part of a series of six Christian virtues. In the majority of collections these prints are found on separate sheets. Bartsch mentions that one of the prints of *Temperance* bears the monogram A.A. - Andrea Andreani - a Bolognese printer of the end of the 16th century, who came into possession of many plates created in the first half of the century, and repeatedly published new print runs.

In this case both plates are printed on one sheet and united into a common composition. Andreani also added his monogram, not on the images themselves but in the middle of the sheet. As a result the empty space around the images has been brought into play and is included in the overall decorative effect of the work. Such a consciousness of the decorative potential of emptiness and of the signature used as an abstract sign recalls Art Nouveau, as in the graphic works of Whistler and Aubrey Beardsley. The experiments of the Art Nouveau were linked with the influence of Japanese woodcuts, but as this sheet shows there was no need to seek examples in the Far East - in 16th-century Italy we can find examples of similar experimentation.

There are many unresolved questions surrounding the series of Virtues. Firstly, there are six of them, in place of the seven canonical virtues - *Justice* is missing, so we do not know if the series remained unfinished or whether one plate has simply not survived. Secondly, only these two Virtues were ever printed on the same sheet, so it is hard to decide if they were carved on one plate (which is very likely) or each engraving had its own separate plate. Thirdly, it is hard as a result to determine the state of the engravings and impossible to determine whether Andreani added his monogram to the plate he acquired or whether he deliberately united the two images, creating a special plate with one frame (which is hardly likely). There are many questions as to the author of the engraving. Bartsch thought it to be the work of an anonymous engraver. Later Antiono da Trenta was mentioned as the possible author. Oberhuber saw in Nicolo Vicentino the author of the engraving on the basis of stylistic similarity with his other works. The author of the drawing for the engravings in this series has never been in doubt, although there are no surviving drawings by Francesco Parmigianino which match this series completely.

AI

*Two chiaroscuro woodcuts with two tone blocks in olive green and yellowish grey and with a common framing. Frame: 188 x 327 mm. Sheet: 219 x 372 mm.*

Bartsch, 1 and 5.
Watermark: Anchor (cf. Briquet, 572).
Signed in the olive green tone block at centre with Andrea Andreani's monogram.
Inscribed verso along left edge above centre in pencil: "B XII. VII. 1", below "Temperance": "VIII.6", below "Hope": "VIII,1".
Publisher: Andrea Andreani.
Provenance: Old property.
Inv.no. GB 1042.
Selected literature: K. Oberhuber, *Parmigianino und sein Kreis: Zeichnungen und Druckgraphik aus eigenem Besitz*, Graphische Sammlung Albertina, Vienna 1963, pp.45-46; Bruce Davis, *Mannerist Prints. International Style in the Sixteenth Century*, exh., Los Angeles County Museum of Art 1988, pp.152-153.

Attributed to **Nicolò Vicentino**
*Hope and Temperance*

**HENDRICK GOLTZIUS**  *Dutch, Mülbracht 1558 - Haarlem 1617*
*Icarus.  1588.  Sheet no. 2 from the series Disgracers, after Cornelis Cornelisz. van Haarlem.*

His fall is deep, as deep as it can only be for one who in a moment of youthful arrogance has transgressed the limits the gods have set for human endeavour. The naked man, a swelling bundle of muscles, who like a modern high jumper is on his way down after having failed his back-turned record attempt, is Icarus.

He was the son of the cunning craftsman Daedalus, who is now chiefly remembered for the labyrinth he built on the island of Crete for King Minos. It was to be the habitat of the monstrous Minotaur, half human, half bull. With great difficulty Daedalus succeeded in finding his way out of the ingeniously constructed labyrinth, but when he implored the king to let him to go to Athens with his son, his request was refused. Nothing could detain Daedalus, however, and as one of the undisputed pioneers of flying, he cleverly used bees' wax to make two sets of fan-like wings out of the feathers of migratory birds. In contrast to Leonardo da Vinci and other later inventors of various flapping-wing machines, father and son actually succeeded in taking off. Despite all warnings, Icarus could not resist the temptation to fly - like a moth - towards the light. He came so close to the sun that the wax melted and he fell into the sea, since then called the Icarean Sea. Probably stunned by what was happening, Daedalus lost his bearings and fluttered westwards, finally alighting in Sicily, where he was well received by King Cocalus.

In Hendrick Goltzius's engraved depiction the Icarus figure is practically identical with one of the numerous male nudes who in Cornelis Cornelisz. van Haarlem's ingenious painting in the Statens Museum for Kunst (c.1588, oil on canvas, 239 x 307 cm, inv.no.1) are falling into a vertiginous abyss. Whether it is God's earth, Hell or Tartarus which is the final destination of the involuntary free fall of these aerialists, is still an open question. In 1621 King Christian IV acquired the painting as "Een Vall der Engelen van Mr. Cornelis" (a Fall of the Angels by master Cornelis), a title which historically might be the artist's own. It refers to the Bible's description of the dragon (the Devil) and his angels who are hurled towards the ground, having been vanquished by Archangel Michael and his host of angels (Apocalypse 12:7-9). Recently (Van Thiel, 1985) the painting has been interpreted, not quite convincingly as far as details are concerned, as *The Fall of the Titans* into Tartarus, the land of shades of Greek mythology, where the worst wrongdoers are punished.

The real content of the painting may be doubtful, but not so the content of the engravings and the'r four Titans, as their names are clearly stated in Latin inscriptions encircling the figures and elucidating the motifs. Tantalus, Icarus, Phaethon and Ixion fall and fall, for they have fallen into disgrace. They are punished for their arrogance and disobedience. To live up to Mannerist demands of variation in attitudes and a constant alternation between light and shade, they tumble headlong in their confined, self-centred small worlds. The series is rightly famous, not just because the sheets are extremely sophisticated, each by itself and all together, but also because the date 1588 (sheet 1) makes them some of the earliest and at the same time most homogeneous instances of the Dutch continuation of this originally Italian style.

JG

*Engraving.*
*Platemark and sheet: diameter*
*c.330 mm.*

Only state.
Hirschmann, 307; Bartsch/Hollstein, 259; Strauss, 258.
Watermark: Fleur-de-lis in a coat of arms with characters WR attached.
Inscribed in the plate, bottom centre: "C.C. Jnue./HG. (monogrammed) sculp./2.", in a circular frame: "SCIRE, DEI MVNVS, ... NOMINA DONAT AQVIS."
Inscribed verso, bottom centre in pencil: "259" ( = Bartsch, 259).
Provenance: Old property.
Inv.no. GB 1045.

Within the engraving's circular border: SCIRE, DEI MVNVS, DIVINVM EST NOSCERE VELLE, SED FAS LIMITIBVS SE TENVISSE SVIS. DVM SIBI QVISQ. SAPIT, NEC IVSTI EXAMINA CERNIT, ICARVS ICARVS NOMINA DONAT AQVIS.

Signed at bottom: CC inue. HG sculp. 2.

Selected literature: Otto Hirschmann, *Verzeichnis des graphischen Werks von Hendrick Goltzius ...*, Leipzig 1921; Walter L. Strauss (ed.), *Hendrik Goltzius, 1558-1617, The Complete Engravings and Woodcuts*, New York 1977; Anne Walter Lowenthal, "The Disgracers: Four Sinners in One Act", in *Essays in Northern European Art Presented to Egbert Haverkamp-Begemann on his Sixtieth Birthday*, Doornspijk 1983, pp.148-53, fig. 1-6; Pieter J.J. van Thiel, "Cornelis Cornelisz. van Haarlem - his first ten years as a painter, 1582-1592", *Netherlandish Mannerism, Papers given at a symposium in Nationalmuseum, Stockholm, September 21-22, 1984*, Görel Cavalli-Björkman (ed.), Nationalmusei skriftserie N.S. 4, Stockholm 1985, pp.76-78, fig.3; Steffen Heiberg (ed.), *Christian IV og Europa, Den 19. Europarådsudstilling*, Copenhagen 1988, pp.301 (text Olaf Koester), 313 (repr.), 314 (cat.no. 1016; text Hanne Jönsson); Henrik Bjerre, " 'Titanernes fald' - og genoprejsning, Omkring restaureringen af Cornelis van Haarlem's manieristiske figurbillede", in *Kunstmuseets Årsskrift 1991*, vol. 61, Copenhagen 1991, pp.70-81; Exh. Ger Luijten, Ariane van Suchtelen e.a. (ed.), in *Dawn of the Golden Age, Northern Netherlandish Art 1580 - 1620*, Rijksmuseum, Amsterdam, Zwolle 1993, pp.15-17 (Wouter Th. Kloek), 331-33 (Bart Cornelis), 335 (Pieter J.J. van Thiel); Hanne Jönsson, "Cornelis Cornelisz. van Haarlem, Titanernes fald", in *100 Mesterværker*, Statens Museum for Kunst, Copenhagen 1996, p.52f. (repr.), (English edition: *100 Masterpieces*, ibidem 1996, p.52f. (repr.)).

*Hendrick Goltzius: Tantalos, Phaeton and Ixion. Engraving.*

**Hendrick Goltzius**
*Icarus. 1588*

## 23 JAN (PIETERSZ.) SAENREDAM *Dutch, Zaandam c.1565 - Assendelft 1607*
*Vanitas. 1599/1604.*

The literal meaning of the Latin word vanitas is emptiness, and in the world of pictorial art it is used about the specific form of still life that probably came into being in Holland at about 1600. The vanitas idea as such can be traced back to Ecclesiastes 1:2, from where the Hebrew expression hebel habalim (the breath of breaths) via Greek was turned into the less expressive Latin phrase vanitas vanitatum (the emptiness of emptiness or endless emptiness as the Danish version of the Bible has it). Even so, vanitas is an ambiguous term with strongly negative connotations of outward pomp and circumstance, which may be further related to the vanity of man and the transience of all things. It is this somewhat broader sense of the vanitas idea we have to do with here.

This technically and artistically perfect engraving by Jan Saenredam is in all probability a non-inverted reproduction, correct in every detail, of a lost painting by the Dutch Mannerist Abraham Bloemaert (1564-1651). The lost original is mentioned in Karel van Mander's *Het Schilder-Boeck* ... (The Book of Painters...), Haarlem, 1604, and is briefly described in three later sales catalogues. A comparison of the various statements gives one an idea of a more colourful total impression than the one the "main motif" seems to warrant.

No text is needed to convey the sombre message of the picture, for it is clear that the total sum of emblems adds up to a memento mori, a reminder of death. Wherever the eye may roam there are simple, but eloquent symbols of the inexorability of death: the sarcophagus at the top (with the arms of the Guild of St Luke in the middle), flanked by smoking lamps which, like the torches below, will burn themselves down, the coffin-maker's and gravedigger's tools, and the skeleton between the hourglasses, which can only measure mortal time, not eternity. Perhaps the ambiguity of a few of the symbols lies in their double function; this is true of the trumpet, for instance, which was used at funerals, but which is also an image of brief glory and the Last Judgment.

As if this was not enough, several inscriptions present admonitions that dispel all doubt. Capitals in Latin, which lapse into Greek, bring a quotation from R. Lubbaeus: "There may be a safer place for everything, but no castle is secure against the sovereignty of death. Whether we carry a sceptre or delve with a hoe we must all pay tribute to death". Quite appropriately the Greek Pindar quotation in the line just above the skeleton can be interpreted in the following way: "We must all remember that we are stretching but mortal limbs". Finally the finely calligraphed italics on the rather crumpled piece of paper, bear – in a queer mixture of Latin and Greek - the somewhat cryptic message: "Are you a visitor to this place? Indeed I am, in the Lydian carriage!" (Here perhaps synonymous with a hearse as the Lydian vehicle was notorious for its slow progress).

The engraving bears no date, but was most probably made at the same time as the painting, which means at some point between 1599, when Saenredam began to work for Bloemaert, and 1604 when it is mentioned by Van Mander. In a sense the picture may be regarded as an allegorical counterpart to the existential questions and answers which at about the same time, in 1602, Shakespeare for the first time made Hamlet formulate – confronted with a skull.

JG

*Engraving.*
*Platemark: 372 x 130 mm.*
*Sheet: 392 x 338 mm.*

Second state of two.
Bartsch, 30 II; Wurzbach, 30 II; Hollstein, 110 II.
Inscribed on the creased scrap of paper below the skull: "ABlommaert Pinx./Joan Saenredam sculp. Robbertus de Baudous. excudebat."; further inscriptions in Latin and Greek in the text frame (see below).
Provenance: Old property.
Inv.no. GB 1046.
Selected literature: Hans Mielke, *Manierismus in Holland um 1600, Kupferstiche, Holzschnitte und Zeichnungen aus dem Berliner Kupferstichkabinett*, Berlin 1979, p.61 (cat.no.87, repr.); Marcel George Roethlisberger, "Abraham Bloemaert's *Vanitas* Representations", in *Delineavit et Sculpsit*, no.5, Leiden 1991, p.20 (repr.); Marcel G. Roethlisberger, *Abraham Bloemaert and his Sons, Paintings and Prints*, 2 vols., Doornspijk 1993, vol.I, pp.101-03, vol.II, pl.101.

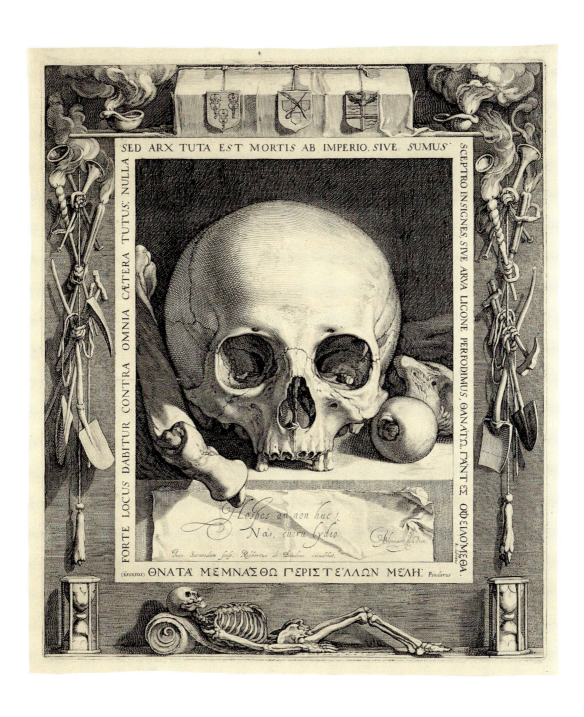

**Jan (Pietersz.) Saenredam**
*Vanitas. 1599/1604*

95

## 24

**PHILIPP UFFENBACH**  *German, Frankfurt-on-Main 1566 - Frankfurt-on-Main 1636*
*The Angel Rolls Back the Stone from the Tomb of Christ. 1588.*

Philipp Uffenbach's etching *The Angel Rolls Back the Stone from the Tomb of Christ* is often mistakenly called *The Resurrection*, but the Resurrection is not exactly what the print shows. The evangelists do not in fact tell us how Jesus rose from the dead, only how the empty tomb was discovered. And it is the scene leading up to this discovery which Uffenbach depicts. As clearly stated at the upper left of the print, it illustrates the words of the Gospel according to St Matthew, Chapter 28, Verses 2-4, "And, behold, there was a great earthquake: for the angel of the Lord descended from heaven, and came and rolled back the stone from the door, and sat upon it. His countenance was like lightning, and his raiment white as snow: And for fear of him the keepers did shake, and became as dead men."

The angel has wrapped his luminous arms around the tombstone to remove it; his face is like a sun, and a powerful light emanates from his eyes, sweeping away the four guards. The earthquake is illustrated by rocks tumbling down the mountain on the right. In a manner which brings modern comic-book clichés to mind, thick bolts of lightning denote the angel's passage from heaven to earth and the explosive force released by it. All that is missing is the onomatopoeic KAPOW!

In Christian pictorial art the treatment of most subjects, including the Resurrection, follows a prescribed norm, but this particular action-packed biblical passage is very rarely illustrated, which might explain why the artist has indicated his biblical source on the print itself. But Uffenbach's highly original choice of motif is not due to any lack of knowledge about the pictorial Resurrection canon, as the background of the etching clearly demonstrates. One of the most frequent Resurrection motifs is the *Three Marys at the Tomb*. Far to the left in Uffenbach's print we see the three women referring to the scene following the one depicted: The discovery of the empty tomb and the angel telling them that Christ is risen from the dead.

And Uffenbach has very subtly incorporated yet another of the traditional Resurrection motifs in his picture: the Gospel according to St John tells us that Mary Magdalene meets the resurrected Christ in the garden surrounding the sepulchre, and at first takes him for a gardener. Therefore, in the traditional depiction of this scene, Christ is often equipped with a spade. Diagonally above the three women Uffenbach has placed a very small figure carrying a spade on his shoulder and standing in front of a garden fence - another stock element of traditional renderings of this scene. There can be no doubt that this figure is Christ himself, and when studied through a magnifying glass, the halo around his head becomes clearly visible.

It is an extremely unconventional and humorous idea to reduce the main character of the Resurrection to a barely visible stick-figure. Uffenbach quite literally pushes the scene's main action and its most common motifs into the background in favour of his own slanted but effective angle. He thus turns the rules of Christian iconography upside down, and, while art historians usually term such 16th-century norm-breaking Mannerism, this differs significantly from the Italian Mannerism with its decadent distortion of the High Renaissance classical harmony. Uffenbach subscribes to a robust, expressive realism, a kind of northern European Mannerism, which brings forth the violent, passionate and mystical aspects of Christianity.

EJB

*Etching.*
*Sheet: 248 x 201 mm.*
*Trimmed inside platemark.*

First state of two, before Franz Aspruck's address was added.
Bartsch, 1.
Signed and dated in the plate, top right with monogram: "PUb / 1588".
Inscribed in the plate, top left: "MATT. 28."
Provenance: Probably acquired before 1835.
Inv.no. GB 1047.
Selected literature: Andreas Andresen: *Der deutschen Peintre-Graveur...*, Leipzig 1874, vol.4, no.2, p.317.

**Philipp Uffenbach**
*The Angel Rolls Back the Stone from the Tomb of Christ. 1588*

## 25

**JACQUES BELLANGE** *French, Nancy c. 1575 - Nancy 1616*
*Balthasar, Melchior, Caspar*

Jacques Bellange worked as court painter in Nancy, the capital of the Duchy of Lorraine, where the records show that he executed portraits, murals and theatre decorations between 1600 and 1617. But very little of his work has been preserved except for some drawings and 48 etchings. These, however, constitute some of the most superb manifestations of late Mannerism and are closely related to works by El Greco, Fréminet and Bloemaert, who - like Bellange - derived inspiration from Michelangelo, Raphael and Parmigianino. In Bellange and the other Mannerists the Renaissance ideal of logic and clarity is rejected in favour of a style founded on distorted forms and perspectives. His art was created for an educated upper class and was the product of an intellectual revolution based on the discovery of new continents and the infinity of space. In contrast to the scientific and humanist interests of the Renaissance and the political and moral aims of the Baroque much Mannerist art was created to satisfy the sophisticated aesthete and to entertain or titillate the scholarly viewer, who took pleasure in puzzling out concealed references to art, literature, events or concepts not contained within the work itself.

The representation of the Magi afforded Bellange ample opportunity of exploiting the whole range of Mannerist devices. According to the Bible it was three Magi who followed the star to the stable in Bethlehem, where they found and worshipped the infant Jesus. They brought him gifts: gold, frankincense and myrrh. The Magi were regarded as the first to recognise that Jesus was the Son of God, and to convert to Christianity. Their gifts were interpreted as an expression of their wisdom. The gold symbolised the royal descent of the infant Jesus, the frankincense his divinity and the myrrh, which was used for embalming, his death. The event was interpreted as a prophecy of the dissemination of Christianity throughout the world, since the Magi became representatives of the continents of the world and of the different ages of man. To give structure to the story they were ascribed names: Caspar, was the oldest king and came from Europe; Balthasar, was in his full manhood and came from Asia, while the youngest was Melchior, from Africa. Bellange focused primarily on their exotic garments. He depicted the figures from three different sides, thus concealing their age to some extent, and as a typical Mannerist feature, he left the figures unidentified by not inscribing their names. This has led to some confusion, not least because Merian names the Magi incorrectly in his highly popular copies of them. The reason for his error is probably connected with the fact that Merian replaced Melchior, who is standing with his back to the viewer and whose face and gift are hidden, with the less enigmatic Balthasar from Bellange's large etching *The Adoration of the Magi*. The collector who provided the versions in The Department of Prints and Drawings with names followed Merian.

The subtle gradations in the play of light and shadow and the masterly characterisation of the materials from deepest black to the lightest of greys must be the result of repeated and very precisely calculated bitings in acid. The scrolled signature is found only on the etching of *The Martyrdom of St Lucy* and the stylistically closely related *Hortulanae*, which is thought to have been executed around 1615.

CF

*Balthasar:*
*Etching.*
*Platemark: 288 x 164 mm.*
*Sheet. 299 x 176 mm.*

Second state of two.
Walch, 26[II].
Watermark: Grapes (Griffiths and Hartley, 1997, p. 128, no. 1).
Signed in the plate, bottom left.: "Bellange".
Inscription added in the plate, bottom left of centre: "le Blond excud".
Inscribed recto, bottom centre in pencil (19th century?), trimmed:"Caspar Rex Tarsi"; verso in pencil (19th century?): "Caspar Rex Tarsis" , in another hand: "1442".

Publisher (all three): Le Blond.
Provenance (all three): Cilius Andersen, Copenhagen; his sale at Chr. Hée's Eftf., Copenhagen, 10.5. 1935, lots 187-189; acquired here.
Inv. no. (all three) 13383.
Selected literature: Nicole Walch, *Die Radierungen des Jacques Bellange: Chronologie und kritischer Katalog*, Munich 1971, 26 II, 27 II, 28 II; Amy N. Worthen and Sue Welsh Reed, *The Etchings of Jacques Bellange*, exh., Des Moines Art Center, des Moines, Iowa 1975, no. 33, 34, 35; Jacques Thuillier, in *L'Art en Lorraine au temps de Jacques Callot*, Musée des Beaux-Arts, Nancy 1992, 34, 35, 36; Antony Griffiths and Craig Hartley, *Jacques Bellange c. 1575-1616 Printmaker of Lorraine*, exh., British Museum , London 1997, no. 29-31.

**Jacques Bellange**
*Balthasar*

99

*Melchior.*
Etching.
Platemark: 290 x 166 mm.
Sheet: 299 x 177 mm.

Second state of two.
Walch, 27[II].
Signed in the plate, bottom
right, trimmed: "Bellan".
Inscription added in the plate,
bottom left: "le Blond excud".
Inscribed recto, bottom centre
in pencil (19th century?): "Baltasar Rex Saba"; verso in pencil
(19th century?): "Baltasar Rex
Saba", in another hand: "144".


*Caspar.*
Etching.
Platemark: 285 x 167 mm.
Sheet: 293 x 175 mm.

Second state of two.
Walch, 28[II].
Signed in the plate, bottom left:
"Bellange".
Inscription added in the plate,
bottom right: "le Blond excud".
Inscribed recto, bottom centre
in pencil (19th century?),
trimmed: "Melchior Rex
Nubiæ"; verso in pencil: "Tres
Magi, Melchior Rex Nubiæ / ces
trois Rois sont de Bellange
Originaux / Ceux graves par Jac
ab heydeá Strasbourg / sont des
Copies", in another hand:
"144".

*Matthæus Merian: Balthasar.*
Etching.

**Jacques Bellange**
*Melchior.*

100

*Matthæus Merian: Melchior.*
*Etching.*

**Jacques Bellange**
*Caspar*

## 26 PIETER PAUL RUBENS ? *Flemish, Siegen, Westphalia 1577 - Antwerp 1640*
*St Catherine of Alexandria. 1620/22 ?*

Almost all extant prints with images by Bruegel the Elder or Rubens were produced, not by the Flemish painters themselves, but by some of the veritable host of professional so-called reproduction- or expert engravers who had specialized in reproducing other artists' works in the three graphic techniques known at the time: woodcut, engraving and etching.

Bruegel's claim to be called a graphic artist rests on one single etching (see cat.19), and Rubens can pride himself of little more, as scholars are reasonably agreed that no more than three prints can be ascribed to him. They are Bust of Seneca (Hind 2; Hollstein 3), Old Woman and Boy with Candle (Hind 3; Hollstein 2) and the present St Catherine of Alexandria (Hind 1; Hollstein 1).

A much needed revision of Rubens's own personal share in the fifteen etchings ascribed to him over the years, was begun in 1923 by Arthur M. Hind. According to him the Catherine sheet was the only autograph Rubens sheet. This statement did not remain unchallenged, however. In 1972 Hans Vlieghe referred to the "spontaneous style" of the depiction as proof that the probable artist was Van Dyck, an idea which Hind also had been playing with earlier.

According to legend St Catherine was young, rich, beautiful and also wise. She incurred the emperor's anger by calling a heathen sacrificial feast ludicrous, she was imprisoned and forced to dispute with fifty specially summoned philosophers and convert them to Christianity, before she was set free again. But this was not the end of her ordeal. She was tied to a spiked wheel to be killed by its rotations, but the Lord heard her prayer and the wheel broke. Even so, she suffered a martyr's death when the emperor had her beheaded. Angels carried her body to the top of Mount Sinai where she was buried, a monastery being built later and dedicated to her at the foot of the mountain.

Here she is, then, high in the clouds, big and beautiful, with billowing skirts and ample Flemish curves, a palm leaf in her hand as a symbol of the victory of faith and the spirit over the spiked wheel and the sharp edge of the sword, images of the evilness of man and physical death.

The sheet bears no date, but it was probably executed when Rubens was decorating the Jesuit church in Antwerp (1620-21), where the motif comes from. If Vlieghe is right in spotting Van Dyck's style in the etching, it must probably have been finished before that artist left for England in October 1620 at the latest.

That Rubens was at least indirectly involved, seems demonstrated by a contre-épreuve of the first state (New York, Metropolitan Museum, Rogers Fund, 22.67.3) with corrections in brown ink which according to some Rubens experts are unmistakably his own. In the second state these corrections are especially reflected in more cross hatchings, and it is not until the third and last state that Rubens is mentioned as the artist. That inscription may have been engraved at a later date to increase the saleability of the sheet. This, however, would not change the basic question: Is the etching by or merely after Rubens?

JG

*Etching with some engraving.*
*Platemark: 295 x 198 mm.*
*Sheet: 319 x 220 mm.*

Third state of three.
Hind, 1923, 1[III]; Hollstein 1[III].
Inscribed in the plate, bottom left: "P. Paul Rubens fecit."
Inscribed verso, bottom right in pencil: "P.P. Rubens".
Provenance: Probably identical with lot 1789 on the sale of C.F. von Rumohr's collection, Leipzig, 1846, 19.10.ff.
Inv.no. GB 1048.
Selected literature: Arthur M. Hind, "Rubens as Etcher", in *The Print Collector's Quarterly*, vol. 10, no. 1, London 1923, pp.61-63, 65, 70, 72, 74, 78; Frank van den Wijngaert, *Inventaris der Rubeniaansche Prentkunst*, Antwerpen 1940, pp.21, 88 (cat.no. 595), 93 (cat.no. 635), pl.29; John Rupert Martin, *The Ceiling Paintings for the Jesuit Church in Antwerp (Corpus Rubenianum Ludwig Burchard, part 1)*, Brussels 1968, pp.145-47, fig. 143; Hans Vlieghe, *Saints I-II (Corpus Rubenianum Ludwig Burchard, part 8)*, Brussels 1972, vol. I, p.116f. (cat.no. 75, 75a), fig. 127f.; Konrad Renger, "Rubens dedit dedicavitque", in *Jahrbuch der Berliner Museen*, vol. 17, Berlin 1975, pp.166, 168, fig. 2.

**Pieter Paul Rubens ?**
*St Catherine of Alexandria. 1620/22 ?*

**27  HENDRIK GOUDT**  *Dutch, Haag 1583 - Utrecht 1648*
  *The Mocking of Ceres. 1610.*

For some artistically decisive years Hendrik Goudt was closely affiliated with the German painter Adam Elsheimer (1578 - 1610). Without him Goudt's pictorial universe would undoubtedly have looked different and would hardly be remembered any longer. The seven engravings he left to posterity are all based on Elsheimer originals.

They met each other in Rome, where Elsheimer had arrived in 1600, staying there for the rest of his short, debt-ridden life. Goudt, who was a very prosperous man, arrived four years later and apparently became Elsheimer's patron and pupil at one and the same time. For two or three years he lived with Elsheimer and his family, but in 1609 he moved to a house in the neighbourhood. Several early sources claim that Goudt demanded Elsheimer to be thrown into a debtors' prison for working so slowly that he could not produce enough paintings in return for the financial help he received. During his imprisonment Elsheimer is said to have contracted the disease that led to his premature death.

In any case, the two men remained in contact. During the last year of Elsheimer's life, Goudt made the present engraving, dated Rome 1610, after one of his paintings. After 1613 we know of no work from Goudt's hand. Perhaps he was suffering from galloping insanity inherited from his mother. Several concordant sources claim, however, that the cause of his illness was a love potion, administered to him by an enchantress who wanted control over him and his worldly possessions.

Another magic potion is brought into play in Goudt's engraving after Elsheimer's lost painting The Mocking of Ceres. The motif comes from Ovid's Metamorphoses (5:438-61), which relates how Ceres, the Roman goddess for the growing of corn, anxiously searched for her daughter Proserpine all over the world, in the frosty night with two pinewood torches lit by the fire of Mount Etna. At a certain point she asked an old woman in a low, thatched cottage for a drink of water to quench her thirst, and was given a sweet drink containing roasted grains of malt. When a young lout scorned her and called her greedy for guzzling the drink, she got so furious that she threw the rest of the liquid in his face. The malt grains made his skin scaly, his arms were turned into legs, a tail grew forth and he shrank to a size smaller than the smallest lizard; finally he scurried into a hole, the weeping old woman stretching her hand at him.

As there is no literary support for letting precisely this part of the story take place at night, Elsheimer himself must deliberately have chosen this dramatic possibility, which in Goudt's congenial black-and-white intrepretation becomes the first "nocturne" in 17th century Netherlandish graphic art. Both the engraving and its style were soon copied, also in France and in Italy.

We know as little about Goudt's early training as an artist as about the rest of his obscure fate. He is supposed to have studied calligraphy, which seems to be confirmed by the bold, sweeping inscriptions of the engravings. It is still an enigma what preceded his sudden emergence in the world of graphic art in Rome in 1608, not only as a technically excellent engraver, but as one of the very best performers of the profession at the time. He still hovers in the twilight where light is engaged in an unequal struggle with darkness - as in his engravings.

JG

*Engraving.*
*Platemark: 320 x 247 mm.*
*Sheet: 328 x 255 mm.*

Only state.
Dutuit, 6; Wurzbach, 5;
Bartsch/Hollstein, 5.
Inscribed in the plate, bottom:
"Scipioni Burghesio./S.R.E. (=
Sacrae Romanae Ecclesiae)/Cardinali amplissimo in deuoti animi festimonium H Goudt [H G sammenskrevet] sculpsit et dicauit Romae. 1610./A Elsheimer [A E sammenskrevet] pinxit."
Futher two columns of four lines in Latin: "Dum frugum genitrix, ... stellio factus Erat./-Janus Rutgers sp [compiled; = scripsit?]".
Provenance: Old property.
Inv.no. 1049.
Selected literature: Wolf Stubbe, "Elsheimers Radierung 'Die Verspottung der Ceres' ", in *Zeitschrift für Bücherfreunde*, XXXVIII, 3. Folge, 1934, p.171ff.; Heinrich Weizsäcker, *Adam Elsheimer, Der Maler von Frankfurt, Beschreibende Verzeichnisse und geschichtliche Quellen*, Zweiter Teil, Berlin 1952, p.139f.; Keith Andrews, *Adam Elsheimer, Paintings - Drawings - Prints*, Oxford 1977, pp.34, 153 (under cat.no. 23), pl.86; Clifford S. Ackley, *Printmaking in the Age of Rembrandt*, Boston 1981, p.76f., repr.; Keith Andrews, *Adam Elsheimer, Werkverzeichnis der Gemälde, Zeichnungen und Radierungen*, Munich 1985, p.34f., 188 (under cat.no. 23), fig.43.

**Hendrik Goudt**
*The Mocking of Ceres. 1610*

**28  GIUSEPPE RIBERA**  *Spanish, Játiva 1591 - Naples 1651*
*The Poet. 1620/21.*

Ribera grew up in Spain, where he probably received his artistic schooling. As a young artist he travelled down through Italy from the north, eventually arriving in Naples after a stay of some years in Rome. Naples was at that time the capital of the Spanish vice-roys, wo ruled southern Italy. Ribera settled here from 1616 and he soon occupied a leading position among the local painters, not least because of his close links to the Spanish viceroys.

Already during his stay in Rome Ribera had seen paintings by Caravaggio and his followers. Caravaggism immediately made a great impact on Ribera's art with regard to both motif and style, but he transformed and radicalised it. The depiction of the destruction of the body is a leitmotif in Ribera's paintings, and his typical subjects are bestial martyrdoms and representations of old philosophers, ascetic hermits and saints with wrinkled, sinewy bodies.

These particular themes are also to be found in Ribera's prints, since his etchings functioned as a kind of testing ground for motifs, many of which were later reproduced in his paintings. His production of prints comprises only 16 etchings that can be attributed to him with certainty, and which were executed in the relatively short period between c. 1620 and 1626. Among these works *The Poet* occupies a special position and is not related to any of the paintings. The motif is part of a classical antique tradition, and its treatment is correspondingly classicising and thereby different from Ribera's other works. The poet's body is concealed, enveloped in extraordinary draperies, which fall in heavy folds irrespective of the limbs they conceal. Only a foot, a hand and the head can be seen and suggest that the laurel-wreathed poet is sitting in a relaxed and pensive pose. Compositionally he is balanced by the tree stump and the stone block, which with the withered branch and the crack in the cube seem at one and the same time to reflect the poet and his mood. Deep shadows fall especially around his face, but also his garments are formed by powerful contrasts between light and dark areas, which constitute a graphic equivalent to Caravaggio's *chiaroscuro*.

Ribera's poet has adopted the characteristic pose of melancholy. This was a state of mind that had particularly interested visual artists since the Renaissance, as melancholy was thought to be closely related to artistic genius. So Ribera's etching forms part of a tradition that includes, for example, Dürer's print *Melancholia* and Raphael's depiction of Heraclitus, "The Weeping Philosopher" in *The School of Athens*. In Raphael's fresco this figure is also leaning against a cube and therefore seems to have been a direct source for Ribera's etching. With Ribera's *The Poet*, however, melancholy is directly linked to the art of poetry for the first time. Many attempts have been made to explain the background for this. Reference has, for example, been made to parallels in verses by Walter van der Vogelweide and Lorenzo de' Medici, and attempts have been made to identify Ribera's melancholy figure with poets like Virgil, Dante or Petrarch. But the idiom of Ribera's poet seems to avoid the specific, establishing, first and foremost, an expressive image of the gloomy, meditative aspect of artistic creativity.

JM

*Etching.*
*Sheet: 160 x 125 mm.*
*Trimmed to and partly inside platemark.*

Bartsch, 10.
Provenance: Old property. Most probably Den ældre Kobberstik-samling, vol. 8 blad 12, 17, 22, 26 or 27.
Inv. no.  GB 1083.
Selected literature: Jonathan Brown, "Jusepe de Ribera incisore", in *Jusepe de Ribera 1591-1652*, exh., Castel Sant'Elmo, Certosa de San Martino, Cappella del Tesore di San Gennaro, Naples 1992, pp. 363-70; cf. Andrea Bayer, *Ibid.*, no. 3.3. (with bibliography).

**Giuseppe Ribera**
*The Poet. 1620/21*

**29  JAN (VAN) BROSTERHUISEN**  *Dutch, Leiden c.1596 - Breda 1650*
*Landscape with Sheep on a Hill.  1640s.*

To call Jan Brosterhuisen a misunderstood genius would be an overstatement. It would be far more reasonable to see him as a versatile talent, appreciated by his contemporaries, but almost forgotten today. His special field was botany, but he was also a teacher of Greek and engaged in music, poetry and architecture, not only as an aesthete and theorist, but also as creative artist himself. He played the organ, and already as a young student he wrote highly praised poems in his mother tongue, which was quite uncommon at the time; he may even have made architectural designs in cooperation with the architect Jacob van Campen, who built the town hall in Amsterdam. Whether Brosterhuisen also worked as a painter we do not know. He was a friend of many of the most prominent learned people of his country, and highly learned himself when he died on 13 September, 1650 after some years of delicate health. Art historical information on Brosterhuisen is sparse and random. The latest decades, however, have seen a renewed interest in his graphic work. It forms but a small part of his activity: it is restricted to 16 etchings of his own, and most of them are known only in a few copies. The sole exception is the series *Praedia* (Small Estates), consisting of six landscape etchings, all in the Copenhagen Department. The sheet illustrated here is no.3 in this series. None of the prints are dated, but probably executed about the mid-1640s.

At that time Brosterhuisen had settled in Amersfoort, where he was engaged in two different forms of translation work. One task was making the antique author Vitruvius's treatise on architecture accessible to Netherlandish readers, the other producing some of the 56 etchings after Frans Post's drawn originals for the folio work *Rerum per octennium in Brasilia gestarum historia* (Amsterdam, 1647); he collaborated with the graphic artist Salomon Savery, but it is still an open question which of them actually made what. Doubt has even increased since it became clear that most of the etchings were later worked over with a burin, probably by Dirk Matham. One thing is certain, however: whether Brosterhuisen worked after his own original or after those of others, nature was always the focal point. The title of the present print, *Landscape with Sheep on a Hill*, is not Brosterhuisen's own, but it might well have been since it reflects the same sense of detail as does his art in general. Everything in the picture has been meticulously executed, each leaf, each straw, and it would all have been equally meaningful, and therefore equally meaningless, had not some of it been bold-faced and some in fine italics. A corresponding, almost consistent emphasis on the strong and weak elements recurs in the sharply outlined areas of light and shade. Generally speaking, Brosterhuisen's art points more backwards than forwards, to Gillis van Coninxloo and other artists of the Frankenthal school, and even farther back. Although new viewpoints and motifs had already become manifest a couple of decades before Brosterhuisen began, he was not the only artist with a retrospective, nostalgic attitude. The same tendency in a slightly varied form is discernible in Johannes Ruischer, Jacob van Ruisdael and Claes van Beresteyn, all born in the 1620s: the poetry of reality transformed into poetic reality.

JG

*Sheet no 3 from the series Praedia, consisting of six etched landscapes.*

*Etching.*
*Platemark and sheet: 168 x 213 mm. Trimmed to platemark.*

Second state of two.
Van der Kellen/Wurzbach/Hollstein, 13[II].
Inscribed in the plate, top left in pen and brown ink: "3";  bottom left of centre: "98".
Provenance: Old property.
Inv.no. GB 1050.
Selected literature: Jan Garff, "Jan Brosterhuisen, (Blade fra Kobberstiksamlingens mapper, 1)", in *Grafik*, I, no.3, p.4f.; Irene de Groot, *Landscape, Etchings by the Dutch Masters of the Seventeenth Century*, London 1979, pls.90-95; David Freedberg, *Dutch Landscape Prints of the Seventeenth Century*, London 1980, p.57f., pls.86-88; Clifford S. Ackley, *Printmaking in the Age of Rembrandt*, Boston 1981, pp.191-94 (incl. pls.128-29).

**Jan Brosterhuisen**
*Landscape with Sheep on a Hill. 1640s*

**30** **CLAUDE GELLÉE,** CALLED **CLAUDE LORRAIN**   *French, Chamagne 1600 - Rome 1682*
*The Rape of Europa. 1634.*

Claude Lorrain has primarily enjoyed wide recognition as a painter of landscapes. As a pioneer in this genre he was the first to specialise successfully in landscape painting. Nature and buildings are the main protagonists in his atmospheric and sometimes large landscape paintings. In accordance with the norms of his time, however, he usually garnished his canvases with small figures from the Old Testament or classical mythology.

Claude Lorrain had a long and productive career as a painter in Rome, but as a printer he was primarily active from the 1620s to the 1630s in the phase when he needed to establish his name as a painter. Although his prints thus played a subordinate role in relation to his painting, his work in the former field was also both innovative and of the highest standard. His etchings seem immediate and painterly, but are in reality often technically very complicated because of his wish to create the subtle nuances of light and shadow so characteristic of his paintings.

The etching *The Rape of Europa* is a repetition of the composition in a painting that Claude Lorrain had executed probably a short time before. This painting, now in the Kimbell Art Museum, Fort Worth, was a tour-de-force by the artist, his hitherto largest canvas and his most ambitious with respect to idea and composition. It is likely that the etching following the painting was inspired by the wish to show this result to a wider public and thus to potential patrons.

The literary source is the story of Jupiter's desire for Europa, the daughter of a king, as told in Ovid's *Metamorphoses* (II, 832-76). Jupiter transformed himself into a white bull and mingled with the king's herd at a spot where Princess Europa was wont to play with her ladies-in-waiting. Jupiter in the form of a bull succeeded in persuading Europa to sit on his back, after which he abducted the terrified princess to the seashore. Claude Lorrain's etching seems to correspond to Ovid's text with respect to the characters and the setting. But its calm and harmonious mood diverges from that of its literary source, and the artist seems to have suppressed any sense that the pastoral idyll ends in rape and ruin.

JM

*Etching and drypoint.*
*Platemark: 200 x 256 mm.*
*Sheet: 223 x 264 mm.*

Third state of seven.
Mannocchi, 14.
Signed in the plate, bottom right on the stone: "Claudio Gille I.N.V.F. Romae 1634". Provenance: P. & D. Colnaghi, London; acquired here 1953 as gift of the Ny Carlsberg Foundation.
Inv. no. 19660.
Selected literature: Lino Mannocchi, *The Etchings of Claude Lorrain*, New Haven and London 1988, 14. H. Diane Russel, *Claude Lorrain 1600-1682*, exh., National Gallery of Art, Washington 1982, pp. 229-302, no. 21.

**Claude Gellée,** called **Claude Lorrain**
*The Rape of Europa. 1634*

**31   REMBRANDT HARMENSZ. VAN RIJN** *Dutch, Leiden 1606 - Amsterdam 1669*
*Christ presented to the People. 1655.*

When Jesus had been taken from Herod to Pilate - according to St Luke (23:1-12) from Pilate to Herod and back to Pilate again - he was finally presented to the people to receive its judgment. The meeting which had taken place shortly before between the "King of the Jews" and the Roman governor of Judaea and Samaria, Pontius Pilate, is described in more or less identical accounts in the three first gospels of The New Testament, but the gospel according to St John has a somewhat different, apparently freer version.

In contrast to other written sources, the Bible's description of Pilate is remarkably positive. He is depicted as a lenient and just man, who for a long time disregards the wild accusations of the chief priests and the elders. Although under increasing pressure, he tries to the very last to have Jesus acquitted by following an ancient custom which allows the people to have one prisoner set free at the Passover. But the Jews adamantly insist on their demand: Barabbas, the murderer, must be set free and Jesus crucified. Pilate washes his hands in front of everybody, saying: "I am innocent of the blood of this man: see ye to it" (St Matthew, 27:24). Then he has Jesus scourged and leaves him to his fate.

It is these dramatic moments just before the sentence is pronounced Rembrandt has depicted here, when the good and the light become engaged in an unequal struggle with the evil and the darkness, which seeps in everywhere. On the dais before the hall we find the three chief protagonists of the fatal drama: the pathetically gesticulating Pilate in splendid oriental outfit, the inaccessible, half-naked Jesus and Barabbas in between. They are surrounded by soldiers armed with spears and swords, and to the very left a good-natured civilian with a pitcher, which presumably contains the water Pilate will use a little later to protest his innocence. The woman with the precious headgear in the window to the very left is usually identified as Pilate's wife, Procla, who is trying to swing the proceedings in favour of Jesus by using the soldier in the other window as a messenger to inform Pilate of the many bad dreams she has had on account of "that just man" (St Matthew 27:19).

It is beyond dispute that the blindfolded figure in the niche top left who holds a pair of scales in her hand, is Justitia, the Roman goddess of justice, but the identity of her counterpart is not so easily established. Most convincing is perhaps the suggestion that she is the cardinal virtue Prudentia (wisdom), here in the shape of an amazon, the indefatigable champion of freedom. Such an alliance between justice and wisdom often found pictorial expression in Rembrandt's day on courthouse facades. By honouring this custom and the established practice of having legal proceedings take place on a platform in the open air, the artist obviously attempted to update the biblical account.

An inconclusive debate has been going on whether the gigantic, partially obliterated torso between the two arches at the bottom is Neptune, the old Adam or the Prince of Darkness, the Evil One.

Before finding its final form, the etching went through several alterations. Almost halfway through the process Rembrandt made a radical change, spiriting away the figures in front of the dais, whose former presence is now only discernible as faint shadows on the wall. Their

*Etching (drypoint).*
*Platemark: c.355 x 451 mm.*
*Sheet: 352/5 x 448/51 mm.*
*Slightly trimmed.*

Last state of seven or eight (depending on the catalogue used). Bartsch/Hollstein, 76[VII/VIII]; Hind, 271[VII]; Biörklund & Barnard, 55-A[VII].
Inscribed in the plate on the doorcase to the right: "Rembrandt f 1655."
Provenance: Old property.
Inv.no. GB 1051.

omission probably served a compositional purpose: the main characters would no longer be lost in a crowd; instead, their presence would be emphasized as the depth of the pictorial space was considerably diminished. At the same time Rembrandt seized the opportunity to distance himself from the picture which must rightly be considered the most obvious model of the present sheet: Lucas von Leyden's engraving from 1510 of the same motif (Bartsch / Hollstein 71). Rembrandt owned a copy of it himself, which he had acquired together with thirteen other prints by his fellow townsman for the then exorbitant price of 1400 guilders.

All major or minor later alterations to Rembrandt's engraving were the result of inner artistic necessity. But behind them all lies a wish to challenge Van Leyden on his own terms, the choice of graphic technique for instance. Most of the approximately 300 prints by Rembrandt were executed as etchings. Only in the present work and in four other cases did he use a drypoint needle. When this needle furrows its way across the plate, small ridges of metal shavings, the so-called burr, will form on both sides of its track. Such a funnel-like extension of the line above the surface, results in prints of great richness, but as the burr is worn down during the printing process, the effect soon loses its original strength. To avoid unnecessary wear of the burr, Rembrandt deliberately limited the number of proofs. In the beginning he almost exclusively used Japanese paper, whose standard size was so modest that he had to piece two sheets together. Since this is neither economically nor aesthetically particularly desirable, he probably made an early decision to adapt the plate to the standard sheet measurement by cutting off a 25 mm edge at the top. Later he began using ordinary white or ivory handmade paper and in extremely rare cases very costly thin vellum. The Copenhagen Department owns two copies of the etching: the above-mentioned last state, and the earlier briefly mentioned, rare fourth state, of which no more than eight prints have been registered so far. This sheet displays the composition as it was just before the crowd of people in the foreground was obliterated.

On account of its format, technique and theme, *Christ presented to the People* has naturally been considered a companion piece to Rembrandt's etching, produced two years earlier, *The Three Crosses* (Bartsch/Hollstein 78; Hind 270; Biörklund & Barnard 53-A). A print of this etching is also found in the Department's ample Rembrandt collection. It is the fourth and last phase of the sheet and demonstrates radical changes in comparison with the three preceding states. Large parts of the motif are almost concealed under heavy draperies of pitch-black ink.

*As in Christ presented to the People*, Rembrandt also here reduced the gallery of figures, although not by obliterating but by concealing them.

JG

Selected literature: Ludwig Münz, *A Critical Catalogue of Rembrandt's Etchings ...*, London 1952, vol. 2, pp.55, 107f. (cat.no. 235), pl.266-68; K.G. Boon, *Rembrandt. f., Das graphische Werk*, Vienna & Munich 1963, p.26f., pl.261-62; Emanuel Winternitz, "Rembrandt's 'Christ Presented to the People' - 1655, A Meditation on Justice and Collective Guilt", in *Oud Holland*, jaargang LXXXIV, Amsterdam 1969, pp.177-98 (incl. 28 repr.); Christopher White, *Rembrandt as an Etcher, A study of the artist at work*, London 1969, pp.18, 61, 75, 87-92, 99, 140, pl.112-17; Idem, *The late etchings of Rembrandt, A study in the developement of a print*, An Arts Council Exhibition, The British Museum Gallery of Prints and Drawings, 20 March - 11 May 1969, London 1969, p.23f. (cat.no. XV); Erwin Mitsch, *Rembrandt, Radierungen aus dem Besitz der Albertina (Die Kunst der Graphik VI)*, Graphische Sammlung Albertina, 223. Ausstellung, 10. Dezember 1970 - 28. März 1971, Vienna 1970, pp.144-46 (cat.no.253-57), pl.76-77; J.P. Filedt Kok, *Rembrandt etchings & drawings in the Rembrandt House, A catalogue*, Maarssen 1972, pp.69-72 (incl. two repr.; cat.no. B 76); Barbara Welzel, "Ecce Homo", in Holm Bevers e.a., *Rembrandt: the Master & his Workshop, Drawings & Etchings*, New York & London 1991, pp.274-77 (incl. two repr.; cat.no. 38).

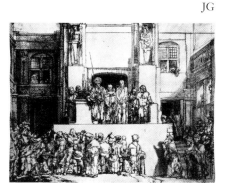

*Lucas van Leyden: Christ presented to the People. Engraving.*

*Rembrandt Harmensz. van Rijn: Christ presented to the People, 1655. Fourth state of seven or eight.*

**Rembrandt Harmensz. van Rijn**
*Christ presented to the People. 1655*

115

**GIOVANNI BENEDETTO CASTIGLIONE,** CALLED **IL GRECHETTO**
*Italian, Genoa 1609 - Mantua 1664*
*Bust of an Oriental in Profile.* *c. 1650.*

The invention of the monotype is attributed to Castiglione. He seems to have been the only artist to take an interest in this technique among the artists of the 17th and 18th centuries.

Castiglione used two different variants of this technique. Either the motif was drawn in printer's ink, so that it appeared in black lines on the white paper, or, as in *Bust of an Oriental*, the plate was covered with a layer of ink, which was worked over with blunt and soft instruments, such as wooden pegs or cloths, so that the motif appeared as white lines and grey areas on a black background. These two variants, black on a white background and white on black, were also combined by Castiglione in technically rather advanced prints, and he even subsequently worked over a few impressions in watercolour or oil.

Castiglione was born in Genoa and worked in Rome, Naples and Mantua. As a painter he specialised in Old Testament scenes of people wandering through a landscape and in antique motifs and allegories inspired by Poussin executed in warm, rich colouring. As an etcher, he shared the interest of his contemporaries Pietro Testa and Salvator Rosa in depicting motifs relating to stoicism. In addition, Castiglione was a very productive draughtsman and executed coloured drawings using a brush and oil pigments, which as independent works of art come close to being paintings.

The figure depicted in *Bust of an Oriental in Profile* with its high cheekbones, beard, hook nose and turban is one that often appears in Castiglione's paintings and etchings, first and foremost in his two series of *Exotic Heads*. In fact the type can be traced back to Rembrandt's and his pupil Jan Lieven's etchings of exotic heads from the 1630s, which had inspired Castiglione.

Today there are about 30 known monotypes by Castiglione. A large part of these repeat motifs that appear in his etchings. This might indicate that the monotypes were produced in connection with the etchings, but originated in the artist's need to escape the particular limitations imposed by that technique, in order to create contrasts of light and painterly effects.

JM

*Monotype in black on thin paper.*
*Sheet: 235 x 197 mm.*
*Trimmed inside platemark.*

Watermark: Coat of arms with three animals, possibly bees, below a cardinal's hat.
Provenance: Old property.
Inv. no. GB 1084.
Selected literature: Leo Swane, "Et monotypi i Kobberstiksamlingen af G. B. Castiglione", in *Kunstmuseets Aarsskrift*, 1926-28, XII-XV, Copenhagen 1928, pp. 217-18, repr. p. 217; Anthony Griffiths, "Castiglione", in *Print Quaterly*, IX, 1992, p. 68, fig. 70.

*G. B. Castiglione: Head of an old Man. Etching*

*Rembrandt van Rijn: Oriental Head number three from the series Oriental Heads. Etching.*

**Giovanni Benedetto Castiglione,** called **Il Grechetto**
*Bust of an Oriental in Profile. c. 1650*

## 33  ADRIAEN VAN OSTADE  *Dutch, Haarlem 1610 - Haarlem 1685*
*The Barn. 1647.*

Some Dutch artists went abroad, occasionally even settling there for good, others - not always the most inferior - stayed within the boundaries of their country, moving from place to place or simply remaining where they were born. Adriaen van Ostade belongs to the last-mentioned group. In 1657 he had to go to Amsterdam to get married for a second time, but otherwise Haarlem and its environs formed the hub of his universe. Here he studied under Frans Hals, as much of a stay-at-home as Van Ostade. Apparently he had no trouble finding his motifs there: life inside and outside the houses - everyday occurrences and festive occasions. Here he died and was buried after a good and joyful, active life without too many financial worries.

Van Ostade's artistic legacy to posterity consists of about 1,000 usually signed and dated paintings, more than 400 drawings and watercolours, and 50 etchings. Most of these are undated and have later been catalogued according to the number and size of figures in them. In this statistic arrangement of the artist's enormous gallery of characters, *The Barn* has somewhat misleadingly been placed in the category of single full-length figures. It depicts a peasant woman who turns her back and bends over her work in a dilapidated farm building. Influenced by Impressionism we, today, will hardly hold the chief motif of the picture to be a sentimental description of a lonely being's hopeless struggle against poverty and picturesque decay, but rather turn our attention to the constant interplay of light and shade on a quiet, sunny day more than three hundred and fifty years ago.

As a graphic artist Van Ostade was undoubtedly greatly indebted to Rembrandt, and in the present etching he is the artistic, if not technical, equal of the great master. Many connoisseurs find the state illustrated here the most felicitous example of Van Ostade's achievement as a graphic artist.

For most of the etchings one or several preparatory works are still extant. In an article from 1987 Leonard J. Slatkes quotes some highly illustrative examples of this and, in another context  (Appendix 1, 1994), lists the 32 etchings for which preparatory drawings and watercolours are known. Neither he nor Schnackenburg (1981) or others, refer to the drawing in the Copenhagen Department illustrated here, which is undoubtedly the artist's own preparatory work for *The Barn*, and which is here published for the very first time. It is a mirror image of the etching, slightly shorter in both directions and as is so often the case: more summary. Many of the details of the foreground are missing: the basket to the extreme left, the stool that has been upset, the pitcher, the hens and the wheelplough. Small and minor differences occur. The upper half of the barn door is not ajar as in the etching, but firmly closed.

There is correspondence in motif, style, technique, and probably also time between the present drawing and another one ascribed to the artist (*A Pig is Killed in a Barn*. Black chalk; frame: pen, black ink, 164 x 256 mm. Gernsheim 3740). In his *catalogue raisonné* as well as in a recent sales catalogue (Christie's, Amsterdam, 10 November, 1997, p.69, lot 130, repr.) Schnackenburg has rejected it as autograph. If the drawing of this Department is an original preparatory work, as seems to be case, this rejection must be revised. The interconnection of the drawings is so strong that the attribution or rejection of one must be decisive for the other.

JG

118

*Etching.*
*Platemark: 157 x 195 mm.*
*Sheet: 163 x 200 mm.*

Sixth state of ten. Davidsohn/Godefroy/- Bartsch/Hollstein, 23[VI]. Inscribed in the plate, bottom left: "A v [compiled] ostade 1647". Inscribed verso bottom left in pencil in Jørgen Sthyr's hand: "30 3" (in a reclining oval); bottom centre: "B 23/F III Tr". Along the borders distinct traces of green water colour. Provenance: Probably (1) identical with a sheet purchased by the dealer Hermann 9.4.1883 or (2) acquired 1845 in an exchange with Holm, titular Councillor of State, who in stead got a duplicate of the Rembrandt etching Bartsch, 21. Inv.no. GB 1052

*(c.1647). Preparatory drawing for the etching. Drawing, Department of Prints and Drawings, Copenhagen.*

*Reversion of the drawing.*

*Selected literature: Paul Davidsohn, Adriaen van Ostade 1610-1685, Verzeichnis seiner Originalradierungen, Leipzig 1922; Clifford S. Ackley, Printmaking in the Age of Rembrandt, Boston 1981, p.159, repr.; Bernhard Schnackenburg, Adriaen van Ostade, Isack van Ostade, Zeichnungen und Aquarelle, Gesamtdarstellungen mit Werkkatalogen, 1 (Text), 2 (Tafeln), Hamburg 1981; Leonard J. Slatkes, "Preparatory Drawings for Prints by Adriaen van Ostade", in Drawings Defined, New York 1987, pp.229-40; Louis Godefroy, The Complete Etchings of Adriaen van Ostade, New Illustrations and first English Translation of the Catalogue Raisonné, together with a reprint of the original French edition, San Francisco 1990, pp.23, 87-89, repr.; S. William Pelletier, Leonard J. Slatkes & Linda Stone-Ferrier, Adriaen van Ostade, Etchings of Peasant Life in Holland's Golden Age, Athens, Georgia 1994, pp.130-33, pl.59-63, Appendix 1, pp.263-68; Christie's, Adriaen van Ostade's Etched Copper Plates, The Property of the Heirs of the late E.H. Kok, Amsterdam, 13 November 1995, p.35, lot 21, repr.*

**Adriaen van Ostade**
*The Barn. 1647*

**34** **CORNELIS BEGA** *Dutch, Haarlem 1631/32 - Haarlem 1664*
*The Tavern. c.1660.*

In art history Cornelis Bega has played no leading part, but been a minor character with a limited, but distinctive repertory. Perhaps it is true that he lived hard, at least we know that he died young. Even so, he found time to demonstrate, but not develop, an indisputable talent, before his artistic career was cut short by death when he was thirty-odd years old.

He came from the liberal Haarlem school, probably a pupil of Adriaen van Ostade; he was clearly influenced by this master, as was also later Cornelis Dusart, who is practically always mentioned in the same breath.

Bega was the son of gold- and silversmith Pieter Janz. Begeyn (Begijn; Begga) and Maria Cornelis, an illegitimate daughter of the Mannerist painter Cornelis Cornelisz. van Haarlem, who was descended from a wealthy family; at his death in 1638 he left a considerable fortune, of which his daughter inherited half. Sufficient means, therefore, enabled Cornelis Bega to set out in 1653 on a tour of Germany and Switzerland. Perhaps he even visited Italy. At any rate he was the first Dutch artist of the 1650s who began working with an entirely novel print technique, monotype, invented in Italy a decade earlier. No later than on 1 September, 1654, Bega was back in Haarlem where he was admitted to the Guild of St Luke, and where he worked until his premature death. Accounts still extant reveal that his funeral was sumptuous.

From Bega's hand we have about 160 paintings, half as many drawings, and about 35-40 etchings. Occasionally he repeats an attitude or a figure, as is the case in the present etching, in which the sitting girl is almost identical with the woman who is seen standing in *The Young Hostess* (Hollstein 33). In several of the prints there are obvious loans from Rembrandt and, in particular, Van Ostade. As far as the latter is concerned, influence seems also to have worked the other way round, as his *The Smoker at the Window* (Hollstein 10) and *Village Romance* (Hollstein 11), both probably from about 1667, must be regarded as kind variants of Bega's etchings, a decade earlier, of *The Peasant at a Window* (Hollstein 19) and *The Amorous Couple* (Hollstein 25); incidentally, it is an odd couple of a young girl and an old man whose starfish-like hand covetously fondles her round breast. The sharp features, big noses, thin lips and usually averted eyes of Bega's peasants from the back of beyond make them differ considerably from Van Ostade's more civilian character gallery. This is further emphasized by the pointed, straight-line figure style and the innumerable dense parallel and cross hatchings, which struggle for elbowroom in the small narrow picture spaces.

The etchings from the period 1658-60 form an exception, however. Especially the very last ones, *The Tavern* among them, differ from the norm by being larger and more intimate. In each of them the scene is practically always the same: in the foreground three or four persons, joined in silent or almost wordless companionship, apparently so confident and strong that everyone and everything else is excluded. Patiently they wait for release, hoping for an answer. And in the semi-darkness or at the very front there is always at least one of these mysterious men with their backs turned.

JG

*Etching.*
*Platemark: 226 x c.174 mm.*
*Sheet: 233 x 180 mm.*

First state of two.
Dutuit, 35; Bartsch/Hollstein, 35$^I$.
Inscribed verso, bottom left in pen and brown ink: "4 d-"; bottom centre in pencil: "P A a̱ 40 bis[?] 80 fr/-6-"; bottom left: "Zu 5573"; bottom right: "Wasserzeichen/Amsterdamer Wappen/ex recueil/T.R.G. Carlyon". Provenance: T.R.G. Carlyon (cf. *verso*; not in Lugt); acquired from C.G. Boerner, Düsseldorf, 1965 (Neue Lagerliste Nr 40). Inv.no. 1965-174.
Selected literature: Barry Pearce, *Cornelis Bega Etchings*, The Art Gallery of South Australia, Adelaide 1977; Clifford S. Ackley, *Printmaking in the Age of Rembrandt*, Boston, 1981, p.256, repr.; Mary Ann Scott, *Cornelis Bega (1631/32 - 1664) as Painter and Draughtsman*, Ann Arbor, Maryland 1984 (dissertation).

**Cornelis Bega**
*The Tavern. c.1660*

**35** **ANTOINE WATTEAU** *French, Valenciennes 1684 - Nogent-sur-Marne 1721*
**SIMON HENRI THOMASSIN** *French, Paris 1687 - Paris 1741*
*Recruits on their Way to join the Regiment.*

In its first state the print of the departing recruits is a pure etching, one of the few executed by Watteau himself. The effect is bright silvery but became somewhat subdued in its second state - the one at hand - where it has been completed by the engraver Simon Henri Thomassin who darkened it by additional engraving. The etching is a copy of a painting and forms part of the second volume of the extensive *Recueil de Julienne* - issued in a hundred copies in 1735 - which presents Watteau's paintings reproduced as etchings and engravings by different craftsmen. The copy of the second volume owned by the Department of Prints and Drawings was probably assembled and bound in the 19th century. The reproduction of paintings as prints is a graphic discipline that dates back to the early 16th century, to Marcantonio Raimondi's engravings of Rafael's paintings. The purpose of these reproductions was to make the paintings known, and therefore they were usually produced on the initiative of the artist himself. In Watteau's case the project was launched posthumously by his friend, art collector Jean de Jullienne. At Watteau's time engravers worked with extreme virtuosity, using both etching and engraving, a combination which allows greater visual subtlety in the translation of the sensuous texture of the paintings to a range of tonal values from black to white, adding nuance to the representation of the silk and velvet of costumes and the delicately blurred light of garden landscapes.

Watteau's depictions of the soldiers' life in the field belong to a popular category of genre painting, especially Dutch genre painting, with which the artist was familiar. In this picture, however, the motif is devoid of the narrative aspect of genre. The nine soldiers are isolated in an interim landscape; they move in a borderland between near and far with no clear signs of their precise whereabouts. These shapes exist less as reference to a seen reality than by virtue of their purely pictorial, or iconic, function as an ornamental and self-reflecting rhythm moving across the picture plane. Their fluttery migration begins at the bank of the shiny pool beneath the rainbow. From here they depart as from a *fête champêtre*, one of those pastoral scenes that were Watteau's preferred motifs. Galantly turning toward each other, gesturing as in a courtly dance, the recruits follow their mounted officer out toward the picture's hidden horizon where clouds are gathering and moving towards them, soon to obscure the rainbow and the light. The work gives form and context to the figure of departure. Its basic theme is one that is also played out in Watteau's best-known painting, *Embarkation for Cythera*, in which the loving couples, linked like a chain of flowers, illustrate the different phases of departure and the movement towards the "little death" on the island of love. But there are no women among these recruits who narcissistically seek out their own image in the other. They are walking toward their regiment and annihilation. Here too, it is as if everything is set on a stage where, as in Racine's tragedies, the important action is taking place off stage. On this pictorial stage everything is carefully arranged and determined by the picture's stylized logic. Even the conventional set-piece tree in the foreground shrinks to rocaille.

JWF

*Etching and engraving.
Image: 207 x 334 mm.
Trimmed inside platemark.*

Second state of three. Inscribed in the plate, bottom left: "Watteau pinxit" and bottom right: "Thomasin sculp". Publisher: Sirois, Paris. Provenance: Marcel Lecomte, Paris; acquired here 1960 as gift of The Ny Carlsberg Foundation.
Inv.no. 1960-59.
Selected literature: Émile Dacier & Albert Vuaflart, *Jean de Jullienne et les graveurs de Watteau au XVIIIe siècle*, Paris 1922, no.178[II]. - Margaret Morgan Grasselli and Pierre Rosenberg, *Watteau 1684-1721*, Washington 1984, pp.122-124.

Watteaux pinxit

A Voir marcher cette Recruë,
On juge bien qu'elle est Recruë;
Par les Vents, et par les frimats;
Leur officier sur sa Mazete
Assi comme sur la sellete
Ne paroist pas êtres moins las.

RECRUE
ALLANT IOINDRE LE
REGIMENT

Se vent A Paris chez Sivir sur le quai Nequê aux Armes de France A.P.R.

Ils maudissent entre eux sans doute,
La dure et fatiguante Route:
Mais au gite allant heberger
Aux depens du premier Village
Ils sauront se dedommager
De la fatigue du Voiage.

Thomassin sculp

**Antoine Watteau**
**Simon Henri Thomassin**
*Recruits on their Way to join the Regiment*

123

This sheet is part of a series of 23 etchings known as *Scherzi di fantasia*, a series which remains an enigma in the work of Tiepolo. We do not know who (if anybody) commissioned the series, what prompted Tiepolo to take up the art of etching, or the artist's purpose in creating the *Scherzi*. Nor do we know the precise dates when the series was created, but newly discovered evidence indicate that work on the *Scherzi* began at the end of the 1740s and that the series must have been completed around 1756.

Since the sheets were only given numbers in the posthumous publication of the engravings undertaken by Giovanni Domenico Tiepolo, the artist's son, it is very difficult to date individual compositions and the order of the scenes is unknown.

The central enigma remains in the meaning and subject of the series. So far not one convincing interpretation of these whimsical scenes has been suggested, and all attempts by scholars to explain them end in a perplexed admission that the *Scherzi di fantasia* are so called precisely because they are just that, the fruit of the artist's fantasy. In one of the most recent studies, the author states openly: "Diese Orte sind geographish nicht genauer lokalisierbar und auch die Zeit ist nicht bestimmbar." (Koln, S. 158).

In this composition, known as *The Philosopher* (all the compositions were given names after Tiepolo's death and these names are somewhat arbitrary) we see a wise man in oriental clothing, seated at the foot of a pyramid. In his left hand he holds a pair of compasses, in his right a book. At his feet is a large sphere, and a little further off is a flaming brand around which a snake is entwined. In the engraving's first state (state I), in the space between the Philosopher and the book were the heads of two youths, and the whole scene had the appearance of some initiation rite. Then Tiepolo, dissatisfied with the poor proportional relationship between the different parts, removed the heads from the plate.

There is no doubt that the Philosopher has some connection with the Orient. Moreover, the sphere, pyramid and torch are all accessories found in the Allegory of Asia in Tiepolo's wall paintings in Würzburg, and thus we cannot truly say that it is impossible to identify where the action in the *Scherzi* takes place - the series is a kind of imagined journey through some generalised vision of the Orient, anticipating Goethe's *West-Östlicher Divan*"(1819).

This sheet is particularly valuable in that it was visibly worked up in pen, undoubtedly in the 18th century. L.C.J. Frerichs considers these additions in pen to be the work of Tiepolo himself (oral communication to the author). This, however, is problematic - the idea of completing the pyramid and filling the empty space of the sky is somewhat rude for Tiepolo. Doubt is also aroused by the presence of a number in the same inks as the other workings. We know that the numbers were added only in the first posthumous publication of the engravings made by the artist's son, and Tiepolo himself would seem not to have numbered the sheets. Be this as it may, whether the pen additions were added by Tiepolo himself during his work on the plates or whether they were introduced as a later correction, they were made by someone from the artist's closest circle and this recent acquisition by the museum provides us with one more detail in the history of the enigmatic *Scherzi*.

AI

*Etching with additions in pen and brown ink.*
*Sheet: 230 x 170 mm.*
*Trimmed inside platemark.*

Second state of three.
Signed in the plate, bottom right:"GB. Tiepolo", above that traces of erased "GB ....".
Inscribed recto, top right in pen and brown ink: "20"; verso, top right in pencil: "N".
Provenance: Hill-Stone Inc., New York; acquired here 1996.
Inv.no. 1996-48.
Selected literature: Aldo Rizzi, *L'opera grafica dei Tiepolo. Le acqueforti*, Milano 1971, pp.72-73, no.23; H. Diane Russel, *Rare Etchings by Giovanni Battista and Giovanni Domenico Tiepolo*, National Gallery of Art, Washington 1972, pp.76-77; *Giambattista Tiepolo 1696-1770*, exh., National Gallery of Art Washington / Ca Rezzonico, Venice 1997, pp.358-361; *Das Capriccio als Kunstprinzip. Zur Vorgeschichte der Moderne von Arcimboldo und Callot bis Tiepolo und Goya. Malerei - Zeichnung - Graphik*, exh., Wallraf-Richartz Museum, Cologne / Kunsthaus Zürich / Kunsthistorisches Museum, Vienna, 1996-1997; Chris Fischer, *Det døende Venezia*, Lommebog 57, exh., Den Kgl. Kobberstiksamling, Statens Museum for Kunst, Copenhagen 1992, pp. 17-20.

**Giovanni Battista Tiepolo**
*The Philosopher*

125

**37  WILLIAM HOGARTH**  *English, London 1697 – London 1764*
*Tail Piece or Bathos.  1764.*

A full understanding and enjoyment of William Hogarth's pictures is often hampered by the fact that today we have no automatic knowledge of their exact references, and targets of irony. It requires some degree of knowledge of contemporary individuals, incidents, whims of fashion, debates on art, and so on, to unlock Hogarth's images and their wealth of detail. To open *Tail Piece*, you have to see it as a travesty of the type of sepulchral monument that presents the deceased surrounded by allegories and attributes, i.e. figures and objects that visualize his character and deeds. Here Hogarth is parodying the overly ornate baroque monuments found in numerous European churches. The character who in this print is quite literally expiring, breathing the word FINIS (Latin: end), is the traditional allegorical figure of Time who often appears on sepulchral monuments. In other words, the image represents the end of Time, or the end of everything.

Time is surrounded by various attributes, each in their own way a visualization of the end of everything: the crown, the shotgun, the broom, the empty purse and the shoemaker's last have all been destroyed, showing that all social activity has stopped; the ruined church tower and the broken bell testify to the end of religion; Cupid's broken arrow to the end of love; the cracked palette, the burning engraving and the scattered fragments of pillars tell us that art, too, is finished; and, finally, the two withered trees and the dead sun god, riding his chariot with its team of dead horses in the sky, show that nature has run its course. All is over. It is The World's End, as it says on the pub sign showing a burning globe.

Hogarth's complex apocalyptic image can be seen as a criticism of the dominant artistic practise of his day. He is clearly mocking academic history painting, i.e. depictions of biblical or mythological scenes, often weighed down by learned allegory decipherable only to art connoisseurs. In *Tail Piece* each detail requires an odd little explanation of its own, and the entire logic of the allegory collapses under its own weight. This is how allegorical history painting brings about its own demise, says Hogarth. It requires too much explanation. In his other graphic works, he countered this tendency by a kind of realism, telling stories of his own time. He wanted to update history painting in an immediately accessible idiom, free of subtle allegorical figures. He was extremely successful in achieving this aim  - at the time. Today, however, Hogarth's pictures have succumbed to the very fate that befalls/befell history painting: his work has become just as inaccessible and weighed down by implicit codes as history paintings can be. Hogarth's pictures have ended up being precisely what they set out to criticize. They are now marked by the passage of Time, have disintegrated - as in the case of this print - atomized into an incomprehensible chaos, alluded to on the testament scroll which Time holds in its hand. In *Tail Piece* Hogarth seems to realize that in time his own work will fall prey to this kind of antiquation. *Tail Piece* is one of his last works and has therefore often been interpreted as his artistic testament, presenting a both blackly humorous and resigned view of his own work: with his death, his work, too, will fall to ruin. Only explanations, decodings and pedagogy will be able to revive it. All pictures age and die. And while this is unfortunate for Hogarth, it spells steady work for the mediators of art.

EJB

*Etching and engraving.*
*Platemark: 319 x 337 mm.*
*Image: 258 x 325 mm.*

Provenance: Old property. Inv.no. GB 1053.
Selected literature: Frederick Antal: *Hogarth and His Place in European Art*, Routledge and Kegan Paul, London 1962, pp. 21, 167f., pl. 143b; Joseph Burke and Colin Caldwell: *Hogarth. The Complete Engravings*, Thames and Hudson, London 1968, no. 267; Hans Sedlmayr: "William Hogarth: 'Das Testament der Zeit'", in *Epochen und Werke, Gesammelte Schriften zur Kunstgeschichte*, Dritter Band, Mäander Kunstverlag, Mittenwald 1982, p. 213ff., repr; Ronald Paulson: *Hogarth's Graphic Works*, Third Revised Edition, The Print Room, London 1989, no. 216, p. 185f.; Ronald Paulson: *Hogarth*, Vol. 3, Art and Politics, 1750-1764, The Lutterworth Press, Cambridge 1993, p. 413ff., pl. 112.

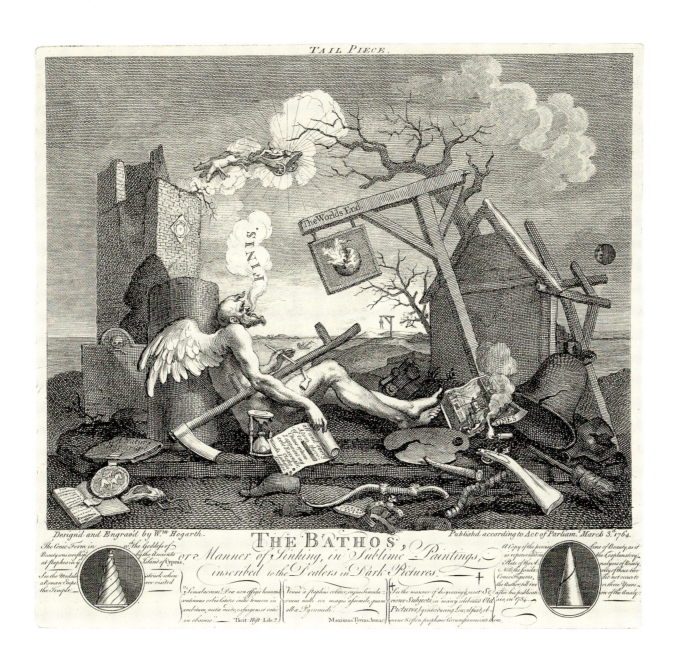

**William Hogarth**
*Tail Piece or Bathos.* 1764

**38  GIOVANNI BATTISTA PIRANESI**  *Italian, Mogliano (?) 1720 - Rome 1778*
*The Triumphal Arch.  From the series Grotteschi.*

This etching, one of a series of four sheets known as *Grotteschi*, depicts something between an architectural fantasy and a still-life. In the foreground lie various objects jumbled untidily - medals, weapons, musical instruments and architectural fragments - recalling the recurrent type of still-life known as the "Vanitas". In the middle ground is a vast, luxuriant structure which recalls both a palace and a triumphal arch. Between the rubbish tip of the foreground and the architectural luxury of the backdrop are a number of human figures. Some are naked, such as the gigantic figure to the left, usually described as a river god, and some are dressed in whimsical costumes recalling Tiepolo's fantasies on themes by Veronese. Is this some real scene or is it but some ghostly assembly?

The term *grotteschi* (the French 'grotesque' is more common in contemporary usage) entered the Italian language in the 16th century. Initially it was used to describe wall paintings discovered in the ancient Roman palaces which had been buried beneath the ground, as well as modern imitations of these works. The most famous were the wall paintings of the so-called "Golden House" of Nero, which provided endless material for the artists of the Renaissance. Grotesques became fashionable and the most famous example of such decorative wall painting became the Raphael Loggias. In the same 16th century, *grotteschi* were 'emancipated' into independent scenes, losing their initial, purely decorative significance. Montaigne, referring to grotesques, was perfectly aware that they were a visual element, but used the term in his essays on literature. With time the 'grotesque' was to become an aesthetic category. In the 19th and 20th centuries we can find many examples of the 'grotesque' in literature and music.

The central law of the grotesque is the absence of any laws and the giving of full freedom to the artist's creative fantasy. At the same time even modern grotesques contain a genetic link with what artists felt at the end of the 15th century when they looked at the ancient wall paintings. Appearing out of the dark from beneath the ground, they were perceived as evidence of secret mysteries, filled with hidden meaning, linked with the forces of the ancient Underworld. The Grotesque was and is the opposite of the world of *ratio*.

The ghostly nature of the world in this work by Piranesi is explained by the fact that a grotesque is not subject to reason. Its clear link with the tradition of the Vanitas was in keeping with the artist's numerous meditations on the majesty of the ancients and on modern decline. Usually the Vanitas was depicted as a disordered collection of luxurious objects which spoke of the vanity of everything temporal.  Piranesi creates an image in similar vein, but here the subject of the Vanitas is culture.

The *Grotteschi* are usually dated to 1745, the time of Piranesi's return to Venice, emphasizing the direct influence of Tiepolo's  prints. That influence is undoubtedly visible, but it is also clear that Piranesi used his Venetian impressions to meditate on the past of Rome, and Andrew Robinson's assertion that this series was probably completed after the artist's return to Rome, in 1747, seems just. The whole series was included in the *Prima parte di architettura*,  printed in 1748-49, and separate sheets of early states made before they were given numbers, like this one, are comparatively rare.

*Etching and engraving.*
*Platemark: 391 x 544 mm.*
*Sheet: 543 x 779 mm.*

Third state of five.
Focillon, 21.
Inscribed in the plate, bottom left: "Piranesi inv; incise, e vende in Roma / in faccia all'Accademia di Francia".
Inscribed verso, top left in pencil: "I 21 / 2".
Originally in a binding from the 18th century together with *Opere varie*, *Carceri* (2.ed.), *Alcune vedute di archi trionfali* and *Trofei di Ottaviano Augusto...* (without the sheets by Francesco Piranesi).
Provenance: Hiersemann, Leipzig; from here shortly after 1918 to "a Danish collector" via Skandinavisk Antikvariat, Copenhagen; acquired here 1925/26.
Inv.no. 14381.
Selected literature: Andrew Robison, *Early Architectural Fantasies. A Catalogue Raisonné of the Etchings*, Washington 1986, pp.15,118-119, no.22; David Succi, *Capricci veneziani del Settecento*, Turin 1988; *Das Capriccio als Kunstprinzip. Zur Vorgeschichte der Moderne von Arcimboldo und Callot bis Tiepolo und Goya. Malerei - Zeichnung - Graphik*, exh., Wallraf-Richartz Museum, Cologne / Kunsthaus Zürich / Kunsthistorisches Museum, Vienna, 1996-1997; Chris Fischer, *Det døende Venezia*, Lommebog 57, exh., Den Kgl. Kobberstiksamling, Statens Museum for Kunst, Copenhagen 1992, pp. 16-17.

AI

**Giovanni Battista Piranesi**
*The Triumphal Arch*

129

**39  FRANZ ANTON MAULBERTSCH**  *German, Langenargen 1724 - Vienna 1796*
*The Last Supper.*

Until recently the Austrian 18th century attracted little attention among art historians. It was thought that French Rococo was the mainstream in Western European painting and the Austrian school was perceived as a provincial version of the belated Venetian Baroque. In the 1970s the situation in Europe was subject to revision and the art of Central Europe, formerly thought to be provincial, was re-evaluated. Maulbertsch and Sigrist, not long before this known only to a few specialists, took up their places in the Pantheon of the history of art.

Initially, great interest was aroused by Austrian monumental painting and sculpture, since the originality of late Catholic culture was most clearly demonstrated in the grandiose scale of these Baroque apotheoses. Then other spheres were opened up, bringing forward some extremely interesting prints by Austrian 18th-century artists.

The greatest influence on Austria was exerted at that time by Venetian art. *The Last Supper* is a reworking of a composition by Giovanni Battista Pittoni, one of the most brilliant representatives of Venetian Rococo. The grandiose porcelain-like fragility of his figures, regardless of whom he was depicting, be it a nymph or a martyr, was extremely popular with European collectors. Maulbertsch, borrowing the whimsical grace of Pittoni, gives the whole scene a totally different character. The combination of the Apostles' exaggerated expressive faces and the affected elegance of the gestures is almost caricature-like. The mystical revelation, its divine nature emphasized by the presence of angels floating in the air, becomes like some theatrical pantomime staged by the court troupe in the style of the Commedia dell'Arte.

The grotesqueness of this scene does not, however, throw into doubt its profound religious feeling. Maulbertsch's exaggeration is far from blasphemous and the caricature effect is created because the artist seeks to convey a state of religous ecstasy in an era when such ecstasy was less and less linked with religion and the Church. The Venetian roots of Maulbertsch's art and his taste for the visionary, so evident in this work, call to mind another artist from a different century - El Greco. The almost hysterical tension of the religious scenes of the Austrian are close to the vision of the Toledo intellectual, but in the 18th century such feelings could not but take on the caricature quality of an anachronism. At the same time we cannot say that Maulbertsch looks only to the past - the elevated expression of his art lays the ground for the Vienna Sezession and in some measure Maulbertsch is a forerunner of Oskar Kokoschka.

AI

*Etching.*
*Platemark: 420 x c.317 mm.*
*Sheet: c.426 x c.322 mm.*

Inscribed verso, bottom right in pen and blackish brown ink: "50x" and in pencil in Emil Bloch's hand: "Johann Domenico . / Tiepolo -".
Provenance: Old property.
Inv.no. GB 1054.

**Franz Anton Maulbertsch**
*The Last Supper*

**40  J.-F. BEAUVARLET**  *French, Abbéville 1731 - Paris 1797*
*Toilet for the ball. 1737. After Jean-François de Troy's painting, dated 1737.*

It is evening, and a small party is about to go out. We do not know who they are, but we know they are going to a ball. These elegantly dressed men and women have arranged to meet first in the boudoir of one of the women. The title of the picture is *Toilet for the Ball*, and it belongs to the genre known at the time as "tableaux de modes", that is to say, depictions of modern, elegant life and manners. The work is part of the large collection of French 18th-century prints, owned by the Department of Prints and Drawings, comprising nearly 9000 prints acquired by Joachim Wasserschlebe, secretary to the Danish Ambassador to Paris in the years 1731-51. The collection is unique in that a great many of these prints probably were purchased directly from their original place of publication and sale.

The artist, Jacques-Firmin Beauvarlet, was an excellent engraver who had specialized in copying other artists' paintings, old as well as modern. Before the invention of photography in the 19th century, graphic reproduction was the only means of "mass-producing" art, and thus of making individual artists and their work known. Beauvarlet based his picture on an original painting by J.- F. de Troy (1679-1752), one of the popular painters of the day who became especially well-known within the Parisian art world for his small, elegant genre paintings.

In French visual art, Rococo is above all the epoch of love. Parlours, interior decoration and exhibitions abounded with depictions of sensual love in its various manifestations. To judge solely by the evidence of these pictures, the life and manners of the aristocracy were governed by an openly displayed, erotic game-playing, saturated with unmistakable meaning - at times more subtly articulated as an underlying, electrifying current flowing among the participants. The desire to satisfy lust was stimulated through conversation, as one may see in *Toilet for the Ball* where the characters are engaged in lively conversation while fixing each other with their eyes. The game is already in full progress, anticipating the pleasures of the ball. The room lies hidden in a presentient darkness while the human figures are illuminated, allowing the viewer - male or female - to become fully absorbed in the crypto-erotic gestures and body language of the depicted characters. Only the opulent sensuality of the overwhelming masses of silk and brocade threatens to burst apart this scene of an otherwise controlled and highly ritualized alliance with desire. At the ball, seduction can continue. Hidden behind a half-mask, and thus at a distance, one can approach the unknown and the dangerous. Longing and an awareness of loss and separation are the driving forces behind the seduction staged within this pictorial reality.

In another picture entitled *Returning from the Ball* - also by Beauvarlet, based on de Troy - the small party is again assembled in a parlour. The gaiety is gone, and a certain fatigue seems to have set in. However, the central female figure and the man on the right appear to be still involved in an erotic intrigue - clandestinely - but we are not told what will happen next. As spectators we are merely, momentarily, witnessing a before and an after the ball.

VK

*Engraving and etching.*
*Platemark: 491 x 369 mm.*
*Sheet: 514 x 492 mm.*

Inscribed in the plate, bottom left: "de Troy pinx . Fc." and bottom right: " J. Beauvarlet sculp."
Provenance: Joachim Wasserschlebe.
Inv.no. GB 1055.
Selected literature: Émile Dacier, *La gravure de genre et de moeurs*, Librairie Nationale d'Art et Histoire, Paris and Brussels, 1925, p. 72, cat.no. 53, pl. XXXVII; cf. Jan Würtz Frandsen, "Lyst og længsel – men hvilken og hvis?", in exh., Lene Bøgh Rønberg (ed.), *Lyst og længsel*, Statens Museum for Kunst, Copenhagen 1995, pp. 38-39.

*J.F. Beauvarlet: Return from the Ball. Engraving and etching.*

132

de Troy pinx. Rc.                                                                                          J. Beauvarlet. Sculp.

**TOILLETTE POUR LE BAL.**
*Tiré du Cabinet de Monsieur Prousteau, Capitaine des Gardes de la Ville.*
*A Paris chez l'Auteur rue St Jacques vis à vis celle des Mathurins.*

**J.-F. Beauvarlet**
*Toilet for the ball. 1737*

133

**41    JEAN-HONORÉ FRAGONARD**  *French, Grasse 1732 - Paris 1806*
*Baccanal. A Nymph Steps over the Arms of two Satyres.  1763.*

Art historians have somewhat despairingly given a very matter-of-fact title to Fragonard's etching *A Nymph Steps over the Arms of two Satyrs*. Although, strictly speaking, the title describes what takes place in the picture, it offers no explanation. For what is really happening? The title's sobriety is in glaring contrast to the pornographic suggestiveness of the tableau. After all, satyrs are classical symbols of desire, their lusty smiles leaving no doubt of their intentions. And the nymph would have to be quite a nymphomaniac to satisfy these two goats. All this lechery is not presented directly, however - the motif is not straight pornography - but shown in a transcribed way: the *ménage à trois* seems to be subject to certain rules. But what are they? Why must the girl step over the satyrs' arms? Is she to be carried on them or rocked in them? Are these figures engaged in some sort of game or foreplay? Just what obscene acts are about to take place? This, regrettably, we shall never know; we can only see that the action is regulated by a ritual of some kind.

This kind of subject matter is not at all exceptional in Fragonard's art. Sensual motifs abound in his pictures, and generally we perceive Rococo - which Fragonard is known to epitomize - as a thoroughly eroticized art. French Rococo art of the mid 1700s is crowded with draped female behinds in piquant boudoir settings, and, according to the 19th-century French writers, the Goncourt brothers, Fragonard was indeed "a poet of the art of love". But simply to view his pictures in this way, as mere sensual intoxication, is to lose sight of the fact that the display of sensuality must be properly set up to have any exciting effect at all. Which seems to be the very point of this etching.

Fragonard indulged in park scenes as a special genre, and this picture is related to them. When he abandoned the overheated Rococo boudoirs, he would most often place his love scenes in old, decaying parks. This pictorial biotope had its origins in a long summer's stay, during 1760, in the garden and landscape surrounding Villa d'Este in Tivoli, outside Rome. Fragonard's love parks are Arcadian, idyllic zones where scenes of a more or less veiled erotic nature are played out, where time is playfully spent on secret *rendez-vous*, elegant socializing or actual games such as blind man's buff, pushing girls on swings etc. The activities that go on in Fragonard's parks are frivolous, but always governed by some sort of love-making rules. There can be no game without rules.

In this etching Fragonard zooms in on one corner of the park, and here he seems to reveal the very method by which he depicts sensuality. We perceive that the vegetation is lush and apparently growing wild, but nevertheless subjected - as a game or a park - to a certain degree of regulation or cultivation, as indicated by the tied-up rushes on the right. The playing of the satyrs and the nymph is not an incident actually occurring in the park itself, but is frozen in a classical relief - even today part of the set-up necessary to the seductive park. The relief is thus a picture within a picture, one more method by which Fragonard places us at a certain cool distance from the sensual motif. Awareness of the regulation of passion seems to be his recurring theme. Hence with Fragonard it is both a question of love *and* of its proper staging. In other words: no loving without playing. The picture shows you how.

EJB

*Etching.*
*Image: c.132 x c.198 mm.*
*Sheet: 140 x 205 mm.*

First state of two, or probably second state of three.
Signed in the plate on a stone, bottom centre: "Frago 1763" (the name is erased, the chiffer 6 is reversed).
Provenance: Herbert N. Bier, London; acquired from him 1953 as gift of Gustav Philipsens Legat.
Inv. no. 19686.
Selected literature: Prosper de Baudicour: *Le Peintre-Graveur Francais...*, Paris 1859, p. 161f, no. 6; Louis Guimbaud: *Saint-Non et Fragonard*, Le Goupy, Paris 1928, p. 209, no. I a; Georges Wildenstein: *Fragonard aquafortiste*, Les Beaux-Arts, Edition d'Etudes et de Documents, Paris 1956, no. III,1°, p. 11; Cornelis Vermeule: *European Art and the Classical Past*, Harvard University Press, Cambridge Massachusetts 1964, p. 128f.; Pierre Rosenberg: *Fragonard*, Galeries Nationales de Grand Palais, Paris 1987 & The Metropolitan Museum of Art, New York 1988, cat.no. 67, p. 155; Dore Ashton: *Fragonard in the Universe of Painting*, Smithsonian Institution Press, Washington D.C. 1988, pp. 17-19.

**Jean-Honoré Fragonard**
*Baccanal. A Nymph Steps over the Arms of two Satyres.  1763*

**42  VALENTINE GREEN**  *English, 1739 Salford near Evesham – 1813 London*
*An Experiment on a Bird in an Air Pump.*  *1769.  After the painting by Joseph Wright of Derby, 1768.*

Before photography became common, graphic art was the most popular medium of visual communication. The graphic technique known as mezzotint, or the "black manner", was formerly much used as a reproductive medium, serving to make the great masters of painting and their works known. Mezzotint reached the height of its flourishing in the late 18th century in England, and is therefore also known as the "English manner". Valentine Green's mezzotints are outstanding examples of this technique. His reproduction of *An Experiment on a Bird in an Air Pump*, a painting by his countryman, Joseph Wright of Derby, was published just a year after the painting was completed in 1768, which testifies to the popularity of this sort of art product with the upcoming bourgeoisie. Mezzotint, as opposed to other graphic techniques such as engraving and etching, is a technique based on tone rather than line and therefore became the contemporary medium best able to translate the many subtle gradations of tone in painting to graphic art. The technique is especially well suited to reproducing dramatic lighting, an effect much used by Wright whose paintings, for that reason, were often reproduced in mezzotint.

Wright's *Air Pump* is one of the most signficant paintings produced in England at the time, reflecting many of the intellectual and spiritual concerns of the day. It shows a philosopher of the Enlightenment giving a lecture on pneumatics - more specifically on vacuum. To demonstrate this phenomenon, he pumps the air out of a glass flask containing a cockatoo which until then had been perched safely in its cage, visible at the upper right. The bird suffocates, and we are in fact witnessing a death scene disguised as an experiment in which an animal is killed in the name of science by means of modern technology. The audience reacts to the experiment with wonder, speculation, disgust, fascination, and so on. The picture seems to point to a dilemma typical of its day: on the one hand, we have the worship of reason and the faith in progress inherent in the philosophy, science and technology of the Enlightenment - the foundation of our modern world. On the other hand, we have nature in the shape of the bird, perhaps here a religious symbol as well, representing - as has been suggested - the Holy Ghost. Wright seems to say that modern rationality can only succeed at the expense of, and by going against, nature and religion. As we know, the importance of this dilemma has not diminished since the 18th-century dawn of modernity. Whether or not Wright's picture is a statement for or against the forward march of technology and science, it is beyond question that a drama is being played out, for the picture is staged using one of the pictorial formulas for high drama, namely the richly contrasting, so-called *chiaroscuro*. Are we seeing progress depicted as a dark deed?

EJB

*Mezzotint and some etching. Platemark: 481 x 585 mm.*

Second state of three.
Signed and dated in the plate, bottom right: "Val. Green fecit, Londini 1769."
Publisher: First Green, then John Boydell, London.
Provenance: Liutenant Mathiesen, Copenhagen; his sale 1.12. 1854, Hotel du Nord, Copenhagen, lot 250; acquired here. Inv.no. GB 1056.
Selected literature: *Fortegnelse over en udmærket Samling Kobberstik og Raderinger...*, [auction catalogue of lieutenant Mathiesen's estate], Copenhagen 29.11.1854, lot 250, p. 10; John Chaloner Smith: *British Mezzotints Portraits*, Henry Sotheran & Co., London 1884, cat.no. 163[I], p. 598f.; Alfred Whitman: *British Mezzotinters, Valentine Green*, A.H. Bullen, London 1902, cat.no. 167[II], p. 126, repr. p.72; Carol Wax: *The Mezzotint, History and Technique*, Thames and Hudson, London 1990, p. 56, repr. p. 43; Timothy Clayton: *The English Print, 1688-1802*, Yale University Press, New Haven and London 1997, p. 193, repr. p. 194.

**Valentine Green**
*An Experiment on a Bird in an Air Pump.  1769*

**43  FRANCISCO GOYA**  *Spanish, Fuendetodos 1746 - Bordeaux 1828*
*Bullfight in a Divided Ring.* 1825.  *From the series Los toros de Bordeos (The Bulls of Bordeaux).*

In his final years, Goya, unorthodox as he always was, would work on the lithographic stone balanced on his easel. He would cover the surface with a uniform grey, afterwards using a scraper and crayons to make the motif stand out in light and dark areas. During the whole process he would be standing up, moving back and forth in order to evaluate the work as it gradually emerged. *Bullfight in a Divided Ring* was made in this way.

In Spain, bullfighting is not only a national sport, it has the status of a cult, with death and the triumph over death as the vital nerve in this drama of cruelty played out in the ring. Here catastrophe may occur at any moment, especially in critical situations, and it is these moments Goya captures, as effectfully as possible, in order to affect the viewer emotionally. The attending crowd and its reactions, conveyed to the viewer, play at least as great a part in Goya's depiction of reality as the bullfight itself. The crowd reflects the drama in the ring, cheering or mocking the bullfighter's passes, his wisdom and courage, or lack of such, in the confrontation with the raging animal which, by its strength alone, arouses fascination and a pleasurable sensation of fear. Goya sees and depicts the bullfight in its entirety as a passionate, give-and-take exchange between the participants, in as well as outside the ring, drawing the viewer into the picture's realistic fictional space as part of the drama.

In *Bullfight in a Divided Ring*, two fights are going on at the same time. In the one, some spectators, at the peril of their own lives, have broken into the ring to experience the drama as intensely and closely as possible. At the lefthand corner, a shouting banderillero approaches to goad the bull. Its neck muscles are bleeding from wounds made by the picador's lance and by banderillas - the barbed darts thrust into it - which the bull has tried in vain to shake off. In the far background, a horse lies dead, its belly torn open by the bull's lethal horns. While this is going on, the fight in the other ring has reached its final act, the bull now so exhausted that the matador is preparing for his last pass. His muleta, the red cape meant to help and protect him, is lying on the ground. He is raising his sword, passing it over the horns, and in the next moment - perhaps - he will have thrust the blade with precision into the aorta, and the bull will collapse, dead on the spot. But Goya arrests the action while the outcome is still uncertain. The scene is pulled into the very forefront of the picture and slightly magnified to mark its importance. The barrier dividing the ring cuts diagonally across the pictorial space, and the arena opens out towards the viewer, inviting him or her to partake in the action along with the other spectators. By using such effects, Goya keeps the viewer in a state of excitement which he deliberately avoids relieving in order to involve him or her all the more in a brutal and spectacular drama of life and death.

VK

*Lithograph.*
*Image: 304 x 414 mm.*
*Sheet: 437 x 690 mm.*

Harris, 286.
Signed in the stone, bottom left of centre: "Goya".
Verso: Bottom left stamp of the Cleveland Museum of Fine Art (Lugt Suppl. 449c) inscribed at centre in pencil: "49.3", to the left of that the same stamp inscribed at centre in pencil: "L.E.P. [?]/6/15/51".
Printer: Gaulon, Bordeaux.
Provenance: Bolzheimer Collection, Munich; acquired here by Richard Zinser; acquired from him by the Cleveland Museum of Art; from the museum back to Zinser; acquired from him 1956 as gift of the Ny Carlsberg Foundation.
Inv.no. 1956-12.
Selected literature: Tomás Harris, *Goya. Engravings and Lithographs*, London 1964, vol. I, pp. 220-222, vol. II, p. 428, cat.no. 286; Pierre Gassier and Juliet Wilson, *The Life and Complete Work of Francisco Goya*, New York 1971, pp. 346-348, p. 364, cat.no. 1710; Werner Hofmann (ed.), *Goya. Das Zeitalter der Revolutionen 1789-1830*, Hamburger Kunsthalle, 1981, p. 290, p. 299, cat.no. 266; Juliet Wilson Bareau, *Goya's Prints. The Tomás Harris Collection in the British Museum*, British Museum Publication Limited, London 1981, pp. 91-95; Juliet Wilson-Bareau and Manuela B. Mena Marqués, *Goya. Truth and Fantasy. The Small Paintings*, Museo del Prado, Madrid, et al., Yale University Press, New Haven and London, 1994, pp. 332-333, p. 375, cat.no. 118; Alfonso E. Pérez Sánchez and Julián Gállego, *Goya. The Complete Etchings and Lithographs*, Munich/New York 1994, p. 236, p. 240, cat.no. 17.

*Bullfight in a Divided Ring. 1825*

139

## 44  J.F. CLEMENS  *Danish, Gollnow 1748 - Copenhagen 1831*
### *The Battle of Copenhagen. c. 1802 - 1805. After C.A. Lorentzen's painting, dated 1801.*

*The Battle of Copenhagen* - or "The Battle of April 1801 on the Roadstead of Copenhagen", which is the official title of this print - records the surprise attack by the English on the Danish fleet. The Danes had been forced to hastily mobilize all available men, and all ships more or less ready for combat. Clemens' etching is based on a painting by C.A. Lorentzen who had witnessed the battle and sketched it as it occurred. The event is seen from a bird's-eye perspective, supposedly from the tower of Vor Frelsers Kirke (Our Saviour's Church). The buildings of Nyholm, at the centre, stretch diagonally into the picture toward a hoisting-sheers still in existence. On the left is the Greenland Trade Department's warehouse, compositionally closing the foreground, while the ramparts on the right afford an unobstructed view over The Sound where the action is taking place, veiled in clouds of gunsmoke. It took Clemens three years to complete this enormous picture, a war report in which he used the techniques of graphic art in order to mass-reproduce an event that would soon assume great national importance. With his delicate line etching, worked over with a deep-cutting burin for precision, Clemens achieved a highly descriptive and dramatic pictorial effect.

The historical background for the battle was England's war against Napoleon, a war in which all of Europe was involved. The Danish government had provoked England by entering into a neutral alliance with, among other states, Russia. On the morning of Maundy Thursday, the 2nd of April, Lord Nelson, second-in-command of the British navy, sailed through the Kongedybet channel just as all the church bells began to ring for Matins. The attack had been expected, but not so soon. The preceding days had been marked by hectic activity on the Danish side. The fleet was in a largely unrigged state, that is to say without sails, ropes, cannon or ammunition. Only two, partly-rigged ships of the line and some smaller vessels were available, and so, at lightning speed, a line of defense was constructed from scrapped ships, hulls of ships of the line with only one side equipped with cannon. Between these were placed barges carrying as many cannon as possible. One fourth of the men were volunteers, of all ages and from all ranks and classes. Nevertheless, the English met with far more resistance than they had expected and suffered considerable losses. Although they were far superior to the Danes in strength and would have ultimately won the battle, Nelson halted the fighting and agreed with the king on a cease-fire to avoid further losses. The Danish people, beginning to experience a sense of national pride, were not far from considering this a victory. They had stood together, helped each other before and after the battle - which thousands had observed - and a high-spiritedness spread throughout the city where the streets resounded with the song "Take up arms, for the enemy is approaching". And when all was over, the heroes of the battle were idolized.

Clemens' picture is a successful piece of propaganda art, which was issued in a large edition and displayed in many good Danish citizens' homes. It is full of descriptive details, such as enthusiastic crowds of spectators and a high-flying Danish flag, but the core of the story's plot is the overwhelming cloud that almost completely obscures the English fleet, as if it were going down in steam and smoke.

VK

*Etching and engraving.*
*Platemark: 586 x 804 mm.*
*Sheet: 668 x 921 mm.*

Swane, 318.
Inscribed in the plate, bottom centre: "BATAILLEN d. 2. April 1801, paa KIØBENHAVNS REED", bottom left: "C.A. Lorentzen pinx:" and bottom right: "I.F. Clemens sculps:".
Provenance: Together with other engravings gift 1929 of The Library of The Royal Academy of Art, Copenhagen, where the main part of these sheets were collected in a portfolio, probably from C.F. Clemens's own collection.
Inv.no. 10793.
Selected literature: Leo Swane, *J.F. Clemens*, Copenhagen 1929, p. 125, pp. 245-246, cat.no. 318; Jørgen Sthyr, *Dansk Grafik 1500 - 1800*, Foreningen for Boghaandværk, Copenhagen 1943, pp.234-235; John Erichsen, *Københavnske motiver 1587 - 1807*, Københavns Bymuseum, Copenhagen 1974, p. 84, cat.no. 136.

*BATAILLEN d. 2 April 1801, paa KIØBENHAVNS Reed.*

**J.F. Clemens**
*The Battle of Copenhagen. c. 1802 - 1805*

## 45  JOHN MARTIN  *English, Haydon Bridge 1789 - Douglas, Isle of Man 1854*
*The Deluge.   1831/39.  From Charles Tilt's 1839-edition of Illustrations of the Bible.*

The end of the world has always been a favoured subject. To the disaster fetishist John Martin, it was an obsession, and his megalomanic staging of death and destruction became a formula for success that secured him stardom on the English art scene of the 1820s and 1830s, as well as the nickname *Mad Martin*. His paintings became major attractions, and to profit from the attention, he reproduced them graphically. Before long his graphic works were so much in demand that they were no longer made as reproductions of paintings but as pictures in their own right. *The Deluge* is an example. It exists in various versions and is characteristic of Martin's choice of themes. He favoured Old Testament scenes where the Lord vents his anger on a sinful humanity. Martin's disaster motifs fascinate because they unabashedly indulge in the entire range of Gothic effects. In *The Deluge* the elements are raging, the horizon is blotted out, a pitch-black abyss opens up to swallow lost souls, there is thunder and lightning, it is raining rocks - as the Lord is in the habit of letting it do at times - and floods are pouring from the heavens. Humans are depicted as terrified masses or in various stages of despair, as in the case of the central male and female figures, placed in traditional pictorial postures of terror - e.g. she in the same pose as the woman in Füssli's famous painting *Nightmare*. The whole image is saturated with imagery, but its power to fascinate does not rest on aesthetic overkill alone, but equally on the pedantic precision with which Martin seeks to depict his scenes of horror. In preparing for this work, for instance, he calculated how high the mountains in the background would have to be, based on the laws of perspective. He placed the sun, the moon and a comet in conjunction, in accordance with a contemporary scientific theory on the cause of the Deluge and, in the same scientific spirit, furnished the picture with trumpeting mammoths and dinosaurs, placed on an island at the far back, to give a historically correct impression of the fauna at this prehistoric time. Nor is the source of original sin, the snake of Paradise, missing. Furthermore, Martin placed Noah's Ark on the only calm surface in the picture. Like some mysterious crate, it floats on a calm sea in the eye of the storm.

There is no doubt that the overwhelming richness of imagery in Martin's pictures explains both why they became so popular and why distinguished critics often considered them vulgar kitsch. A genuine work of art, as we all know, should not rely on an unrestrained use of *gimmicks*. On the contrary, if one wishes to be taken seriously, a certain restraint would seem to be required. This is true not only with respect to visual art, but characterizes the generally ascetic relationship of high culture to images - especially within the Christian, Protestant culture - not only at Martin's time, but in our own as well. *The Deluge* is a slap in the face to such pictorial puritanism: Martin's image poses a fundamental question concerning our concept of imaging: Can an image be too much of an image? And, if so, when exactly is it too much?

EJB

*Mezzotint with etching.
Platemark: 267 x 352 mm.
Image: 197 x 289 mm.*

Seventh state of eight.
Inscribed in the plate, bottom centre: "Designed and Engraved by John Martin / THE DELUGE".
Provenance: Paul Prouté, Paris; acquired here 1987.
Inv. no. 1987-425.
Selected literature: Thomas Balston: *John Martin, 1789-1854, His Life and Works*, Duckworth, London 1947, no. 9a 11.6; Cf. Lynn R. Matteson: "John Martin's 'The Deluge', A study in Romantic Catastrophe", in *Pantheon* 1981, XXXIX. Jahrgang, p. 220ff.; J. Dustin Wees with Michael J. Campbell: *"Darkness Visible"*, *The Prints of John Martin*, Williamstown, Massachusetts 1986, cat.no. 34, p. 46, CW no. 97; Michael J. Campbell: *John Martin, Visionary Printmaker*, York City Art Gallery 1992, CW 97 vii/viii, p. 134.

**John Martin**
*The Deluge.   1831/1839*

143

**46  JEAN-BAPTISTE-CAMILLE COROT**  *French, Paris 1796 - Paris 1875*
*The Dreamer. January 1854.*

A *cliché-verre* is a photographic contact print on paper which has been pre-pared with a light-sensitive emulsion, a method which greatly interested French artists around the middle of the 19th century. Corot's graphic art is a highly respected part of his total work, but he never took much interest in the technical processes involved. He left the etching and printing to others, such as the engraver Félix Braquemond, who was later to advise Edouard Manet (see Manet, cat.50). In most cases, Corot's *cliché-verres* were executed as dense textures of hatchings, but occasionally, as here, he would cover the plate with oil paint and then bring out the image by removing the paint from certain areas which on the print appear black, brownish or brownish-purple because the light-sensitive paper darkens on exposure to sunlight. Whichever method he employed, matter rather than form seems to be the essential in Corot's pictures. His late landscapes, especially, emerge from a formless obscurity; the twilight originating in the foreground of the pictures seems not only to fill them completely but to reach, through the field of vision, into the viewer's mind. Corot pays no attention to individual line, but lets the arbitrary sum of his hatchings form masses with no real shape or outline - masses which, in the act of percep-tion, assume the soothing shape of the familiar in the beholder's conscious-ness. But the formation of the picture is a process that is not finished with the completion of the composition. It is visibly a function of the picture. The perception of Corot's late landscapes could be described by reference to the model used by gestalt psychologists at the beginning of the century to explain the function of sight: the eye allows the chaotic complexity of the world to take shape in the conscious mind as recognizable figures, in a movement from formlessness to form. Corot's landscapes exist precisely by virtue of their proximity to formlessness. This quality conveys a dreamlike unreality, seeming to cover the familiar in a veil of strangeness and to test the apparent shadowy innocence of trees and buildings. If one moves close to the pictures, their forms dissolve into nothingness, and thus, by existing at this borderline of chaos, they are able to articulate what the psycholo-gists called a "pre-gestalt experience", an experience of being close to the primary, to the origins of the world, to matter. It is this quality which later made Corot useful to Cézanne whose paintings attempt to show how the world takes shape in the process of perception. But whereas Corot's land-scapes seem regressively oriented, pointing back toward unarticulated mat-ter, Cézanne's paintings move forward from this stage toward gestalt, toward form as conditioned by the consciousness of sight.

Corot's pictures articulate an original state, made visible and given form, not just because his landscape motifs describe an ideality rooted in the classical tradition of landscape painting, but also because they make the regression toward a primary formation of images their true aim, achieved by pictorial or iconic means free of all external reference. The landscape motif simply serves as a pretext for the artist.

JWF

*Cliché-verre on thin, smothe paper.*
*Image: c.150 x c.198 mm.*
*Sheet: c.170 x c.220 mm.*

Reprint; pl.3 from the portfolio *Quarante clichés-glace de Corot - Daubigny - Delacroix - Millet - Rousseau*, Paris 1921.
Copy/edition: 22/150.
Delteil, 43.
Signed in the plate, bottom left: "COROT".
Verso: Le Garrec's stamp in vio-let and inscribed in pen-cil:"22/150".
Publisher: Maurice Le Garrec, Paris.
Provenance: Le Garrec, Paris; acquired here 1922.
Inv.no. 8932.
Selected literature: Loys Delteil, *Le peintre-graveur illustré, Tome cinquième. Corot*, Paris 1910, no.43; Claude Bouret, *Corot. Le génie du trait*, (Bibliothèque Nationale de France), Paris 1996, pp.30-32, no.65.

**Jean-Baptiste-Camille Corot**
*The Dreamer. January 1854*

**47** **EUGENE DELACROIX**  *French, St.-Maurice-Charenton 1798 - Paris 1863*
*Arabs of Oran. 1833.*

In 1832, the French King Louis-Philippe sent a delegation to Marocco, led by Count Charles de Mornay. The purpose of this diplomatic expedition was to negotiate a non-agression pact with the Maroccan Sultan. The year before, Algeria had been colonized by France. Delacroix was invited to accompany the expedition, and throughout the six months of its duration he recorded his experiences and observations in his many sketchbooks. Delacroix had a great talent for seeing the picturesque in the places he visited, and his work gives us an insight into the exotic cultures of Marocco and Algeria. Delacroix was himself overwhelmed by the world he encountered, and the journey was to become all-important in the development of his work. Oriental scenes soon became Delacroix's preferred motifs, and many of his later paintings are based directly on sketches he made on this - his only - journey to the Orient.

On the way home, the expedition made a short halt in the town of Oran in Algeria, giving Delacroix the opportunity to make a drawing of two Arabs. Later, after his return to France, he used this drawing as the basis for the etching at hand, and for other works. The *Arabs of Oran* motif is thus known in several versions with different techniques. It is characteristic of Delacroix that he often varied his compositions and worked them over repeatedly, eliminating certain elements or adding new ones.

This etching shows Arabs in a desert landscape. The one in the foreground is regarding us, wrapped in his dark, woolen cape, while the seated Arab seems detached, absorbed in his own thoughts. Delacroix's presence seems neither to have affected nor interested them very much.

Delacroix was a great admirer of the dignity of the Arabs and would often compare them to the Roman senators of antiquity. He seems to deliberately attach such importance to the two Arabs in his picture by underscoring their monumental character.

The compositional emphasis on the diagonal lines is characteristic of Delacroix. The particular dynamics of this etching are generated by the countermovement of two diagonals: the one stretching along the path with the two figures turned away from us and continuing out toward the minaret at the horizon, the other starting at the reclining Arab and the gun in the foreground.

The motif attracts the viewer by its spontaneity and sense of recorded life. *Arabs of Oran* differs from the artist's earlier works inspired by the Orient in that it is a composition based on reality rather than on literary sources, a reality firmly grounded in Delacroix's visual and sensual memories of his journey.

LS

*Etching on thin paper laid down on larger sheet.
Image: 145 x 191mm. Platemark: 177 x 216 mm.*

Fifth state of six.
Delteil, 20$^V$.
Signed in the plate, bottom right: "EugèneDelacroix", and top right with monogram reversed: ED in a circle.
Inscribed in the plate below the image, bottom right: "Sarazin Imp, Paris"; bottom left: "E. Delacroix sculp", and bottom centre:"ARABES D'ORAN / Paris. Publié par CADAR & LUQUET. Editeurs, 79, Rue Richelieu"; above the image:"197."
Printer: Sarazin, Paris.
Publisher: Cadart et Luquet, Paris.
Provenance: Winkel & Magnussen, Copenhagen 4.5.1956, sale 399, lot 215; acquired here.
Inv.no. 21649.
Selected literature: Loys Delteil, *Le Peintre Graveur Illustré, Tome Troisième. Ingres & Delacroix*, Paris 1908, no. 20$^{IV}$; *Themen und Variationen. Arbeiten auf Papier*, Städtische Galerie im Städelschen Kunstinstitut, Frankfurt am Main 1987-1988, cat.no. H19-H21, pp. 152-155; *Delacroix in Morocco, Institut du Monde Arabe*, Paris, 1995, cat.no. 55, pp. 185, cat.no. 60, pp. 192, cat.no. 70, pp. 200.

ARABES D'ORAN.

Paris, Publié par CADART & LUQUET, Éditeurs, 79, Rue Richelieu

**Eugène Delacroix**
*Arabs of Oran. 1833*

**48 EUGENE ISABEY** *French, Paris 1803 - Paris 1886*
*Souvenir de Saint-Valéry-sur-Somme. Planche 4 from the series Six Marines, 1833.*

Isabey's graphic work is not extensive. Nevertheless, he holds a prominent position among the early French lithographers who introduced the new and revolutionary method of print-making from stone in the period between 1820 and 1850 - a group of artists including Théodore Géricault, Eugène Delacroix and Honoré Daumier. Isabey was unsurpassed when it came to making the crayon used on the polished and grainy slate produce tonal values ranging from deep black through light grays to pure white. He engaged himself in satisfying the growing demand for grand topographical descriptions of places and towns, a flourishing industry, especially in England. Thus, as a sketching tourist, he traveled through Auvergne, Brittany and - like the English water-colourist Richard Parkes Bonington - Normandy. Isabey and Bonington are the best known among the many artists, now mostly forgotten, who contributed picturesque prospects of towns and romantically perceived landscapes of "ancient France" to the 25 volume work entitled *Les Voyages pittoresques et romantiques dans l'Ancienne France*.

Isabey's prospects may in part have laid the foundation for the perception of ancient France which we later find in Victor Hugo's novels, not to mention his drawings, and which we encounter in caricature in Gustave Doré's illustrations for Rabelais' *Gargantua* and Balzac's *Contes drolatiques*. Isabey's landscapes are often characterized by a grand solemnity which underscores the fantastic or even awe-inspiring character of the locations. He follows a tradition reaching back over more than a century to Poussin's heroic, ideal landscapes of the 17th century. In these, the imaginative pathos is all-important, whereas Isabey is concerned with topographically defined localities. But in this lithograph, depicting the banks of the Saint-Valéry-sur-Somme, the reality of a well-established location is undermined and disturbed in the pictorial transformation, and another reality - as seen later in Proust's writing - emerges from memory. The image evokes the sense of awe which the English romantics and the philosopher Kant termed "the sublime": a state of mind in which the realization of one's own powerlessness brings a sense of fear mingled with joy and pain, which Isabey may have seen staged pictorially in contemporary graphic reproductions of William Turner's pictures of English landscapes.

The site is not the actual locality, despite the title's assurance of its reality and accessability. Its topos lies at the horizon and can only be reached, through the artist, in the viewer's own imagination. The leaning mast of the shored boat can be seen as the sign leading into the picture. Like the needle of a compass, it takes the bearings of an immensity which - rather than the topographical description - may be the picture's essential theme, becoming visible as suddenly as the flash of light from the building in the picture's middle plane. This metaphysical effect relies on a visual and absolute contrast, formed by the deep black of the boat's hull. The boat can be seen as the picture's dynamic centre of meaning, the form through which it becomes possible to grasp the immensity of the sublime, as defined by Kant.

JWF

*Lithograph.*
*Image: 302 x 242 mm.*
*Sheet: 431 x 335 mm.*

Second state of three, with full text.
Blind stamp, oval, bottom left for V. Morlot.
Printer: Ch. Motte, Paris.
Publisher: Morlot Galerie, Vivienne No. 26, Paris / Mc Lean, 26 Hay Market, London.
Provenance: Deposit 1922 from Det Danske Kunstindustrimuseum, Copenhagen.
Inv.no. GB 1057.
Selected literature: Atherton Curtis, *Catalogue de l'oeuvre lithographié de Eugène Isabey*, Paris 1939, no.66[II].

SOUVENIR DE S! VALERY SUR SOMME.

**Eugène Isabey**
*Souvenir de Saint-Valéry-sur-Somme. 1833*

**49**  **CAMILLE PISSARRO**  *French, Saint Thomas 1830 - Paris 1903*
*Square in Rouen: Place de la République.*  *c. 1883.*

Camille Pissarro was the most prolific print-maker of all the impressionist painters creating 126 etchings, 66 lithographs and a number of monotypes. Pissarro was interested in the technical processes of printmaking and, together with Degas, adopted innovative methods exploring them for their pictorial effects.

The circulation of Pissarro's prints is limited as he only printed a few impressions of each plate. The Department of Prints and Drawing's *Square in Rouen: Place de la République* is the second copy out of only five. However, Pissarro's family made a posthumous printing of this plate (40 impressions) in 1907 before cancelling it.

Most of Pissarro's prints portray rural landscapes, however there are also a number of city landscapes, like *Square in Rouen* which was inspired by his trip to Rouen in 1883. Pissarro made several sketches of this city which he later developed in a number of drawings, prints and paintings presenting the viewer with a topographical record of his wanderings. The majority of Pissarro's city landscapes depict old, narrow streets; *Square in Rouen* is one of his few scenes representing a wider urban expanse.

Pissarro selected a high viewpoint from which he could observe the various activities of the tramway, pedestrians, and horse-drawn carriages. The influence of Japanese woodblock prints can be seen in the depiction of rain puddles, the delicate translucent tones of gray and the compositional devices. For example, the figures placed near the surface of the picture plane confront the viewer with the two-dimensional space of the sheet and emphasize the flat design of the image. The severe cropping of the figures and horse in the foreground also accentuates the flatness of the square which appears to have no center. The relatively isolated motifs are united by an overall gray tonality which Pissarro achieved by scratching the plate in parallel lines resulting in a modelling of tone as well as the effect of glistening rain puddles.

Both the compositional devices and the technical processes communicate the busy and bustling activity of city life. The scene is a fleeting moment in which everything is in movement: carriages and pedestrians are hurrying by and the dominant horse-drawn tramway in the foreground is already well on its way out of the picture. The rain puddles emphasize the transitoriness of the observed image and details are omitted in order to capture the motion of the square. Pissarro's *Square in Rouen* represents a typical expression of the impressionist aesthetic and the evanescence of modern life.

JeG

*Etching on copper.*
*Platemark: 152 x 172 mm.*
*Sheet: 299 x 345 mm.*

Second (final) state.
Copy/edition: artist's proof 2/5.
Delteil, 65[II].
Signed bottom right in pen and black ink: "C. Pissarro" and inscribed above that: "Place de la Republique / à Rouen";, bottom left in pen and black ink over pencil: "no 2".
Provenance: Marcel Lecomte, Paris; acquired from him 1959 as gift of the Ny Carlsberg Foundation.
Inv.no. 1959-122.
Selected literature: Loys Delteil, *Le peintre-graveur illustré, Tome dix-septième. Pissarro, Sisley, Renoir*, Paris 1923, no.65; Barbara Stern Shapiro, "Pissarro as Print-maker", in *Pissarro*, London 1980, no. 181; Annegret Rittmann, *Die Druckgraphik Camille Pissarros*, Frankfurt a.M. 1989, pp.138-39, no.94, repr.

no 2

*Place de la République
à Rouen
C. Pissarro*

**Camille Pissarro**
*Square in Rouen: Place de la République. c. 1883*

## 50 EDOUARD MANET *French, Paris 1832 - Paris 1883*
*The Dead Toreador.* 1867/68.

Manet's etching repeats the lower section of a contemporary painting entitled *Episode of a Bullfight*, the composition of which he had found unsatisfactory. He trimmed it in order to concentrate on the figure that must initially have been the painting's essential theme. What he achieved was monumental and aesthetic isolation. Manet also worked extensively on the etched version which exists in as many as seven states. Of its first state, only three copies are known. These can be traced to two French artists who at mid-century were involved in advancing the status of graphic art as original work, namely Félix Braquemond and Edgar Degas, and to the critic Philippe Burty. Burty owned two copies that were later acquired by Degas. Today, one of these is owned by the National Museum, Stockholm, the other by the Copenhagen Department of Prints and Drawings. The third one, according to Guérin, was printed by Braquemont, as were perhaps the two others, and is still in private ownership. Around 1860, Degas and Manet began an aquaintance characterized by mutual criticism. Thus Degas reputedly remarked of his colleague that Manet was a perfect example of how the study of nature is determined by convention. He was nevertheless quite interested in Manet's experiments with graphic art, and in addition to *The Dead Toreador*, he owned *Le Gamin* in its second state (Harris 31 II). Also this is now owned by the Department of Prints and Drawings in Copenhagen.

Degas was right in noting that Manet conveyed his own impressions through studying the old masters. His figuration imitates a reality that is often - in its concentration and staging - inspired by Velazquez. This is also the case with *The Dead Toreador*, based, as has been established, on a painting of a dead soldier, previously ascribed to none other than Velazquez. Around 1860, when Manet first started working with etching, he had looked to yet another Spanish master for guidance. His own collection of graphic art included aquatints by Goya, whose technical skills had been described by Théophile Gautier in *Cabinet de l'amateur* as early as 1842, and this so interested Manet that in 1867 he reworked several of his early plates - among them *The Absinth Drinker* - with aquatint, probably with the assistance of Braquemond. In *The Dead Toreador* Manet employs Goya's method of combining line etching with various degrees of aquatint graininess in order to reproduce the subtly defined tonal range of painting. By means of the plane effects of aquatint and hatching, he demonstrates that a picture is a two-dimensional interpretation of the depth of reality. Robbed of all narrative content, the visual representation becomes a pictorial discourse on what a picture is. It becomes a painting about the reality of painting, or a graphic work demonstrating the artistic means available to graphic art: line and plane. The picture, in its painted as well as its graphic version, seems to be more concerned with aesthetic and pictorial problems than with problems of signification. The latter are made diffuse by the isolation and theatrical stasis which Manet creates by cutting away all that might justify the - in all events clearly postulated - iconography of the figure. It is precisely the theatricality which suggests that a picture is anything but synonomous with the reality from which it springs. When he exibited the final version of the print in 1867, Manet had changed its title - despite the references of costume - to the more neutral *The Dead Man.*

JWF

*Aquatint and etching on thin yellowish Japanese paper. Image: 97 x 195 mm. Sheet: c.145 x c.263 mm.*

First state of seven.
Moreau-Nélaton, 13[II]; Guérin, 33[I]; Harris, 55[I].
Signed in the plate, bottom left: "Manet".
Inscribed bottom left in pencil: "6", bottom right: "247/7" and above: "5[?]0".
Provenance: Philippe Burty, Paris; his sale 4.-5.3.1891, lot 247/7; Michel Manzi, Paris; from him to Edgar Degas; Degas sale 6.-7-11.1918, lot 245; from him to Duval Fleury, Paris; Wilhelm Hansen, Copenhagen; acquired from him 1923. Inv.no. 9163.
Selected literature: Etienne Moreau-Nélaton, *Manet. Graveur et lithographe*, Paris 1906, no. 13[II]; Marcel Guérin, *L'Oeuvre gravé de Manet*, Paris 1944, no. 33[I], Jean C. Harris, *Edouard Manet. The Graphic Work. A Catalogue Raisonné.* Revised Edition, San Francisco 1990, no. 55[I]; Colta Ives, Susan Alyson Stein and Julie A. Steiner e.a., *The Private Collection of Edgar Degas. A Summary Catalogue*, The Metropolitan Museum of Art, New York 1997, no.837 (here erroneously catalogued as second state).

**Edouard Manet**
*The Dead Toreador.  1867/68*

153

**51 EDGAR DEGAS** *French, Paris 1834 - Paris 1917*
*The Bath. 1879/83.*

Degas produced about 80 monotypes, all of them made during two brief periods of his career. He would work on a metal plate, either in a dark field manner - covering the entire plate with paint and then partially removing it to make the motif emerge from the dark ground - or in a light field manner, whereby the motif gradually takes form as more paint is applied. From such a plate, only a single satisfactory print can be made. Sometimes, however, Degas would let the plate go through the press one extra time, thus producing a weaker print which subsequently could be used as the basis for a new picture.

In *The Bath*, a motif he also worked with in other media, Degas used both the above mentioned techniques. He first covered the whole plate with paint and then removed it with a rag from certain areas, for instance the inside of the bathtub. In other areas, such as the wall and floor, he applied the paint with a rag, his fingers or a sponge. Lastly, the contours of the body and the dress were traced with a brush. The result is a richly differentiated surface where the whole tonal range of light and dark forms a blurred contrast to the few clearly drawn lines. Like his pastels, these monotypes are characterized by spontaneity, showing Degas quickly registering and capturing a moment in time. He offers a glimpse into the private world of others through his own impressions of what he perceives.

Degas concentrated his subject range to brothel scenes, bathing scenes and a number of unique landscapes depicted during the early 1890s. Although the first two categories are drawn from modern urban life, he considered himself an artist in the classical tradition. He once said that if he had been painting 200 years earlier, his subject would have been *Susannah and the Elders*. Instead, he now painted what he himself called "Women Bathing". At this point in the history of art, the bath scene had developed from such well-defined biblical scenes as the bathing Bathsheba or Susannah to a firmly established, general category of bathing women - *Baigneuses*.

Like other contemporary artists, Degas worked with the female nude as a natural motif in his exploration of different visual media, endlessly fascinated with experimentation. He made use of the spontaneous quality of the monotype in more explicit motifs - depicting living, contemporary women as life had formed them. These women have a personality of their own, and - whether ugly, old, sensual or youthful - they are all portrayed in their own environment, as opposed to the idealized nude placed in an imaginary world. What is most remarkable about Degas' bathing women is that they are not oriented towards the viewer, as in the pornography of the time; they are completely absorbed in themselves. And they seem at any moment about to turn even further away from the viewer's space. In *The Bath*, the woman is drying herself with her back turned and at the same time seems to be bending over forward in a movement that further emphasizes her introversion.

Judging by the way he presented them, contemporary critics were of the opinion that Degas was repulsed by women. Today, his works seem rather to convey a deep fascination with women, depicting them in a radically new artistic idiom.

*Monotype on laid paper.*
*Image: 213 x 159 mm.*
*Sheet: 317 x 232 mm.*

Provenance: Degas sale, 22.-23.11.1918, lot 217; acquired here by Wilhelm Hansen, Copenhagen; acquired from him 1925.
Inv. no. 9161.
Selected literature: Eugenia Parry Janis, *Degas Monotypes, Essay, Catalogue & Checklist*, Fogg Art Museum, Harvard University, Cambridge Mass. 1968, cat.no.41; Jean Adémar et Françoise Cachin, *Edgar Degas gravures et monotypes*, Paris 1974, no.132; Hanne Finsen (ed.), Richard Kendall, Michael Wivel, *Degas Intime*, Ordrupgaard, Copenhagen 1994, cat.no.54.

IO

**Edgar Degas**
*The Bath.   1879/83*

155

**52 PAUL GAUGUIN**  *French, Paris 1848 - Fatu Iwa, Marquesa Islands 1903*
*Human Miseries. 1898/1899.*

The woodcut *Misères Humaines* is part of the series *Souvenir de Bretagne*, produced by Gauguin during his final stay on the Marquesa Islands. The series consists of fourteen prints, each issued in thirty copies. The prints were made very simply, without the use of specialized tools. Gauguin transferred the motif to very thin paper by pressing the paper against the block of wood with a blunt instrument. The use of a simple technique was part of his overall search for an original primitivity, the search which had brought him to the South Sea Islands in the first place. He wanted to get away from Western civilization and its corrupted world views in order to find a purity of imagery, an absolute zero point, free from the numerous layers of meaning and reference of Western pictorial art.

In *Misères Humaines* we see a young, seated woman with distinctly Polynesian features. Her dark hair encircles her head which is resting on her hands. The right side of the picture is framed by a tree bulging with fruit, which Gauguin has placed in a French landscape with a Brittany woman in the background, working the earth. She is wearing the headcloth which all Brittany women must use after they marry. Although the print was made several years later, far away under different skies, it refers, by way of the working woman and the character of the landscape, to his stay in Brittany and to the European world. Like Gauguin's many depictions of a Polynesian Virgin Mary, this woodcut represents a search for a state of primal innocence, symbolized by the Polynesian woman. In Gauguin's artistic idiom, the native woman forms a contrast to the European woman who in his eyes is the product of a corrupted world.

The woman in *Misères Humaines* appears in many other works by Gauguin, notably in the woodcut *Les Misères humaines*, part of the Volpini series (Guérin, 5) produced during the artist's stay in Arles in 1888. In this later woodcut, however, the woman's expression is thoughtful rather than sad, as it is in the earlier work where she is shown with a man in a situation that suggests an underlying sexual conflict, a recurring theme in Gauguin's late work.

To a woman from Brittany, uncovered hair was synonymous with sexual provocation. Here, transformed into a Polynesian woman and placed under a paradisal fruit tree, she becomes the allegorical image of a state of primal innocence, existing before sexuality became associated with shame. The picture is thus a symbolic expression of the sexual conflict inherent in European culture and, at the same time, represents the conflict between European civilization and the primitive society.

This cultural and geographical confrontation brings the symbols and signs of one world into contact with those of another. In an artistic idiom built out of a complex network of cross-references and meanings, Gauguin couples the Polynesian mythical world with the Christian world view. As in this woodcut, where the two worlds that were the pivots of Gauguin's life and career are brought together within one universe.

IO

*Woodcut on transparent Japanese paper, laid down on strong paper.*
*Image: c.194 x c.303 mm.*
*Sheet: c.199 x c.312 mm.*

Copy/edition: 27/30.
Inscribed bottom left in pen an greyish black ink: "n⁰ 27".
Provenance: Mogens Ballin, Copenhagen; acquired from him 1912/13.
Inv.no. 6417.
Selected literature: Marcel Guérin, *L'oeuvre gravé de Gauguin*, Paris 1927, vol. 2, cat.no. 69; Richard Brettell, *The Art of Paul Gauguin*, National Gallery of Art, Washington and The Art Institute of Chicago 1988, pp.428-445.

*Paul Gauguin: Human Misery. Litograph.*

**Paul Gauguin**
*Human Miseries.  1898/1899*

**53   J. F. WILLUMSEN**   *Danish, Copenhagen 1863 - Cannes 1958*
*Fertility.  1891.*

J. F. Willumsen did quite a bit of experimentation with a variety of art forms. The graphic arts is an area which he took up several times throughout his career and some of his most radical development can be seen unfolding in his prints. Early on, Willumsen took up the technique of etching for a period of six years (1885-1891) and these prints reveal his transition from a naturalistic style in *Marriage* (Ægteskab,1886) to a more simplified, synthesist expression *in Promenading Lady* (Dame, der spadserer, 1889) and *Aborre Parken*, (1890). This reorientation took place after travels in France and Spain and culminated in the thorough understanding and personal adaption of Symbolism in *Fertility* (Frugtbarhed, 1891).

It was during Willumsen's stay in Paris that he quickly found his way to an understanding of avant-garde development while at the same time working in a personal, and even brutal, style. *Fertility* is nothing less than Willumsen's manifesto of modern art and as such it can be compared to the French art critic Albert Aurier's manifesto of symbolist art: *Le Symbolisme dans la peinture: Paul Gauguin*. They were produced simultaneously and as Roald Nasgaard has pointed out, Willumsen's print can be interpreted as a visual illustration of Aurier's text. *Fertility* is ideological and symbolist, as described by Aurier, in that the images do not function naturalistically nor descriptivly but perform solely as signs for ideas. In other words, the meanings of the images are symbolic and dependent on their decorative form. The final statement of the etching relies on the interaction of the images according to an independent pictorial logic which gives the picture its own reality and completeness.

The pregnant woman (Willumsen's wife expecting their first child) placed beside a sprouting ear of grain is symbolic of the process of propagation. These symbols refer not only to plant and human life but to the idea of the continual renewal of the forms of art. As Nasgaard suggests, this print can be understood as suggesting a cosmic interpretation of the unity and analogy of the eternal procreative forces of earth, body and spirit. But the immediate didactic purposes of the print concern questions of art directly related to post-impressionist Parisian development. Willumsen makes this clear in the inscription: "L'art ancien a son ancienne langue que le monde peu à peu a appris à comprendre  Un art nouveau a une langue nouvellement formée que le monde doit apprendre avant de la comprendre –".

*Fertility* created a scandal both because of its simple, straightforward style and its subject-matter in which Willumsen transforms and defiles two traditionally positive symbols: art's ideal female beauty is exaggeratedly disfigured by the new life it nourishes and the farmer's pride in the harvest-ready ear of grain is destroyed by nature's chaotic process of germination. This print was first viewed by Willumsen's Danish contemporaries at The Independent Exhibition's (Den Frie Udstilling) initial show which established an alternative to the official exhibitions at Charlottenborg. Most of the works exhibited at The Independent Exhibition could have made it through the Charlottenborg censorship, but not Willumsen's humble little etching which raised an outcry of indignation in the press and amongst the public making *Fertility* one of the most controversial works in Danish art history.

JeG

*Etching, aquatint and roulette.*
*Platemark: 243 x 342 mm.*
*Sheet: 247 x 342 mm.*

One state only.
Signed and dated in the plate bottom left in pencil: "J.F. Willumsen jvier 1891".
Printer: The artist.
Publisher: The artist.
Provenance: Lykke Slott-Møller; acquired from her 1938.
Inv.no.: 13933.
Selected literature: Sigurd Schultz, *J.F. Willumsen. Grafiske arbejder*, Copenhagen 1943, no.17; Sigurd Schultz, *Willumsens grafik. Ny fortegnelse*, Copenhagen 1961, no. 17; Roald Nasgaard, *Willumsen and Symbolist Art 1888-1910*, New York 1973.

L'art ancien a son    ancienne langue que
le monde peu    à peu a appris à comprendre
Un art nouveau a    une langue nouvellement
formée que le    monde doit apprendre
avant † de la    comprendre †

J.F. Willumsen j.vier 1891

J. F. Willumsen

**J. F. Willumsen**
*Fertility. 1891*

159

## 54 HENRI DE TOULOUSE-LAUTREC *French, Albi 1864 - Saint-André du Bois 1901*
### *Miss May Belfort. Large sheet. 1895.*

*Lithograph, olive green.*
*Image: 481 x 337 mm.*
*Sheet: 587 x 419 mm.*

First state of thirteen; very rare.
Wittrock, 114[I].
Signed on the stone bottom left
with Lautrec's monogram;
Lautrec's monogram stamp in
red, bottom right (Lugt 1338).
Inscriptions: Recto, bottom left
in red chalk: "Etat 5 ep. No 1";
bottom left Kleinmann's blind
stamp (Lugt 1573). Verso, bottom right in pencil: "Miss Mary
[sic] Belfort/2 etat tirée à 5 ep.
2 D 119 9212", and bottom
left: "Miss Belford [sic]".
Printer: Ancourt, Paris.
Publisher: Kleinmann, Paris.
Provenance: Acq. 1926 as gift of
the Ny Carlsberg Foundation.
Inv.no. 10075.
Selected literature: Wolfgang
Wittrock, *Toulouse-Lautrec. The
Complete prints*, Sotheby's Publications, London 1985, vol. 1, p.
290, cat.no. 114; Götz Adriani,
*Toulouse-Lautrec. Das Gesamte
Graphische Werk, Sammlung Ger-
stenberg*, Dumont Buchverlag,
Cologne 1986, p. 171, cat.no.
123; *Toulouse-Lautrec. Prints and
Posters from the Bibliothèque
Nationale*. Queensland Art Gal-
lery 1991, p. 36, cat.no. 12.

Toulouse-Lautrec was always on the lookout for whatever was new and shocking in the Parisian night life in order to use it as subjects for pictures as procovative and entertaining as the reality he depicted. He moved with ease in the borderland between the elitist and the popular, creating a type of image that with its eye-catching and immediately readable signs appealed to a mass audience across class barriers. He found the material for his work primarily in the corrupt and titillating night life of Montmar-tre, an environment which - unlike the established high culture - sanc-tioned almost any kind of mental or physical recreation. Among the caba-ret and concert-café stars cultivated by Lautrec ( most notably Jane Avril and Yvette Guilbert) was also Miss May Belfort, an Irish chanteuse whom he discovered at Les Decadents in 1895. English-speaking singers were the height of fashion on the Parisian stage in those years, and Lautrec made as many as six lithographs, three paintings and a poster of her. Even to an audience who had been exposed to a great deal, her stage appearance must have seemed bizarre. But for just that reason it was also appealingly new and different - able, for a short while, to capture the imagination. Dressed in a ruffled gown and a large bonnet, and carrying a kitten in her arms, she would sing children's songs in a lisping voice, adding an unmistakable erot-ic twist to the content. One of her successes was "Daddy wouldn't buy me a bow-wow", and the audience could hardly mistake her interpretation of the lines "I've got a little cat/And I'm very fond of that..."

Many of Lautrec's lithographs are sketchy observations made and later recorded, images of recollected moments frozen in simple, or sometimes more elaborate, quickly-drawn lines. Most of the May Belfort lithographs belong to this category. Lautrec usually gave her the immediately recog-nizable attributes, like the cat and the bonnet. Most often she is seen in profile, as in this very rare print where Lautrec, by means of a few lines and with the minimal use of artistic effects, has captured the surroundings, her stance and her whole general appearance. Any viewer familiar with the May Belfort iconography will quickly identify the cat by the tip of its tail - the only sign of its presence. The diffuse background represents the stage area, and a piano - no more than a suggestion - is outlined as a purely abstract form to the left. As is often the case with Lautrec, expression and content are reduced to a minimum to emphasize what is essential. Lautrec had the lithograph printed in a very limited edition, thus giving it the status of an original. He kept working on the motif, however, but on a new stone, to which he transferred the singer's figure and also incorporated the pianist, a spectator and part of the stage decor. In this later print, the viewer's attention is directed toward the foreground figures as well as the singer, whereas in the first version the focus is strictly on the singer and the melancholy expression she used for some of her songs. This melan-choly is also evident in the only lithograph that depicts her with neither cat nor bonnet. May Belfort was considered attractive by her contempo-raries, but with Lautrec's usual talent for distorting his models' features and emphasizing their less obvious or flattering aspects, she appears here, seen through Lautrec's special optics, as a weary *femme fatale* without props and without the false baby-look.

VK

*Henri de Toulouse-Lautrec: Miss May Belfort with her Hairs down. Litograph.*

**Henri de Toulouse-Lautrec**
*Miss May Belfort. Large sheet. 1895*

**55** **WASSILY KANDINSKY** *Russian, Moscow 1866 - Neuilly-sur-Seine 1944*
*Plate VIII of the* **Kleine Welten** *portfolio. 1922.*

Kandinsky's portfolio *Kleine Welten* (Small Worlds) was issued in 1922, shortly after he began teaching at the Bauhaus in Weimar, and records the progress of his work over ten years - from the early, expressive abstractions of 1912-14 (plate III) to the "cool" abstract murals in the foyer of the Jury-freie Kunstausstellung in Berlin in 1922 (plate VII). Plate VIII is a fascinating example of how Kandinsky's abstraction is the result of a process wherein the representational figures of his early paintings gradually become reduced to purely pictorial or iconic elements. It was the stated aim of the pioneers of abstract art to purify painting by ridding it of all narrative and directly mimetic elements. Painting was to focus on the inexplicable in a world thoroughly explained by positivistic science, and lead in a spiritual direction. It was to express, by its own means, an essential, ultimate reality. Recent research has demonstrated, however, that the iconological dimension - that is to say, the inherent sign language of figurative art, including landscape painting - has not been swallowed up by the iconoclasms of the avant-garde. To Kandinsky, forming an image meant constructing a language of meanings that could be understood in the way that music, preferably symphonic music, is understood. This he discusses in his treatise *Über das Geistige in der Kunst* (Concerning the Spiritual in Art, 1912). But also the iconography of individual figurative complexes, their significance as pictorial gestalts, is brought over into his apparently non-objective compositions. Thus, although Kandinsky, like other modernist artists, was concerned mainly with problems of aesthetic articulation by means of form and colour - discussed theoretically in *Punkt und Linie zu Fläche* (Point and Line to Plane) - his works are by no means emptied of all other meaning than that which the symphonic dynamics of form and colour generates.

On the contrary, plate VIII lives up to its title, indicating that each of the 12 plates represents a microcosm. The image is closely related to Kandinsky's apocalyptic compositions dating from 1912-14. By means of purely iconic elements, it represents a state of chaos, balanced between birth and destruction. This reading can be taken further by incorporating the picture's representational elements, such as the complex of building abstractions at the upper left and right, which seems to be whirling into space in a galactic explosion. On the lower left three parallel lines can be seen, which are actually remnants of the loving couple who appear in several earlier paintings. Other recurring figurative elements - such as a boat with oars and Kandinsky's characteristic icon, the dragon-slaying Saint George - almost dissolve in pictorial energetics, generated by counter-movements. The iconological references are primarily to Doomsday and Resurrection, both themes which appear frequently in the years leading up to the First World War and have therefore inevitably been interpreted in relation to the European catastrophe and the utopian ideas that arose around it, not least in the field of art. Kandinsky's own vision of how to arrive at a harmonious balance in "Das grosse Geistige" should be seen in the context of this period at the beginning of the new century, marked by a general sense of doom and a longing for transcendence.

*JWF*

*Woodcut.*
*Image: 273 x 232 mm.*
*Sheet: 361 x 305 mm.*

Copy/edition: 64/230.
Büttenausgabe.
Signed, bottom right in pencil: "Kandinsky".
Signed in the plate, bottom left with monogram: "VK".
Printer: Staatliches Bauhaus, Weimar.
Publisher: Propyläen-Verlag, Berlin.
Provenance: Jupin, Copenhagen; acquired from him 1936.
Inv.no. 13672.
Selected literature: Hans Konrad Roethel, *Kandinsky. Das graphische Werk*, Cologne 1970, pp.452-453, no.14, repr.171; cf. Vivian Endicott Barnett, *Kandinsky. Werkverzeichnis der Aquarelle*. Erster Band 1900-1921, Munich 1992, p.484, no.550.

**Wassily Kandinsky**
*Plate VIII of the Kleine Welten portfolio. 1922*

163

**56  PIERRE BONNARD**  *French, Paris 1867 - Le Cannet 1947*
*Double page of Paul Verlaine's,* **Parallèlement**. *Paris 1900.*

When Bonnard in Paris, after two years of work, had completed the 109 lithographs for Verlaine's collection of erotic poems *Parallèlement*, he had not only learned to release his own art-nouveau figuration, typical of its time, in a new and fluid style of drawing; he had also found a whole new way to embellish an *édition de luxe*. This art form was since to flourish and reached a high point in the first half of this century. The book had been commissioned by the editor Ambroise Vollard on the occasion of Verlaine's death in 1896, and became the first of Vollard's many luxury editions. It was to become an epoch-making work, but because Bonnard used lithography, still an unappreciated art form, and disregarded contemporary tastes and decorum in respectable book design, it was far from successful. Furthermore, Verlaine's poems were controversial in their insistent celebration of sensuality and a sexuality of *jouissance* that refused to recognize accepted norms, moving freely and unselfconsciously between lesbian and heterosexual pleasure.

Bonnard's drawings spread across the pages of the book, reaching around Verlaine's poems in rosy visions of voluptuously tangled sheets and closely embraced female bodies. Bonnard's model for these drawings was his life-long partner Marthe, a delicately built woman he had met on the street in 1893, and since then photographed, drew, and painted with untiring sweetness and sensuality. Shortly before he began the Verlaine illustrations, Marthe's luminous body had served as the model for Peter Nansen's *Marie* (1898), a novel about love across class barriers. And two years after *Parallèlement* he drew Marthe as Chloé, often from model photographs, in many of the 151 lithographs for Vollard's edition of the classical pastoral novel *Daphnis et Chloé*, published in 1902. In the work of the classical Greek author Longus, as in Verlaine, sex is as natural a practise as any other human manifestation of life, but Bonnard's depiction of it in its cool, pastoral innocence is very different from the decadent urban passion of *Parallèlement*. Nor does Bonnard follow up the total disregard of pictorial rules that characterizes his Verlaine illustrations but in each drawing confines himself to the traditional square or rectangle.

These three *livres d'artiste* show the young Bonnard's range as erotic artist in the French bourgeois tradition, with his roots in Rococo as well as in the modernity of impressionism. His art falls clearly within a French bourgeois framework, and - as in the case of Proust - is preconditioned by it as much as it is determined by a conscious desire to expose the limits of convention. In all these drawings, the female body can be seen as a sign of the hedonistic joy characterizing his work as a whole. Whether it be Marthe, the landscape of Ile-de-France, or later, Le Midi under the sunny skies of Southern France, or just a plate of fruit, the figures of the images convey this delight in sensual experience, the *jouissance* which he lets shine through everything; this desire for earthly, transitory existence and the dream of permanence makes the moment translucent and shapes its image. In his aesthetics, and in his search for timeless harmony, Bonnard reveals a spiritual affinity with Dunoyer de Segonzac. Bonnard's pastoral vision has its later counterpart in Segonzac's etchings for Vergil's *Georgica*.

JWF

*Lithograph (rose-sanguine).*
*Dimensions of the book: 305 x 250 mm.*

Copy/edition: 110/200.
Van Gelder wove with the watermark: "Parallèlement".
Printer: Auguste Clot, Paris.
Publisher: Ambroise Vollard, Paris.
Provenance: F. Helms, Paris; acquired from him 1936.
Book inv.no. 12.272.
Selected literature: Charles Terrasse and Jean Floury, *Bonnard*, Paris 1927, no. 40; Claude Roger-Marx, *Bonnard lithographe*, Monte Carlo 1952, no. 94; Francis Bouvet and Antoine Terrasse, *Bonnard. The Complete Graphic Work*, London 1981, no.73, p.106-139; Colta Ives, Helen Giambruni and Sasha M. Newman, *Pierre Bonnard. The graphic Art*, New York 1989, pp.162-172.

LES PASSIONS.....

Ces paſſions qu'eux seuls nomment encore amours
Sont des amours auſſi, tendres & furieuses,
Avec des particularités curieuses
Que n'ont pas les amours certes de tous les jours.

Même plus qu'elles & mieux qu'elles héroïques,
Elles se parent de ſplendeurs d'âme & de sang
Telles qu'au prix d'elles les amours dans le rang
Ne sont que Ris & Jeux ou beſoins érotiques,

Que vains proverbes, que riens d'enfants trop gâtés,
— « Ah! les pauvres amours banales, animales,
Normales! Gros goûts lourds ou frugales fringales,
Sans compter la sottise & des fécondités!»

119

**Pierre Bonnard**
*Parallèlement. Paris 1900*

**57  GEORGES ROUAULT**  *French, Paris 1871 - Paris 1958*
*Jésus sera en agonie jusqu'à la fin du monde...  Planche from Miserere. 1948.*

During the First World War years, Georges Rouault made a number of drawings which he initially intended to use as the basis for a series of prints entitled *Miserere et Guerre*. The idea for this series grew out of Rouault's deeply felt response to the ravages of war. He was searching for a way to express the pain and inhumanity of the time and turned to the Christian faith for support and inspiration. Rouault did not succeed in seeing these prints published, however, until after the Second World War. His close friend, the art dealer and publisher Ambroise Vollard, kept the drafts until his own death in 1939, and it was not until 1948 that a reduced number were published under the abbreviated title *Miserere*. With the horrors of the Second World War, Rouault reexperienced the feelings that had affected him as a young artist in Paris. In these early years, he had belonged to the group of artists around Henri Matisse and *Le Fauves*, but as time went on, he increasingly distanced himself from the art of the avant-garde, while his concentration on Catholicism intensified.

Rouault's work as a graphic artist was characterized by a unique, experimental spontaneity which influenced his choice of method and technique. For the *Miserere* series, he transferred his original, brush-designed motifs to copper plates by the process of heliography. By this method, a photographically transferred copy of the motif is etched onto a copper plate prepared with powdered asphalt. The resulting prints are straight reproductions, but Rouault subsequently reworked the plates, using different traditional techniques, for instance sugar-lift aquatint. To produce plate 35 of the series, Rouault used a variety of techniques. The print owned by the Department of Prints and Drawings is an intermediate impression. It shows that he used roulette, drypoint and scraper on the plate, and, after the intermediate impression, continued with crayons. Through this mixture of techniques, he achieved many different effects in the one print; working with the roulette, he lightened dark areas, while the use of crayons created a contrast to the sharp contours of the aquatint.

Rouault portrayed society's extremes, the prostituted women and the poor, and generally found his subjects among outcasts and tragic characters. He also showed a great interest in the world of the tragicomical, with clowns and other circus characters as a recurring motif. Rouault emphasized the emotional aspect of their situation. His criticism of society was not all negative, but to a great extent based on his assurance that there was hope in the future for those who suffered, and that salvation could be reached through pain and hardship. This hope was founded on deeply religious ideas which gave Rouault an appropriate motif in the figure of the suffering Christ.

In an overall view of Rouault's graphic oeuvre, the Christ motif is essential, with its focus on the human aspect of Christ as the victim of brutality whose pain and suffering on the cross exceeded all earthly experience.

SP

*Heliogravure with aquatint, scraper, roulette and drypoint, painted in brush, black colour and pastel.*
*Platemark: c. 583 x 414 mm.*
*Sheet: 644 x 500 mm.*

Watermark, bottom right: "Ambroise Vollard" and bottom left: "Arches".
Signed and dated in the plate, bottom right: "GR/ 1922/ 1922/ 1922R*/ GR". (* the chiffers 9- and 2 may also be read as G and R).
Provenance: Erling Haghfelt, Copenhagen; from him c.1961 to P.A. Spleth, Copenhagen; gift 1984 of P. A. Spleth.
Inv.no. 1984-147.
Selected literature: George Rouault, *Miserere* (Foreword by Anthony Blunt), London 1951, repr.; W.A. Dyrness, *Rouault. A vision of Suffering and Salvation*, Michigan 1971, repr.; Allan Wofsy, *Georges Rouault. The Graphic Work*, London 1976, no 142, pp. 49; F. Chapon et I. Rouault, *Rouault. Oeuvre Gravé.* Monte Carlo 1978, no. 88a and e, pp. 266-67.

**Georges Rouault**
*Jésus sera en agonie jusqu'à la fin du monde...  1948*

Dufy's woodcuts for Guillaume's *Le Bestiaire, ou cortège d'Orphée* mark a newly awakened interest in the art of illustration, not only in Dufy but in the French modernists generally. *Le Bestiaire* was first published in 1911, printed in 120 copies. Of these, twenty-nine were sold before the censors intervened and confiscated the rest of the edition due to the "obscene" character of two of the woodcuts. One of these rare copies of *Le Bestiaire, ou cortège d'Orphée* has its place in the fine collection of French *livres d'artiste* in the Department of Prints and Drawings.

*Le Bestiaire* is in the tradition of the 15th century incunabula and can be considered a modern bestiary. A *bestiary* was the medieval equivalent of a handbook of natural science, containing descriptions of real as well as imaginary animals. The appearance and behaviour of each animal was described and a commentary containing Biblical quotations served as warnings to the Christian believer against errors of faith and immoral conduct.

In the short, cunning poems of *Le Bestiaire*, Apollinaire portrays the animals which, according to myth, were attracted by Orpheus and his music. Dufy, in his woodcut illustrations, not only characterizes the individual animal but also imaginatively and creatively explores the formal and sensual potential of the motif.

Like Apollinaire, Dufy plays with the meanings of the Medusa figure. Medusa (in French: Méduse) was one of the three Gorgon sisters, whose ugly face with its staring eyes and snake hair turned anyone who looked at her to stone. But Dufy bases his illustrations on another meaning of the French word *Méduse* which (as the English medusa) is also the zoological designation for a jellyfish.

Dufy thus depicts the Medusa as a jellyfish, searching and probing as it stretches forth its long tentacles in the water. By means of his stylized depiction of the jellyfish's physical appearance, the interplay of the black and white areas, constantly varied in their interrelationship, he creates a clearly structured whole. The tentacles of the jellyfish can be interpreted as the snake hair of the mythical Medusa. Just as the sight of the Medusa turns the beholder to stone, Dufy's composition is petrified into a homogeneous entity, bringing together the decorative elements of the vegetation and the snake-like tentacles of the jellyfish.

The frozen dynamics of the pictorial surface testifies to Dufy's eminent grasp of the ornamental beauty of his motif. From classical content to modern form.

LS

*Woodcut on Imperial Japanese paper.*
*Image: 202 x 195 mm.*
*Sheet: 325 x 249 mm.*

Copy/edition: 82/120.
Printer: Renauld at Gauthier-Villars, Paris.
Publisher: Deplanche, Editeur d'Art, Paris.
Provenance: Gemuseus (?), Basle; acquired here 1949 as gift of the Ny Carlsberg Foundation.
Book inv.no. 18712.
Selected literature: Dora Perez-Tibi: *Dufy*, London 1989, pp. 52-62; Riva Castleman: *A Century of Artist's Books*, The Museum of Modern Art, New York 1994, pp.55, cat.pp. 119.

# La Méduse.

Méduses, malheureuses têtes
Aux chevelures violettes
Vous vous plaisez dans les tempêtes,
Et je m'y plais comme vous faites.

G

**Raoul Dufy**
*Page of Guillaume Apollinaire's, Le Bestiaire, ou cortège d'Orphée. 1911*

**59 PABLO PICASSO** *Spanish, Malaga 1881 - Mougins 1973*
*Page of* Vingt Poëmes de Góngora. *1948.*

*Vingt Poëmes de Góngora*, a collection of poems by the Spanish poet Luis de Góngora y Argote (1561-1627), was illustrated by Pablo Picasso in 1948. He wrote out twenty of the sonnets in his own hand, using drypoint, and added marginal illustrations. For each sonnet, using both drypoint and sugar-lift aquatint, he also made a full-page illustration in which the motif was a woman - with the exception of one, a portrait of the poet based on a painting by Velazquez. Included as the last part of the book were French translations, by Zdislas Milner, of each of Góngora's sonnets. The patriotic Picasso was greatly fascinated by this Spanish baroque poet whose work was enjoying a renaissance in the 1930s, strongly advocated by Garcia Lorca, a distinguished poet himself, who called Góngora "the father of modern poetry".

Sonnet IX is a heroic poem, an unreserved tribute to a French general, and Picasso embellished its margins with simple, sharply drawn profiles. The almost militaristic air of these drawings may reflect a desire to create a visual equivalent of the poem's dramatic and glorifying description of war. The print presents a striking contrast to the accompanying full-page illustration. The woman in plate XX is seen from the front, looking out at the viewer. Her hair falls softly around her oval face, and her mild expression is enhanced by a delicacy of the naturalistic representation.

Her direct look adds intimacy to her presence, an intimacy often found in Picasso's work. In the greater part of his oeuvre, women are presented within a private and intimate sphere, as part of his own passionate worship of them. These depictions reflect his lifelong, ambivalent relationship to women, containing elements of adoration as well as debasement, often explained as manifestations of his extreme temperament.

In this work, Picasso emphasizes the visually attractive and traditionally feminine aspects of the woman, especially her decorative appearance. One nevertheless senses a certain tension in the picture, a wish to arrive at something other and more than just a beautiful visualization of a woman. Picasso overdraws her face with a cubistic profile, one of his common icons used to indicate an exploration and dissolution of simple spatial unity. With this touch, he creates tension between the expressive and the beautiful.

The book's female motifs explore an intimacy, intensified by closeness and presence, which in some cases is almost tactless. The sense of intimacy is also a natural consequence of the fact that Picasso consistently chose to illustrate literary works which were especially meaningful to him. At this stage, the texts he illustrated were either commissioned, or written by a close friend, or, as here, the work of a poet who had a great influence on Picasso. Thus the intimacy manifests itself on several levels, as part of the artistic process and as an important aspect of his special affinity to the work. This is felt throughout *Vingt Poëmes de Góngora* and connects the separate parts of the book so that they form a unified whole.

SP

*Aquatint and drypoint.*
*Sheet: c. 380 x 285 mm.*

Copy/edition: 66/275.
Inscribed verso, bottom left in pencil: "B.XX".
Watermark drawn by Picasso: *Góngora*.
Printer: Roger Lacourière, Paris.
Publisher: Ambroise Vollard, Paris.
Provenance: Antiquarian Axel V. Nielsen, Copenhagen; acquired from him 1956 as gift of Fonden af 7. januar.
Inv.no. 21701.
Selected literature: Abraham Horodisch, *Picasso as a Book Artist*, London, 1962, pp. 67-72, repr.; Patrick Cramer (ed.), *Pablo Picasso. Les Livres Illustrés*, Geneva, 1983, pp. 138-141, no. 51; Hans Naef and John Buchland-Wright, "Picasso. Illustrations to the sonnets of Góngora", in *Graphis*, no. 24, vol. 4, 1984, pp. 310-319, repr.; B. Baer: *Picasso. Peintre-Graveur*, Tome IV, Berne 1988, no. 738-778, pp. 30-72, repr.

*Pablo Picasso: Sonet IX from Vingt Poëmes de Góngora. Line etching and aquatint.*

**Pablo Picasso**
*Page of Vingt Poëmes de Góngora. 1948*

**60  GEORGES BRAQUE**  *French, Argenteuil 1882 - Paris 1963*
*Nature Morte II, Cubiste.*  1912.

*Nature morte II* is one of nine etchings made by Braque between 1909 and 1911, with diligent use of drypoint. Of these, *Nature morte II* and *Nature morte I* make up a pair. All demonstrate the artist's preoccupation with purely pictorial or iconic elements and their relationship to the visible reality which pictorial art until then had claimed to represent. In this print, the visual problematics concern an arrangement of objects. The motif is a juxtaposition of static objects that serve as a pretext for the picture, or rather, as the basis for an artistic discourse on how to represent the changeable, three-dimensional reality, of which we ourselves are a part, within the limits of a flat, rectangular surface. The artist enquires into the existence and function of the image through its own means of expression, and, by limiting himself to a few, static objects, he is able to suggest a larger context: the metaphorical, referring beyond the picture's own reality. Along with Picasso, who in 1907 presumably taught him the techniques of etching, Braque arrived at a form of representation soon to be termed Cubism, a multifaceted representation of solid objects based on splitting up their various surfaces. Shortly thereafter, Edmund Husserl, the founder of modern phenomenology, demonstrated that we are only able to see objects, because we have a previous experience of them as three-dimensional, inhabiting the space in which we ourselves constantly move. We *know* what the backside of an object hides from our view. Husserl termed this characteristic of our perception of the world "das Mitgemeinte". Cubistic representation is based on a similar approach, and it is symptomatic that Braque and Picasso only at the initial stage of their cubistic period worked with the diffuse spatial views of landscape; they soon chose to concentrate on observing the close world of solid objects, attempting to render it transparent. Cubistic representation is based on splitting open the closed forms of objects, allowing them to merge and intersect, letting what cannot be seen in reality - the "backside" of things - take shape and spread across the pictorial surface. The image is thus not representational in any traditional, mimetic sense. As a work of art, and in its descriptive distance from what it describes, it serves as a model for understanding how we perceive the phenomena that shape our reality. The image makes visible what our acquired manner of perceiving tends to obscure, namely that we always only see the world in fragments. It is our consciousness which makes the phenomena in front of us form the coherent whole that appears to us to be the world. Thus the cubistic image formally expresses the dimension of time, as understood by the period's most distinguished French philosopher, Henri Bergson, i.e. time as subjective duration, or *durée*. But Braque was soon to abandon cubistic representation. His few etchings were hidden away in his studio and forgotten, only a couple of them having been reproduced and published immediately after being made. With the exception of one, they existed only as single prints until 1953-54, when they were published by Galerie Maeght in Paris.

JWF

*Etching and drypoint on tinted Arches paper.*
*Platemark: 326 x 455 mm.*
*Sheet: 500 x 600 mm.*

One state only.
Copy/edition: 33/50, printed 1953.
Signed, bottom right in pencil: "G Braque".
Printer: Visat, Paris.
Publisher: Maeght, Paris.
Provenance: F.C.Boldsen, Copenhagen; his sale at Arne Bruun Rasmussen, Copenhagen 3.-4.3.1955, lot166; acquired here.
Inv.no. 21179.
Selected literature: Maeght, *Dix ans d'éditions 1946-1956*, Derrière le miroir, Paris 1956, no.4; Engelberts, *Georges Braque. Oeuvre graphique original*, Geneva 1958, no.10; Gerd Hatje, *L'Oeuvre graphique de Georges Braque*, Stuttgart/Lausanne 1961, no.10; Jennifer Mundy, *Georges Braque Printmaker*, London 1993, pp.9-15.

**Georges Braque**
*Nature Morte II, Cubiste.  1912*

173

**61  AKSEL JØRGENSEN**  *Danish, Copenhagen 1883 - Copenhagen 1957*
*Fyraften (End of the Working Day). 1909 (1935).*

In Martin Andersen Nexø's novel *Pelle Erobreren* (Pelle the Conqueror), "The Ark" is a tenement house where the lowest strata of the working class have settled, a motley crew of the unplemployed, unskilled and unorganized, of criminals, unwed mothers and whores. Brutality and generosity exist side by side in the Ark which is finally destroyed in a blaze of fire. The novel was published between 1906 and 1910, while Aksel Jørgensen was working on a series of socio-realistic woodcuts depicting the living conditions of the urban proletariate. In a book entitled "Life and Art", published in 1959, Aksel Jørgensen writes: "Naturalism and realism meant being on the side of all living creatures under all conditions and in all things, and above all it meant an immense sympathy for human beings in their complete degradation, in their total ruin, such as the social conditions of the time were." By the turn of the century, the social-democratic workers' movement was fairly consolidated and well on the way to creating its own political and and cultural institutions. Urbanization and industrialization burgeoned, real wages increased, and as a result living conditions improved generally. The child mortality rate dropped, and building speculation had been more or less curbed. But there was still substantial poverty and social insecurity among large parts of the working class.

The new, densely populated quarters of Copenhagen were a conglomeration of tenements, industries, places of entertainment and more or less ill-reputed bars. This was the world Aksel Jørgensen moved in, and where he found his models, depicting them in a simple, expressive style - influenced by such artists as Munch - as the basic types of the proletariate. His image of reality is one in which all superfluous, narrative detail that might distract from the clear message of his work has been eliminated. In many of his woodcuts, the physical surroundings are not even suggested, whereas the people stand out as the dominating figurative element. *Fyraften*, by way of an exception, integrates its human figures in a more detailed urban space with streets, pavements, and a factory in the background, a significant element when it comes to decoding the image. The compositional focus is on the three waiting children. There were numerous stories of children sent off to intercept their fathers outside the factory gate before he had time to drink up the week's wages, and it is probably this situation which the picture reproduces with great simplicity of effect and without resorting to propaganda.

This woodcut is a reprint, made in 1935 by Aksel Jørgensen himself, and was acquired by the Department of Prints and Drawings that same year, along with several reprints of his other early woodcuts. Thus the department's collection of Jørgensen's graphic work was considerably expanded, which was badly needed considering that - almost three decades after his 1909 breakthrough - he was still only represented by a few prints. The first editions of his woodcuts were probably purchased by an avant-garde public familiar with a radically new, pictorial idiom. The working class itself preferred trivial art - quite apart from the fact that the prints were too expensive for them. Besides, the workers probably did not wish to surround themselves with pictures of a poverty and misery they knew only too well.

VK

*Woodcut.*
*Image: 466 x 226 mm.*
*Sheet: 607 x 422 mm.*

Reprint by the artist 1935. Signed and dated, bottom right: "Aksel Jørgensen/1909". Inscribed, bottom left in pencil by the artist: "Eget tryk" and "No 20".
Provenance: Acquired from the artist 1935 as gift of C.J. Thomsens legat.
Inv.no. 13351.
Selected literature: Aksel Jørgensen, *Liv og Kunst*, Arbejdernes Kunstforening, Copenhagen 1959, p. 6; *Aksel Jørgensen - Det grafiske værk*, Fortegnelse ved Lars Kærulf Møller, Silkeborg Kunstmuseums Forlag, 1989, p. 9, p. 163, no. 10.

**Aksel Jørgensen**
*Fyraften (End of the Working Day).  1909 (1935)*

**62    JEAN ARP**   *French, Strasbourg 1887 - Basle 1966*
*Double page of Tristan Tzara's* **Cinéma calendrier du coeur abstrait, maisons.** *Paris 1920.*

Arp's graphic works are an essential aspect of his total oeuvre. Graphic art was a discipline he pursued in sequential form, in series of prints usually made in connection with poetry written by himself, or his poet colleagues, and published as books or albums. The graphic oeuvre consists mostly of black-and-white woodcuts, carved by the artist himself. His association with Tristan Tzara dates back to the founding of the first Dada group and the Cabaret Voltaire in Zürich in 1916. The two artists continued working together throughout the 1920s, and Arp contributed original graphic works to several of Tzara's collections of poetry, as did Max Ernst. In the early 1920s, Arp was exploring basic principles of figuration and meaning, working with the activation of elementary functions of sight and conceptualization which, at the same time, was being pursued scientifically by Hermann Rorschach in his psychological test plates with their meaningless forms which may be subjectively interpreted to assume figurative meaning. Arp was of the Platonistic view that art should point to a spiritual dimension, an ultimate reality. But, like the phenemenologist Edmund Husserl, he also knew that the world exists as a "for-me" rather than as an "in-itself". Arp's method of figuration is based on a fundamental principle of contemporary gestalt theory, namely that in the act of seeing - in our perception of wholes (gestalts) which we compile from smaller elements of form - we do not merely scan the world as recognizable figures viewed against a background. The world comes into being as we see it, and - what is equally important - sight and consciousness simultaneously *interpret* what we see. The world appears different to me than it does to anyone else, and what is seen depends not only on *who* is seeing it, but *from where* it is seen. A more recent psychology of perception has proposed that the individual interpretation of visual impressions is subject to laws determined by time and topos, and that sight itself is also subject to a certain historicity, a historically determined changeability.

The principle at work in Arp's small woodcuts - where the image, as if in transition, takes form as you perceive it - is based on how sight combines individual elements of the figurative complex arbitrarily. This principle of arbitrariness articulates a view of the self and the world, of nature as constant coming-into-being and transition, which links Arp to the German romantic philosophers, and which he has also given poetic expression, for instance in the poem *Sekundenzweiger* (published in 1924): "dass ich als ich/eins und zwei ist/dass ich als ich/drei und vier ist/...". Identity is unstable. Like everything else in the world, it is subject to time and change. As we look, the image comes together and strikes us with a precision that holds many images within it, and which Arp termed "indistinct distinctness". Like the Cubists before him, he was preoccupied with the constantly changing appearance, to sight and consciousness, of the phenomena of the world, and it was in part this preoccupation which made him important to the young practitioners of geometrical Concrete Art. But Arp was able to add a humorous subtlety to his pictures, as foreign to Cubism as it is to postwar Concrete Art: a life-affirming carnival mood and a fool's wisdom that was the very essence of Dadaism both during and after the war, the evil effects of which the artist had felt on his own body and spirit.

JWF

*Woodcut no. V out of XIX.*
*Image: c.122 x c.168 mm.*
*Sheet: c.250 x c.205 mm.*

Copy/edition: 70/150.
On wove paper from the early 19th century with the watermark "Giorgio Adamo Beckh in Norimberga".
Arntz, 63.
Signed below the colophon in pencil: "ARP TRISTAN TZARA".
Printer: Otto von Holten, Berlin.
Publisher: Dépôt au Sens Pareil, Paris.
Provenance: Sali Guggenheim; her sale at Christies, London 2.5.1995, lot 301; acquired here.
Inv.no. 1995-102.
Selected literature: Wilhelm F. Arntz, *Das graphische Werk*, Haag, Obb. 1980, no.59-77.

8
les carreaux d'étoffe et de feuillage accentuent
l'excuse des quatre paysages et la diversité
parmi les poteaux de béton en construction coulent
au-dessus de la foule entrecoupée par la nature
jardinier de jaspes sanguins
voilà un ballon
brasserie à danse de ventre imprévue s'est tue
un poisson énorme
un autre
les couleurs sont des chiffres qu'on tue et qui sautent
carrousel
comme tout le monde

**Jean Arp**
*Cinéma calendrier du coeur abstrait, maisons. Paris 1920*

Tristan Tzara was one of the founders of the Dada movement in 1916, a provoker of opposition to the senselessness of world war. He belonged to the notorious Zürich group which included Jean Arp (see cat.62) and Richard Huelsenbeck. In January 1920, he came to Paris and, only a year later, was excluded from the Surrealist group by its chief ideologist André Breton. In the course of the 1920s, Man Ray portrayed Tzara three times in his penetrating, close-up style. The earliest portrait has the appearance of a staged photograph. Ostensibly it captures Tzara during the reading of a sound poem in Zürich in 1916. But the portrait can be read as much more than documentation. Tzara appears seated on a ledge, in a room of uncertain size and definition. The uncertainty is parly due to the projected image of a semi-naked woman, the dimensions of which seem to call all others into question and dissolve the room's largest wall. The position of the poet himself is also defined by a lack of definition. He appears to be situated on the threshold between two rooms, at a point of transition between the formless darkness, on which he has turned his back, and a light geometric space which, at floor level, is absorbed by the darkness welling out behind him. The photograph also exists in a trimmed version. Despite Tzara's admonishment in a 1920 manifesto to - "Take a careful look at me! I am an idiot, I am a fool, I am a mystic" - it is the person portrayed who is eyeing the viewer in two of these three photographs. He scutinizes the viewer through his monocle which - in the close-up of 1924 (or 1926?) - makes Tzara's eye the focal point. Thus the observer, in viewing the portrait, is captured by the lens of the monocle as if it were Man Ray's own photographic lens. In his Tzara portraits, the artist has turned the picture into a mirror in which the observer sees himself, precisely because the other is looking at him. The portrait reverses the ordinary relationship between picture and viewer, where the viewer believes himself to be the one whose eye controls the situation. Unlike the jubilant baby facing Lacan's mirror, the viewer does not see himself as a gestalt, that is to say as a whole figure whose appearance (as with the child) is an unexpected contradiction of a sense of not being able to function as this external whole. On the contrary. And the eye is the pictorial sign that causes the balance to shift. The dark of the eye creates yet another transitional state, a sense of unease which makes the observer conscious of his own existence. The darkness seems to be an otherness, projected by the person portrayed. In the copy of the photo owned by the Department of Prints and Drawings, this "Unheimliche" seems to materialize just behind and under the poet, as well as in the axe, in the transitory symbols of time and space, the clock and the ladder, and above all in the ephemeral, threshold figure of the unattainable - the woman - who with her castrating look joins forces with Tzara. Or is she looking out at us through him, as his alter ego? The portrait is an image of transition. In Dostoyevski, the idiot is the one who knows the truth. It is the fool whose unruly mask can show us the true face of things. The photograph is thus, while a portrait of the *Dadaist* Tzara, a great example of surrealistic imaging where, in the words of Pierre Reverdy in the periodical *Nord-Sud* 1919, "the juxtaposition of unrelated objects creates the picture's potential meanings and determines its poetical power."

JWF

*Photograph.*
*Image/sheet: 294 x c.234 mm.*

Copy/edition: Artist's proof. Signed bottom right in pencil: "MR".
Inscribed bottom left in ballpoint: "E.A.".
Verso: Atelier stamp, bottom centre: "Epreuve Originale / Atelier Man Ray / Paris" and to the right of that the stamp: "Reproduction interdite / sans autorisation écrite / de 77 l'ADAGP / 9 et 11, rue Berryer / PARIS-8ᵉ / 924-03-87", at top edge in another hand in pencil: "TRISTAN TZARA 1920".
Provenance: Galleri Östermalm, Stockholm; purchased here 1985 by Herbert Melbye's Fund. Inv.no. 1985-380.
Selected literature: *Man Ray. L'Occhio e il suo doppio*, Roma 1975, no.66, repr. (here dated c.1922); *Man Ray. L'immagine fotografica*, a cura di Janus (Edizioni La Biennale di Venezia), Venice 1977, no.16, pp.182-183, repr. (here dated 1921); Arturo Schwarz, *Man Ray. The rigour of Imagination*, London 1977, no.407, p.252, repr. (trimmed version, dated c.1921).

**Man Ray**
*Portræt af Tristan Tzara. c.1921*

**64  MAX ERNST**  *German, Brühl 1891 - Paris 1976*
*Une semaine de bonté ou Les sept éléments capiteaux. Quatrième cahier. Oedipe. 1934.*

The meanings signified by the image emerge in its very areas of conflict, in the contrasts created by the relationship of its individual parts to each other. This is one of the principles of Max Ernst's collage technique which, during the twenties and thirties, formed the basis for his so-called "collage novels". The stories in these novels are open and paradoxical to such an extent that there is no limit to how they may be interpreted. Another principle derives from the phenomenological assumption that it is impossible to distinguish between sight and memory. Memory, it is claimed, will always determine the appearance of the seen. A forgotten memory will invariably and inevitably insert itself between the observer and the observed. Ernst composed his collages from fragments of widely different and unrelated realities, lifted from illustrated journals and scientific publications of all kinds. His collage books are intended to demonstrate that the world is deep and cannot be penetrated, as claimed by positivist science. The individual page of a collage novel can be viewed in isolation or in the context of the whole. The example chosen is from the album representing the element of blood. Here, two worlds are concentrated within an indefinable pictorial space. The anthropomorphic gestalt of the male figure has 19th-century Parisian naturalism as its referent. The woman, in her liquid nakedness, belongs to the mythological space of the art of the Salon exhibitions. She is held back and fixated, pierced through her right foot by his knife. The event is set in a space which seems to have little depth and at the same time to recede boundlessly. For is this an outdoor yard, or a quay on the Seine, or should the background be interpreted as pure air? Or, as watery intransparency perhaps? His appearance signals that he belongs in both elements, for he has the head of an eagle, and his throat and neck are fish bones and mollusks. She, too, fluctuates between air and water. He, sealed-off and indefinable, possesses the same anonymity as she, naked, averted, violated and vulnerable, defined solely by the nest of eggs, as he is defined by the knife. The image is without a horizon but not without a centre. The centre is where the two figures intersect, at the point where horizontal and vertical meet, in the sex, in a penetration, the nature of which is revealed in the knife-through-foot image - in other words, in a metonymy that can be viewed as a counter-image of another frequent, surrealistic sexual image, the *vagina dentata*. The two gestalts are united in a balance that is anything but absolute, since she seems about to slide away from him - despite his forcible efforts to keep her pinned down. The violent aggression, the penetration by the knife, seems to be what really connects these figures, but is also what forever separates them. Both are without identity, or their identity is indefinite and polysemous. Especially the man's bird physiognomy seems to lack awareness of what the body is doing. The man's body is in reality headless, and the figure can be interpreted as an *acéphale* (headless person) and an automat, stock figures of desire and the unconscious in surrealist iconography. The bird/fish/mollusk head fixes on the observer sidelong, independently of the body's frontal gesture. The observer is being observed by whatever he or she is observing - by a blind unconscious force, by a Nothingness, the power of which gleams in the staring eye, and toward which the floating woman's averted look is directed.

JWF

*Line block after collage on Navarre paper.*
*Image: 192 x 138 mm.*
*Sheet: 280 x c.214 mm.*

Copy/edition: 277/800 + 16.
Publisher: Éditions Jeanne Bucher, Paris
Provenance: Arne Bruun Rasmussen, Copenhagen, sale no. 204, 8.3.1967, lot 459; acquired here.
Book inv.no. 40412.
Selected literature: Jean Hugues, Poupard-Lieussou, *Max Ernst. Ecrits et oeuve gravé*, Tours/Paris 1963, p.10, no.11; Werner Spies, *Max Ernst - Collagen. Inventar und Widerspruch*, Paris/Cologne 1974, p.194-195 and no.429 (preparatory collage repr.); Werner Spies, Sigrid und Günter Metken, *Max Ernst. Werke 1929-1938*, Cologne 1979, no.2034 (preparatory collage repr.); Werner Spies and Winfried Konnertz, *Max Ernst. Books and Graphic Works*, Stuttgart 1979, no.16.11.

**Max Ernst**
*Page of Une semaine de bonté ou Les septs éléments capiteaux.  Oedipe. 1934*

181

**65  RICHARD MORTENSEN**  *Danish, Copenhagen 1910 - Ejby 1993*
*Sirmione vert.  1955.*

*Sirmione vert*, like its counter-piece *Sirmione bleu*, is a fine example of the particular kind of geometric concretion which distinguished Mortensen from the other artists associated with the Galerie Denise René in the Paris of the fifties. Like Victor Vasarely's, Mortensen early graphic works were transformations of already existing paintings. He had learned about the American technique of serigraphy a few years before, and through André Bloc had met the Cuban serigraphist Wifredo Arcay who was to be his preferred printer till his return to Denmark in 1964. Mortensen had approached this technique, new in Paris, with a certain scepticism, but soon discovered that here he had a near-perfect medium when it came to bringing his colours up to the plane-conscious brilliance he achieved in his mid-fifties paintings.

The two Sirmione prints constitute the third phase in one of the sequential developments characteristic of Mortensen's way of working. Previously, he had produced the paintings *Sirmione I-III*, 1953, and *Suite à Sirmione I-II*, 1954, on which these prints are based. The topographical reference is to the town of Sirmione, one of the many places Mortensen visited on his constant travels, situated on the needle-sharp point that shoots into Lake Garda from the south. Just as their titles have a topos in common, these compositions have in common the development of a structural variation of a basic image. The theme - in this image brought out non-representationally in an interplay of line, shape and colour - is one central to Mortensen's work. Pictorial design and meaning form a synthesis that can be summarized verbally as one of the central concepts of concretion: equilibrium - in French *équilibre* - that is to say, a visualized balance to which Mortensen attached existential importance, and which for him meant physical and psychic harmony. For him the precondition for drawing and painting was a free-floating mental state, a feeling of liberation from the world of objects, which, when transferred to the picture, would radiate from it and transmit to the viewer, flowing through the sense of sight into his or her consciousness. Kandinsky's obsession was to establish equilibrium through the balance of order and chaos. Mondrian's was exclusively equilibrium. But while the latter engaged in a utopian search for an absolute balance which in its reductive purity would exclude the tragic conflicts of the "Lebenswelt", Kandinsky realized the aloofness of this idea. To him, equilibrium meant a dynamic state, moving between genesis and destruction. Nor is Mortensen's equilibrium static. Because of the structural ambiguity of the image, dependent on the psychology of sight, the observer's grasp of the gestalts, the contrast between figure and ground, is subverted. Thus it is possible for the observer to reinterpret the form-given colour as its contrasting, formless ground. In Mortensen's work the balance constantly tips over into another and different one. The centre is everywhere and consequently nowhere. As intention and longing, the balance shifts towards the ideal horizon of the image, where it dissolves into nothingness in the brilliant colours of the composition. Equilibrium is the visualized dream of a life in harmony with oneself and one's surroundings, a dream which the artist, throughout his long life, sought to realize as structure and *formes-couleur*. The many topographical titles of his paintings stand as markers of the places where this dream came into view.

JWF

*Serigraph in eight colours after the painting Suite à Sirmione I, 1954 (Moderna Museet, Stockholm).*
*Image: 414 x 309 mm.*
*Sheet: 650 x 500 mm.*

Copy/edition: 35/100.
Signed bottom right in pencil: "Mortensen 55".
Printer: Wifredo Arcay, Paris.
Publisher: Éditions Denise René, Paris.
Provenance: Galerie der Spiegel, Cologne; acquired here 1992.
Inv.no. 1992-291.
Selected literature: Jan Würtz Frandsen, "Produktion og re-produktion. Et serigrafi af Richard Mortensen", in *Kunstmuseets årsskrift MCMXCII*, Copenhagen 1992, pp.150-153, English summary p.166; idem, *Richard Mortensen. L'Oeuvre graphique 1942-1993. Catalogue raisonné*, Copenhague 1995, p.87, no.20.

**Richard Mortensen**
*Sirmione vert. 1955*

## 66   ASGER JORN   *Danish, Vejrum 1914 – Århus 1973*
*Message essoristique. 1972. Planche 7 of the series Études et Surprises.*

Jorn occasionally quoted the famous, Danish scientist Niels Steensen as having said, "Beautiful are the things we see, more beautiful the things we understand, but most beautiful by far are those which we cannot comprehend". Much seems to indicate that Jorn's paintings quite literally are incomprehensibly beautiful, at least judging by what has been written about them. Books, articles, catalogues and reviews very rarely provide clarification, but seem to suggest that his images are beyond comprehension. An eye opening analysis of his work (whether the painted or the written) is in short supply. Nevertheless, a brief, initial user's guide for Jorn's work may be outlined:

Jorn has defined art, or the aesthetic, as being what he terms unfamiliar, incomprehensible, meaningless, or without value - but without opposing it in any absolute sense to the known and familiar. What is known is constantly changing under the influence of what is not known. There is a dynamic relationship between the incomprehensible in art and what is known and comprehensible in our everyday life. Thus the function of art is to add new values to the already existing ones on which we base our existence. "...The ability to create values depends on the ability to engage in what is without value...", as one of Jorn's *bon mots* states it. Jorn's art is therefore a theory and a demonstration of the constant occurrence of these shifts in values. He himself has named this the "theory of change in aesthetics", and the big question is then: how is this theory expressed in his art?

To demonstrate this dynamic relationship, Jorn composes his images of roughly three elements: *figures*, *arabesque*, and *ground*. Regardless of their level of abstraction, all of Jorn's works contain lumped concentrations of form (figures), either completely abstract - as in the woodcut opposite - or - in his earlier works - recognizable as faces, animals or fable creatures. These multi-coloured formations are outlined by undulating, interwoven lines (arabesques), and the whole medley is set against calm, monochrome, neutral areas (ground) along the edges of the image. His figures are to be very broadly understood as objects, individuals, cultures, concepts, or states of consciousness; the undulating lines represent the paths of energy transporting values to and into the figures; each colour is to be understood as a value, and the mixtures of colour as the shifts in values which Jorn wants to describe. The rapid colour shifts occurring in the figures thus demonstrate how objects, individuals, cultures, concepts, or consciousness change under the constant influence of new and unknown values, while the monochrome backgrounds must be understood as areas where values are still stable and unaffected by the continuous bombardment from what is not known.

In general this description can be said to apply to any one of Jorn's images. To understand more precisely how these metamorphoses of value take place, one must study the sophisticated and systematic method by which Jorn mixes his colours, looking both at his paintings and at his written work on the subject. Jorn's very elaborate theories on colour seem to be the key to his theory about change. However, a discussion of this, besides going beyond the present scope, would not be very meaningful, since no one has as yet really understood what Jorn's theory of colour is all about. The whole thing still remains incomprehensibly beautiful...

EJB

*Woodcut in nine colours.*
*Platemark: 323 x 249 mm.*
*Sheet: 555 x 443 mm.*

Copy/edition: 48 / 75 + 4.
Signed, bottom right in pencil: "Jorn 72".
Inscribed, bottom left in pencil: "48/75".
Printer: Clot, Bramsen & Georges, Paris.
Publisher: Atelier Clot, Paris 1972.
Provenance: Acquired at the artist's exhibition at Galleri Børge Birch, Copenhagen 1972. Inv.no. 1972-140.
Selected literature: Asger Jorn: *Naturens Orden, De divisione naturae. Silkeborginterpretation contra Københavnerinterpretation*, Borgens Forlag, Copenhagen 1962, pp. 109, 139; Asger Jorn: *Held & Hasard, Dolk & Guitar*, Borgens Forlag, Copenhagen 1963, a.o. pp. 20, 25f., 35-37, 46, 110; Ursula Schmitt: "Jorn als Graphiker", in Wieland Schmied (ed.): *Jorn*, Erker-Verlag, St. Gallen & Kestner-Gesellschaft, Hannover 1973, p. 26; Jürgen Weihrauch (ed.): *Asger Jorn, Werkverzeichnis, Druckgrafik*, Galerie van de Loo, Munich 1976, no. 411, p. XII; Nana Jorn / Asger Jorn: "Af et interview", in *Asger Jorns grafik*, lommebog 2, Den kongelige Kobberstiksamling, Copenhagen 1976; Hans-Ulrich Lehmann (ed.): *Asger Jorn, 1914-1973, Das graphische Werk, Die Schenkung Otto van Loo*, Kupferstich-Kabinett der Staalichen Kunstsammlungen Dresden 1994, p. 34, no. 275.

**Asger Jorn**
*Message essoristique. 1972*

**PALLE NIELSEN**  *Danish, b. Copenhagen 1920*
*From the series* The Deserted City.  *1973.*

This untitled etching is one of nine in *The Abandoned City* series, executed in the years 1973-1976. The series depicts a city after the disaster which we find ominously forewarned, or in full eruption, in some of Palle Nielsen's other series, notably *Orpheus and Eurydice*, *The Enchanted City* and *Pandemonium*. In *The Abandoned City* this disaster has emptied the city of its inhabitants, and it is now seriously falling to ruin. The main figure in the picture, the gigantic ventilating plant, has ended up in the water, pacified like a defeated and badly bruised sea monster. Perhaps what we see is the flotsam from a shipwreck, or the remains of an exploded factory; exactly what has happened is left uncertain.

The picture speaks of chaos and drama, but by means of numerous minute, fine lines expressing extreme painstaking and precision. There seems to be a contradiction between the story and the way in which it is told. Does not the choice of a highly controlled technique tone down the content? Or does this control create an even greater sense of tension and unease? Such ambiguity seems characteristic of Palle Nielsen, is quite simply an important element of his style. Almost without exception, his work is executed with the same measure of control and precision, both in relation to line and to the overall composition - despite the fact that his subject matter is always existentially dramatic. One envisions the artist sitting in his studio, filled with anger and despair at the state of the world, quietly placing each small line with great care - a care which can be seen as a stylistic attempt to create order in a chaotic world, and at the same time pointing out the powerlessness of the artist to actually intervene in the world's affairs. It is this ambiguity, of artistic expression as opposed to content, which gives this, and much of his other work, a dreamlike quality of indefinability, here beautifully serving to enhance the silence which reigns in the post-disaster emptiness, in the heart of the city after it has been turned inside out.

As in most of Palle Nielsen's other series, the overriding theme is the downfall of civilization. In illustrating this theme he often depicts a city, but never any specific city. Nielsen's cities appear to be composites of a multitude of European capitals, which is why these nameless cities seem familiar and yet not quite definable. Nielsen himself describes the experience of his city series as "wandering through a well-known world, a world composed of recognizable elements, but still strange". The same ambiguity characterizes this landscape of fragments. On the one hand, we find familiar elements of everyday life, represented by the ventilating plant, as well as particular forms which we recognize as recurring elements of Nielsen's pictorial world. Hidden in the confusion of pipes, we find the classical pillar and the black (port)hole that normally belong to his monstrous rotundas. On the other hand, we are presented with these familiar forms in a highly disturbing context. The disaster has not occurred on a distant planet of no consequence to us. On the contrary, it has struck the familiar, which makes it that much more frightening. It is a very scary story.

LWK

*Etching.*
*Platemark: 251 x 313 mm.*
*Sheet: 339 x 379 mm.*

Inscribed in the plate, bottom right: "138".
Inscribed bottom left in pencil by the artist: "138 6/9/73 2.tilstand. (kun m. klud)"; bottom right: "Den forladte by".
Provenance: Acquired 1979 from the artist.
Inv.no. 1979-14.
Selected literature: *Omkring Orfeus*, Lommebog no.7, Den Kongelige Kobberstiksamling, Copenhagen 1978; Kristian Romare, *Den fortryllede by*, Copenhagen 1990, pp.126-168.

**Palle Nielsen**
*From the series The Deserted City. 1973*

**68  ALLAN KAPROW**  *American, b. Atlantic City 1927*
*Yard. 1990.*

The car tire, as it appears in splendid isolation in Allan Kaprow's offset print, can in many ways be seen as a modern icon of Western consumer society on a par with, for instance, Andy Warhol's well-known pictures of soup cans and coca-cola bottles. During the early sixties, Kaprow - like Andy Warhol and many other artists - was working out of the desire to liberate art from the self-referential, abstract formalism that had dominated the American art scene during the preceding decades, to reestablish a connection to concrete reality and ordinary human experience by making use of objects and images of modern urban culture. For many artists this new-found interest in their familiar surroundings resulted in a new kind of realism, expressed in traditional media such as painting and sculpture, but for Kaprow, who seemed more interested in the meaning of life than in the meaning of art, it led to a radical, and in many ways paradoxical confrontation with the nature of art.

Much of Kaprow's work as an artist was in the form of writings which, even as early as the late 1950s, concentrated on a redefinition of the artist's role. Inspired by the avant-gardist composer John Cage - who at an early point demonstrated the aesthetic potential of the trivial by incorporating everyday noises into his music - and under the influence of eastern philosophy, notably Zen Buddhism, Kaprow, in all his writings, expressed his dislike of habitual thinking and insisted that the artist's search for awareness should be based on his own actions and observations in the immediate, everyday environment. The modern artist, he dictated, must abandon the specialized sphere of art with its fixed rituals, abstract mystifications and hankering for the extraordinary and instead direct his full attention toward the trivial phenomena of existence in order to throw light on the true nature of life and experience.

In practice Kaprow sought to realize his ambitions by experimenting with new art forms, such as environments that included the most insignificant objects and ordinary procedures. In *Yard*, made by Kaprow for an exhibition at Martha Jackson's Gallery, New York, in 1961, the public was encouraged to walk into the back yard of the gallery which had been filled with car tires for the occasion. By making the spectator an active participant in this odd art experience, by using what most of all resembles a Brechtian alienation effect, Kaprow wanted to shift attention from the passive contemplation and admiration of the art object to the viewer's own actions. For according to Kaprow's teachings, even the most insignificant acts can be viewed as a verification of existence and a precondition of awareness.

Originally, this offset print was probably made as a poster for the event described above, but the state presented here was produced to support the Sidney Biennial in 1990.

CKC

*Offset in two colours. 999 x 599 mm.*
*Reprint of poster from 1961.*

Copy/edition: A, 43/60.
Signed bottom right in pencil: "Allan Kaprow", and inscribed to the left of that: "43/60".
Printer: Sinnott Brothers, Sydney.
Publisher: Edition Block, Berlin. From a portfolio with 21 works by different artists, made for *The Readymade Boomerang*, the 8th Biennal in Sidney, 1990. The portfolio is edited by René Block, Berlin, assisted by Susan Shehadie, Sydney. Signed on the title page below in blue speedmarker: "René Block".
Provenance: Acquired 1991 via Edition Block, Berlin.
Inv.no. 1991-230 (10).
Selected literature: Allan Kaprow, *Assemblages, Environments, and Happenings*, New York 1966; Barbara Haskell, *Blam! The explosion of Pop, Minimalism, and Performance 1958-1964*, New York 1984; Jeff Kelley (ed.), *Allan Kaprow. Essays on the blurring of art and Life*, Los Angeles 1993.

*Allan Kaprow during the Installation of Yard in the backyard of the Martha Jackson Gallery, New York 1961. Foto: Robert R. McElroy.*

**Allan Kaprow**
*Yard.  1990*

**69  DAVID HOCKNEY**  *Engelsk, b. Bradford 1937*
*In Despair*:  *1966.  Page of Illustrations for Fourteen Poems from C.P. Cavafy, London 1967.*

David Hockney has often used quotations and literary references as a source of inspiration and as a means of underscoring the messages he wants his art to convey. He has drawn on a wide range of different writers, from Alfred Jarry to the Brothers Grimm to such poets as Blake, Auden and Walt Whitman, the self-declared homosexual who at an early point in Hockney's career became the indirect and symbolic exponent of his own experiences and sexuality. Also the Greek poet C.P. Cavafy could in this respect be considered a sort of mentor, occasionally cited by Hockney prior to 1966-67, when this graphic work was executed, consisting of illustrations for a large group of Cavafy's lyrical poems. It comprises 13 etchings for a selection of 14 poems, all focusing on homosexual love.

The appeal of Cavafy's poems lies not so much in the individual images as in the mood they establish. They create an atmosphere of sophisticated hedonism and nostalgia, in which longing for past experiences and for brief, superficial but memorable encounters play a large part. Time is experienced kaleidoscopically, because such memories constantly interrupt and accompany the situations in which Cavafy places his characters. This is also the case in the poem *In Despair* - written in 1923 - where the protagonist, feeling degraded and full of pain, seeks to revive the memory of a long lost lover by engaging in a series of casual relationships. The poem centers on desire and lust, polarized by a nagging sense of guilt, however, nourished by society's condemnation of the homoerotic relationship. This conflict is a recurring theme in Cavafy's poetry and - if we are to believe the epilogue in one of the other poems - provides the fuel for his work.

Cavafy's style is straightforward, realistic and free of the trappings of symbolism. Hockney translates this style to a simple, very suggestive line, also with emphasis on the realistic. In other respects, he stays less close to the original. The Alexandria of the early 1900s - Cavafy's home and the frame of his poetry - is transformed into a modern urban environment, because Hockney wants to give the viewer a visual equivalent - based on his own life and background - of the more general experiences suggested by the poems. In fact, he simply continued developing a set of motifs that had preoccupied him in the preceding years: scenes showing two undressed male figures in a domestic interior - in a bath, in a living-room, or, as here, in a bedroom - repeated in most of the etchings like variations on a musical theme. Thus the work at hand can be seen as an extension of Hockney's general efforts to express a particular homosexual sensibility. It seems strangely modern, and in many respects is comparable to the highly subjective and confessional art that has dominated the 1990s.

CKC

*Book with 13 etchings for poems by C.P.P. Cavafy. Chosen by David Hockney and translated by Nikos Stangos and Stephen Spender. Platemark: 360 x 230 mm. Sheet: 468 x 332 mm.*

Copy/edition: B 483/500. Handmade paper from J. Barcham Green Ltd. ("Handmade Crisbrook Waterleaf 140 lb Imperial") and H.V. Seir Limited ("Hevisier art Drawing 75 lb Imperial").
Signed in pencil on the last page: "David Hockney 483/500", below in print: "London 1967".
Lay out: Gordon House, London.
Printer and Publisher: Editions Alecto Ltd., London.
Provenance: New Art Gallery / Peter Kattrup, Odense; acquired here 1970.
Inv.no. 1970-211.
Selected literature: Marco Livingstone, *David Hockney*, London 1987, pp.85-89; Nikos Stangos (ed.), *David Hockney by David Hockney*, London 1976, pp.102f, repr.p.138.

**David Hockney**
*In Despair.  1966*

**70  PER KIRKEBY**  *Danish, b. Copenhagen 1938*
*Rebeccas billedark (Rebecca's Scrap Sheets).*  *Sheet no.5, 1973-74*

When Per Kirkeby's paintings are discussed, it is often pointed out that he paints them *layer upon layer*. And Kirkeby himself has said that all this sedimentation creates in the end a picture of *memory*, not any specific memory, but memory in the general, abstract sense. But how is this really to be understood? What does memory look like? This series of six offsets, entitled *Rebeccas billedark* (Rebecca's Scrap Sheets), suggests an answer:

The prints are based on what appear to be two sheets of scraps, probably belonging to the artist's daughter, Rebecca. The scraps are pictures of comic-book-style animals, children's faces, angels, flowers etc. Kirkeby has more or less accurately copied these scrap figures line by line, with a brush or as silhouettes. From these figurative copies he made offset plates, to which he added other plates with non-figurative designs. All the plates were then inked, each in a different colour, and randomly combined in the finished prints of the series. Each colour used in the finished prints represents a separate plate. In the print shown here, there is first a violet colour, quite accurately tracing the scrap sheet figures, and printed on top of that are two silhouettes, one a silvery grey, the other a chrome yellow. This print presents the least complicated combination of colours/plates. Sometimes as many as eight plates are used in one print, making the different layers of colour barely distinguishable - as in the print reproduced here in black and white. The other prints in the series represent stages between these two extremes. The violet plate is used as the bottom layer in five of the six prints, serving as the figurative foundation of the series, gradually blotted out as new layers are placed on top of it.

What does this procedure tell us about memory and what it looks like? First of all, the series seems to show that corny scraps are an important part of our world of images. From our earliest childhood, these cheap, visual clichés of popular culture are imprinted on our memory. They may be scraps, or they may be illustrations in comic books, children's books, or school books, photos in advertisements, pictures on record covers, etc. Secondly, the series clearly shows that these images in our memory are arbitrary and interchangeable. Memory is like a heap of scrap sheets that can be placed in random order, as Kirkeby has done with the offset plates. The principle of layering demonstrates that images in our mind intermingle as in a double-exposure photograph, or a dense, chaotic jungle - to indicate two metaphors central to Kirkeby's work. Thirdly, and finally, at the very centre of memory, as the print shows, there is an empty space not covered by the scraps/plates. This area seems to represent the parts of our inner store of images that are so peculiar as to defy description. All that can be seen at the relatively empty centres of the prints are indefinable, abstract forms and some weak impressions of children's drawings, not tracings of scrap figures but rather representations of the individual's hesitant attempts at making personal interpretations of the visual clichés on which our world of images is based. Thus Kirkeby's depictions of memory show a dynamic contrast between a half-empty, indescribable centre and an outer frame crowded with familiar images. The point seems to be that even our most personal and unique memories emerge from a sea of clichés.

Such a dynamic of contrasts is a recurring basic structure in all of Kirkeby's works.

EJB

*Offset in three colours.*
*Image: c.480 x. c.540 mm.*
*Sheet: 560 x 616 mm.*

Copy/edition: 34/100.
Signed bottom right in pencil: "Per Kirkeby 1974".
Inscribed bottom left in pencil: "34/100".
Printer and publisher: Permild & Rosengreen, Copenhagen.
Copy/edition: 34/100.
Provenance: acquired from the artist in connection with an exhibition in Den Kgl. Kobberstiksamling 1974.
Inv.no. 1975-427.
Selected literature: Ane Hejlskov Larsen: "Erindringens ukendte udseende, Per Kirkebys egne kommentarer", in *Per Kirkeby, Tavler*, Sophienholm 1988, pp. 18-22.

*Per Kirkeby: Rebeccas billedark, no.1. Offset.*

**Per Kirkeby**
*Rebeccas billedark.   1973-74*

**71**  **BRUCE NAUMAN**  *American, b. Fort Wayne 1941*
*Pay Attention.  1973.*

Among a series of colour photographs, made between 1966 and 1970 and collected in an album, there is one of Nauman sitting in a kitchen, spreading marmelade on large letters made out of bread and eating them. The letters on the plate partially form the word "WORDS", the "W" is already consumed. EATING MY WORDS, as the picture is appropriately entitled, describes a concrete, sensual act that not only mentally, but also physically, takes this statement at its word. "These are my words and I'm eating them". The words quite literally belong to the person eating them. We are dealing with what might almost be called a cannibalistic approach to language.

Much can be done with words, as Nauman has shown in his attempts to locate himself and the other by means of language - the fluid, immaterial, obstinate, ambiguous, concrete means of language - in a gesture that first and last is intended to establish contact and communication. By manipulating language in all conceivable ways, he subverts its habitual use. He exposes the conventions of language that determine our behaviour and experience of the world - whether they be worn-out phrases, vulgarities, or subtle puns - by rearranging the letters of words to create new meanings, disconnected from the immediate, logical context. He creates images of and with specific words, involving the viewer and forcing a reaction to the messages he sends out.

And it is precisely this field - the interplay of artist, work, and viewer - which Nauman explores in PAY ATTENTION, as he very directly sets the agenda for the viewer's experience of the work. He tops it off with a crude word from the everyday reservoir of vulgar language by writing "PAY ATTENTION MOTHERFUCKERS"; the words are then printed in multiple copies and circulated. He has used capital letters in bold-faced type, in some places making corrections; on the whole the print is sloppily made, marked by fingerprints and ink smears which he has not attempted to remove before printing it. Like an advertisement slogan, the message addresses the consumer directly. The technique is the same, but the tone and style are very different indeed. Not only the commanding content, but also its formal expression, demand a much more active participation to decode the message. The corrections, and the fact that the image is reversed, require full attention from the person looking at it and obeying - doing what is seen. At least for a brief moment - the time it takes the receiver to decode the message - Nauman activates the viewer and holds his or her attention. In PAY ATTENTION, as in so many of his other word-pictures, Nauman succeeds in linking sensation to consciousness. Looking is not a passive act, nor is the person looking invisible. This, among other things, seems to be what you can infer from the artist's direct address.

VK

*Lithograph.*
*Image: 951x 706 mm. Sheet: 972 x 718 mm.*

Copy: Artist's proof IV. Edition: 50.
Signed and inscribed bottom right in pencil: "B Nauman A/p IV 73"; To the right of that two blind stamps: c and II in circles. Inscribed verso, bottom left in pencil: "AP IV"; below that a black stamp for Gemini G.E.L., and below that in pencil: "BN. 72-492".
Printer: Jim Web, assisted by Ron Olds.
Publisher: Gemini G.E.L., Los Angeles (BN72-492).
Provenance: Galerie Fred Jahn, Munich; acquired here 1993 via the printer Niels Borch Jensen, Copenhagen.
Inv.no. 1993-55.
Selected literature: Christopher Cordes, *Bruce Nauman. Prints 1970-89*, New York 1989, p. 18, p. 118, cat.no. 16;
Paul Schimmel, "Pay Attention", in Joan Simon (ed.), *Bruce Nauman*, Walker Art Center, Minneapolis 1994, p. 69.

**Bruce Nauman**
*Pay Attention. 1973*

195

**RICHARD PRINCE**  *American, b. Panama 1949*
*Cowboys and Girlfriends.  1992.*

The photographic series *Cowboys & Girlfriends* consists of nine "Girl-friends", three "Cowboys", a plate showing all nine girlfriends, and one with the three cowboy photographs juxtaposed. Prince works primarily with appropriation, that is to say, he uses images and texts lifted from different (mass) media, either photographing them directly or using them in a more or less edited form. In this case, the girlfriend pictures have been taken from biker magazines, while the cowboy pictures are photographs of Marlboro advertisements. Prince has worked with these two groups of pictures since the early '80s, making several different versions, both individually and, as here, in combination.

The series touches on several levels in the relationship between the authentic, or "genuine", and the construed. On the one hand, we are presented with the picture of a perfectly styled cowboy, a glossy stereotype of the very symbol of America. The cowboy is associated with the "good old days", when a real man was a strong, brave and just cowboy. He stands as the symbol of the nation's mythical past, and consequently of authenticity. On the other hand, this cowboy is a romanticized, commercially constructed image, from Prince's viewpoint tending toward abstraction. The abstract quality is partly due to what he calls the "lack of an author", the fact that the photographer is anonymous, and is further emphasized, he explains, by his own total lack of personal connection to these pictures. Furthermore, this is not a picture of an arbitrary, individualized cowboy, but rather the essence of a cowboy, the cowboy as concept. The pictures of the girlfriends, however, are not at all cool or slick. Quite the contrary: these pictures have been cut at a crooked angle, they are out of focus, and the choice of background or of the girl's pose is often rather unfortunate. Next to the Marlboro pictures, they seem quite amateurish. These are not stereotypes but individual girls, portrayed with pride and love, photographs of the kind you carry around in your wallet for more or less sentimental reasons. They depict actual situations and people, not dream images. And yet they are not without ambiguity, for both the girls and the photographer are clearly unable to escape from the aesthetics of the fashion magazines, the pin-ups, and the conventional images of the biker culture. These pictures are about personally constructed identities that are still to some degree subject to social constructs, whether subcultural or more general. So even in these photographs, the "genuine" and the construed meet, as well as what might be called the concrete and the abstract.

The juxtaposition of the two groups of images creates an accumulation of conceptual pairs: the stereotypical/the personal; the slick and glossy/the emotional; the old, authentic America/the modern, urban cowboy; the abstract/the concrete. At a first glance, each of the two groups seems to represent clearly distinguishable concepts, but Prince's juxtaposition of them creates confusion. The critic Daniela Salvioni has very appropriately called this aesthetic strategy "seamless collage", a form of collage in which the juxtaposition of different "texts" blurs the distinctions between them, making apparently unambiguous concepts dissolve and letting a (perhaps quite predictable) ambiguity stand out clearly.

LWK

*14 colour photographs in a black canvas portfolio. Sheet: 508 x 610 mm.*

Copy/edition: F/26.
Signed below the colophon in pen and white colour: "R. Prince. 1992 F."
Printer: Aaron Klein at Ultimate Image, New York.
Publisher: Patrick Painter Editions, Hong Kong, 1992.
Provenance: Galleri Asbæk, Copenhagen; acquired here 1994.
Inv.no. 1994-119.
Selected literature: Lisa Phillips, *Richard Prince*, New York 1992, pp.37-41, pp.95-101; Daniela Salvioni, "Richard Prince, *Realist*", in *Parkett*, no.34, 1992 pp.98-102. Heinz-Norbert Jocks, "Richard Prince: "Ich hatte nunmal beschlossen, Warhol zu hassen, entgegen meinen Zeitgenossen, die ihn abgöttisch liebten"", in *Kunstforum*,  vol.136 February-May 1997, pp.284-287.

**Richard Prince**
*Cowboys and Girlfriends. 1992*

197

**73  GÜNTHER FÖRG**  *German, b. Füssen 1952*
*Bauhaus.  1993.  Planche from a series of  7 photogravures after the artist's photographs, taken in 1991.*

With undiminishing concentration, bordering on the obsessional, Günther Förg has persistently photographed cool, rational, modernistic architecture - as in this series of prints of the Bauhaus in Dessau, a sequence of seven photographs which he transferred to photogravure after having seen examples of this technique at Niels Borch Jensen's workshop. In photogravure the motif is transferred from film onto a metal plate. The coating on the plate hardens on exposure to light, the unexposed dark areas are washed out and etched to form cavities in the plate which is subsequently inked and printed. Niels Borch Jensen developed this technique to allow an even finer tonal variation of greys than was previously possible.

The series is typical of Förg's photographic work which belongs in the tradition of the so-called "straight photography", created in the USA around 1915, and adopted by the Neue Sachlichkeit in Germany. This type of photography shows a preference for the anonymous and unadorned photograph with a frontal view of its motif. But Förg's work, although he stays within the framework of this tradition, differs with respect to both form and subject. His photographs resemble snapshots, seeming subject to chance, a quality emphasized by crooked angles and foreshortenings of perspective that make all lines crash. He combines flat areas and spatial depth in a way that accentuates both, very much the opposite of what he practises in his paintings where the flat areas dominate, transformed to pure surface.

Förg goes in search of classical modern buildings by the very greatest architects, such as Mies van der Rohe, Le Corbusier and Walter Gropius. But he has also photographed Ludwig Wittgenstein's functionalistic villa in Vienna, and his largest project to date is an extensive photo series of Italian fascist architecture, mainly of the '30s, which in many cases has been allowed to decay. The Bauhaus was designed in 1925-26 by Gropius who was also head of the school for a number of years. Constructed in glass and concrete, the architecture of the school reflects the ideas underlying its training and its understanding of the function of art in society. Architects, painters and designers were to work together and influence industrial production for the benefit of the masses. The building was constructed functionally in accordance with the need for workshops, studios and dormitories; rooms for working, for instance, were fitted with large, spectacular windows from which the daylight poured in. When Hitler came into power in 1933, the Nazis closed down the school, putting a stop to the avant-gardistic and for a while strongly marxist-oriented teaching.

Förg is preoccupied with materials, light, and surfaces that reach into space and extend out of it. In *Bauhaus* the rational concept of the architecture is paralleled by the emptiness dominating the pictorial space. The choice of motif is loaded with significance. Today, the modernists' romantic, utopian ideas of a better world have lost credibility, but these Bauhaus photographs convey a certain nostalgic longing for lost innocence, reinforced by the somewhat old-fashioned appearance of the photogravure, its grainy and unsharp quality adding a sense of material presence to the depiction.

VK

*Photogravure.*
*Image: 367 x 283 mm.*
*Sheet: 395 x 303 mm.*

Signed, bottom right in pencil: "Förg 93" and inscribed bottom left in pencil: "12/15".
Copy/edition: 12/15.
Printer: Niels Borch Jensen, Copenhagen.
Publisher: Maximilian Verlag. Sabine Knust, Munich.
Provenance: Niels Borch Jensen, Copenhagen. acquired here 1995.
Inv.no.: 1995-84.

12/15                                  Förg 93

**Günther Förg**
*Bauhaus. 1993*

**MIKE KELLEY**  *American, b. Detroit 1954*
*Without Title.  1994.  Planche from a series of 13 pictures.*

Mike Kelley's artistic production has very appropriately been called a laby-rinth without an exit. His oeuvre is overwhelming in its heterogeneity, and you can very easily become disoriented. When you think you have found the exit, it turns out to be the entrance to a new labyrinth. It is almost impossible to get out, once you have gone in. Kelley consistently pursues lawlessness in his art – aesthetically, politically, socially and philosophical-ly – and is constantly changing direction, subverting anything resembling rules and norms along the way, simultaneously guiding and confusing the viewer. Trevor Fairbrother has pointed out that Kelley shows a certain affinity with Nathaniel Hawthorne who in 1844 published a satirical sketch, entitled "Earth's Holocaust", in which some reformers decide to rid the world of all misery and evil. All symbols of evil are thrown into a huge bonfire: old privileges, princes' robes, alchohol, coffee, tea and tobacco, weapons, money, books, the Bible and the church. Thus all ought to be well, but one small detail has been overlooked: they have forgotten to throw the human heart into the fire. Like Hawthorne, Kelley treats authority and the values of civilization disrespectfully. Fully convinced that no salvation exists, neither here nor in the hereafter – at least not for the sceptic Mike Kelley – he exposes a many-sided reality, not in order to transform it but simply to see what it looks like. His aesthetic investigation of the nature of the world extends in all directions. Every medium seems to appeal to him, no genre is left unexplored. He cultivates the banal, exalts the humble, makes what is tasteless tasteful, complicates what is sim-ple. His art is filled with question marks and resists all simple, unequivocal decodings.

Most often Kelley gives a more or less obscure title to his works, but the work at hand is simply named *Untitled*, to ensure that the viewer will first of all relate to the picture itself. Seen from a distance, its abstract forms look like silent planets, floating weightlessly in the infinite universe, pos-sessing an immediate, meditative beauty of their own. But if you move closer, you discover that they are only large wooly lumps of accumulated filth and dirt, with loose hairs sticking out here and there. They look like mutations of the stuffed animals and dolls which abound in Kelley's art. He buys them used, dirty and smelly, bearing unmistakable signs of having been hugged and kissed. Kelley in various contexts exploits their potential as objects of affection and love, indeed of all kinds of feelings projected onto them. While the key words for Kelley in these works are identifica-tion and empathy, he goes in the complete opposite direction in his pic-tures of the tangled lumps. It is impossible to identify with, or even humanize, these accumulations of dirt that repel the viewer and leave him or her in a vacuum. Kelley plays on the viewer's uncertainty and conse-quent sense of irritation at not being able to find any convincing meaning in them whatsoever. These dirt objects, placed within a clinically beautiful space, can mean everything and nothing, which is perhaps the very point of the work.

VK

*Photograph (gelatin silver print).*
*Total dimensions: 787 x 573 mm.*

Copy/edition: 4/5.
Signed, numbered and inscribed verso, bottom left in pencil: "# II 4/5 M. Kelley 1994".
Publisher: Patrick Painter Edi-tions, Vancouver/Hong Kong.
Provenance: Acquired 1995 via Patrick Painter Editions.
Inv.no. 1995-101.
Selected literature: José Librero (ed.), *Mike Kelley 1985-1996*, Museu d'Art Contemporani de Barcelona 1997, p. 136, cat.no. 12, repr. totally p. 74.

*Mike Kelley:  Almost White.*

*Mike Kelley: Without Title. 1994.*

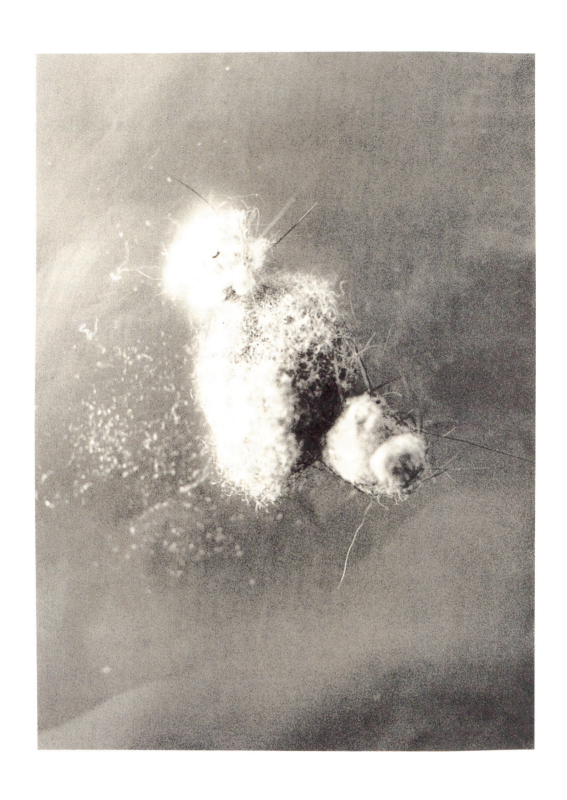

**Mike Kelley**
*Without Title. 1994*

**75   ERIK A. FRANDSEN**   *Danish, b. Randers 1957*
*Grundbilleder (Basic Images).   1988.   From a series of 18 planches.*

Erik A. Frandsen is without doubt the most outstanding graphic artist of his generation, not least due to the fact that the series of prints he regularly publishes bear all the distinctive marks of fine, traditional graphic art. An example is *Grundbilleder* (Basic Images), a series published in 1988, consisting of eighteen colour etchings in three units of six prints each. The series is an exquisite example of craftmanship in printing, impressed on the finest hand-made paper at Niels Borch Jensen's exclusive graphic workshop. The very limited edition is signed and numbered by the artist himself, as is right and proper. Often Frandsen's graphic work is presented in expensive, hand-made albums which you open respectfully, as if handling a rare, old folio. His series of prints are in other words endowed with an aura; they behave as if they were real art. Here we have none of the aesthetics of ugliness or sloppiness which Danish art of the 80s is often accused of cultivating.

But all of this attractive flashiness is not, of course, an end in itself, but a stylistic means played off against the subject matter of his images. For we are presented with a world that is in sharp contrast to the elegant finish of *Grundbilleder*, a chaotic, violent, frightening, disintegrated world. We see parts of naked torsos, frantically extended arms, limbs in panicky flight, and fear-ridden, sad or distorted faces. The existentially exposed beings inhabiting this splatter universe appear against a wet, soiled background, while aggressively drawn lines race across the pictorial surface. However, it never becomes clear exactly what horrors are taking place, because the bizarre oblong format limits the field of vision, making it impossible to view these scenes in their entirety. The special format is due to the fact that the eighteen plates were cut from three large plates, used the previous year for three other etchings. Thus *Grundbilleder* contain fragments of other motifs, which makes their frightening content less distinct, more understated. But why does this series only show us glimpses of the horror instead of confronting us with it directly? The attractive get-up seems to divert our attention, forcing our gaze away from the essential and toward the trappings. The pictorial content is suppressed by its external appearance, the horror is covered over by elegance.

This built-in contrast may explain the not exactly modest title, *Grundbilleder*, which seems to suggest that these images represent some sort of fundamental law of aesthetics, namely that human beings feel a need to aestheticize the horror of existence. *Grundbilleder* seems to succumb to this urge. The world is terrible, but art ignores this fact, pretends not to notice. Art has become perverted, it has turned its back on things (latin: pervertere: turn away). It is in danger of becoming reduced to costly collector's items, incapable of confronting the problems of reality. If this is true, the series of *Grundbilleder* is pronouncing a death sentence on itself and on art. However, by identifying with the problem, it also makes clear to the viewer that the problem is just as much his or hers. *Grundbilleder* freely indulges in an exclusive, escapist aesthetics by which we, as viewers, are initially seduced into beautifying and ignoring the horror played out right under our noses. But subsequently our eyes are opened to the fact that we are subject to this urge. And this basic existential condition is what *Grundbilleder* is about.

EJB

*Etching, drypoint and aquatint. Each sheet is printed with two plates, one with the motif, one with the colour of the sheet.*

Platemark: 320 x 990 mm.
Sheet: 615 x 1006 mm.
Copy/edition: 6/10.
Signed, bottom right in pencil: "Erik A Frandsen 88".
Printer: Dan Albert Benveniste at Niels Borch Jensen, Copenhagen.
Provenance: Acquired from the artist 1995.
Inv.no.: 1995-93.
Selected literature: Peter S. Meyer: "Udtryk med ny betydning", in *Kristeligt Dagblad* 19.4.1989; Ole Nørlyng: "Bund og grund", in *Berlingske Tidende*, 19.4.1989.

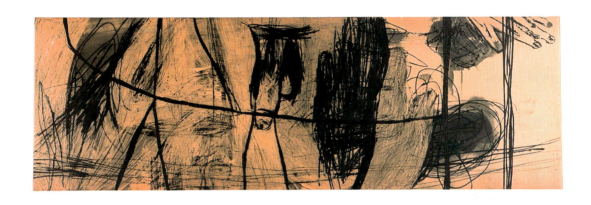

**Erik A. Frandsen**
*Grundbilleder.* 1988

203

## 76  WOLFGANG TILLMANS  *German, b. Remscheid 1968*
*From the series* New Inn Yard August 96, 41+1, 1990-1996. *1996.*

Greatly in demand within the art world and published in international music and fashion magazines, the work of the young German photographer Wolfgang Tillmans has received considerable exposure up through the 1990s. He has become especially known for his depictions of the colourful youths populating the underground scenes of large German and English cities in the 1990s. These works are very personal portrayals of friends, lovers, and situations within the environments he inhabits. Because of its broad, comprehensive scope, his work has been considered representative of a whole generation, an icon on a par with the Canadian writer Douglas Coupland's famous portrait of Generation X.

Tillmans' camera seems to fasten predominantly on the more positive aspects of youth and subcultures: the dynamic atmosphere of dance halls and club scenes; the intimacy and love of freedom within gay and squatters' environments; the general involvement in social and political questions - racism, gay rights, squatters' rights, and the transportation of atomic waste.

Portraiture interests him especially. The portrait is in essence a direct confrontation between the observer and the observed, and often encourages posing, or staging. The attention automatically falls on the portrayed person's conscious attitudes and dress - external signs that reveal identities and affiliations, and collectively define the various subcultures, cutting across a social and cultural system considered to be oppressive. Physicality and sexuality are also conspicuous, a constant focal point of Tillmans' indiscrete gaze and especially notable in the bizarre tableaux which he himself choreographs. These seem to have been made in an atmosphere of playfulness which, along with the uninhibited and self-assured performance of the people portrayed, adds to the positive and life-affirming quality of his depictions. In this respect his work differs significantly from the depictions of urban subcultures by photographers who mainly focus on the problematical and the "unhappy consciousness" as the basic condition of life at the margins of society.

Unwilling to let his work be limited by a narrowly defined and identifiable style, Tillmans has over the years produced pictures in almost all genres. The breadth of his work is demonstrated in his photographic series, the presentational form he prefers. It is also evident in *New Inn Yard*, owned by the Department of Prints and Drawings. This series, consisting of 41 photographs and a postcard - a double portrait of Suzanne & Lutz, a pair who frequently appear in Tillmans' early work - is a comprehensive example of his work from the 1990s.

CKC

*A series of 41 photographs and one postcard. Further a certificate and a plan for the hanging shown in 12 photographs.*
*Images: 100 x 150 mm.*

Signed on the certificate below in pencil: "Wolfgang Tillmans London, August 1996".
Provenance: Acquired from the artist 1996 via Galleri Nicolai Wallner, Copenhagen.
Inv.no. 1996-66.
Selected literature: Burkhard Riemschneider (ed.), *Wolfgang Tillmans*, Benedikt Taschen Verlag, Cologne 1995; Annelie Lütgens (ed.), *Wolfgang Tillmans. For when I am weak I am strong*, Kunstmuseum Wolfsburg 1996.

*Wolfgang Tillmans: Suzanne & Lutz, Bournemouth. 1993. Postcard after photograph.*

**Wolfgang Tillmans**
*From the series  New Inn Yard August 96, 41+1, 1990-1996.  1996*

# ALPHABETICAL LIST OF REPRESENTED ARTISTS

A SIGHT FOR SORE EYES II
76 Prints from The Department of Prints and Drawings
The Royal Museum of Fine Arts, Copenhagen
© Statens Museum for Kunst 1998
© Wassily Kandinsky; Pierre Bonnard; Georges Rouault;
   Raoul Dufy; Pablo Picasso; Georges Braque; Jean Arp;
   Man Ray; Max Ernst;  Richard Mortensen;
   Bruce Nauman / COPY-DAN, BILLEDKUNST 19980338
© Photographs: Hans Petersen and DOWIC Fotografi


Translation from Danish:
Ernst Dupont (JG); John Kendal (CF, JM, MBR);
Annette Mester (CKC, EJB, IO, JeG, JWF, LS, LWK, SP, VK)
Translation from Russian: Catherine Phillips (AI)
Graphics and layout: Thora Fisker
Reproduction: Skogs Boktryckeri AB, Trelleborg
Paper: Biberist Allegro demi-matt 150 gs.
Type: Janson Text, Linotype-Hell AG
Printed by: Skogs Boktryckeri AB, Trelleborg
Bound by: Förlagshuset Nordens Grafiska AB, Malmö

Printed in Sweden
ISBN 87-90096-16-9